To Elg)

MW00878322

The Road From
MOROCCO

a memoir

From my heart
to yours .
With love)
Wafa,
9/13/14

WAFA FAITH HALLAM

Copyright © 2010 Wafa Faith Hallam
All Rights Reserved
ISBN: 1452808082
ISBN-13: 9781452808086

First Publication Date: January 10, 2011
Second Publication Date: July 31, 2012

In loving memory of you, Mother!
Your beautiful and serene face graces this book cover and guides me on my path.

ACKNOWLEDGMENTS

If there ever were a time when I felt the need to acknowledge others, it would undoubtedly be now as I finish the final revisions to my memoir. This book would not have been completed were it not for the love and encouragement of friends and family members along the way.

The first to read my prose and voice words of praise and unbridled support was Marie Volpe. Without my dear Marie, this project would not have seen the light of day. Not only did Marie read my first chapters, she also shared them with others—particularly Angela and Lillian—who went on to further encourage me in my budding attempt. I thank you all for helping me with my initial efforts.

Many months later, as I doubted and anguished, I met Barry Sheinkopf and joined his writing workshop in Englewood, NJ. Thank you, Barry, for believing in me and reigniting the spark. Your friendly and professional guidance made all the difference in the world.

In the final stages of my writing, it was my sweet and gentle friend, Anne DeMarzo, whose infinite kindness and generosity allowed me to finish my manuscript. Anne took a leap of faith and opened her home and heart to lend me, a perfect stranger then, a cozy winter nest to complete my task.

Last but not least, I am grateful to my daughter, Sophia, and my sister, Nezha, for their invaluable love and support throughout the tortuous, and often punishing, process of memoir-writing.

Sophia, you endured countless displays of frustration and gloom and lived through long periods of soul searching even as you had to contend with your own adolescent trials and tribulations. Thank you, my darling, for showing so much forgiveness and understanding when it was needed most.

As to my loving sister, words are not enough to express the depth of my gratitude as you went out of your way at every turn to help revive my deficient memory, always with compassion and humor.

Wafa Faith Hallam
June 2010

CONTENTS

It's going to take a lot of awareness for you to understand that perhaps this thing you call "I" is simply a conglomeration of your past experiences, of your conditioning and programming...

When you're beginning to awaken, you experience a great deal of pain. It's painful to see your illusions being shattered. Everything that you thought you had built up crumbles and that's painful. That's what repentance is all about; that's what waking up is all about.

<u>Awareness</u>, Anthony de Mello

PROLOGUE

The Calling

My eyes were suddenly drawn to the stunning face of Penelope on the cover of the DVD I had rented a couple of days before. In the midst of a flaming garland, her black hair, up in a loose twist, was adorned with a large red poppy and framed her charcoal-dark eyes and crimson lips. The bright, fiery tableau contrasted with the forlorn expression on her eerily familiar pale face, a ghost beckoning me.

I was home alone that night in late April 2007. It was well past midnight, and I had decided to call it a night when, like the faint flutter of a butterfly, an idea flickered in my mind: watch *Volver* tonight...

The spirit of *Volver*, as a New York Times's reviewer had aptly put it, was "buoyant without being flip, consoling without ever becoming maudlin," and while I loved its humorous outlandishness—the peculiar return of a presumed-dead mother, among other things—it touched me at a level that I could not really fathom. The unrelenting adversity and hardship of its themes, however, were not what moved me; rather it was the intricate relationships between its superbly talented female characters that most affected me, their humanity. As the credits scrolled down on my TV screen, so my tears silently rolled down my cheeks.

My heart was filled to the brim with melancholy and compassion when an indescribable yearning took hold of me. Out of nowhere, the urge to tell my mother's story overcame me. *My mother's life story!* All my life, I had heard her wishing out loud to tell it. She was absolutely certain it had to be told, as if there were something invaluable to be learned from it. And there I was, experiencing *her* desire almost physically, as if she were channeling it through me. I stared at Penelope's image once more, and her uncanny resemblance to my gorgeous mother's in her prime, many years ago, hit me.

I jumped out of bed and went rummaging through the drawers of my dresser, looking for a small tape recorder I had taken with me to Morocco when I moved there in December 2003.

**

Mere weeks after we had settled in the sunny white house on the ocean, I had gone to her room, thrilled at the thought of surprising her.

"Mom, I have something here I want to show you," I exclaimed in French as I approached her bed. "But first I'm going to help you get out of bed. It's so beautiful out there."

It was already mid-morning, and her room was still in semi-darkness.

"What is it, honey?" she asked in a weak voice.

"It's a surprise," I answered. "It's something you've wanted to do for a very long time."

I pulled down the covers and helped her sit on the edge of the mattress, her feet dangling above the floor. I reached for the walker, placed it in front of her, within her reach, and turned to the large bay window to draw the curtains wide for the sun to stream through.

Just beyond the large terrace and across a short stretch of barren ground, the sea met the sky in a palette of blue shades bordered with a frothy ribbon of waves breaking over the rocky bluff. The glorious vista never failed to take my breath away.

"Here you go. Now, how about you show me you can pull yourself up on your own?" I challenged her cheerfully.

"Yeah, sure," she snickered. "Why don't you hand me my sweater?" She gestured toward the chair by the bed.

"Mom, you sound like it's an impossibility for you to ever stand up on your own again. You should at least try, don't you think?"

I handed her the cardigan she pointed to and helped her insert each arm through the sleeves. At sixty-five, she looked frail and listless. A dark cotton scarf hid the scalp wounds still discernible through her thinning gray hair; her eyes had lost their twinkle and mirrored her vanished appetite for life. Her trademark seductive grin had been replaced by the sad, fleeting hint of a smile.

"What's the surprise you have for me?" she asked ignoring my remark.

"Hold on. Let's first sit down comfortably. You'll need to wait a bit longer," I teased her.

Slowly, she placed both hands on the walker while I stood by her side and leaned over to lift her up, taking in her sweet scent.

Once seated side by side, I took the small recorder out of my pocket and gave it to her.

"This is a tape recorder I bought especially for you to narrate your life story." I grinned and waited for her to say something.

If she was pleased, she didn't show it. She kept turning the little object in her hand as if not knowing what to make of it.

"Isn't that what you always wanted; to tell the world what you went through? Well this is *our* project now. You record everything for me, and I'll write it for you," I insisted.

"What for?" she muttered at last. "It would take too long, and I'm too weary. Besides, you already know the whole story..."

She handed the recorder back to me with a disillusioned air.

"No, no, no, no... I don't want to hear that. It's a fascinating narrative and I'm sure there is much more that you haven't told anyone." I took back the recorder and patted her knee. "You never know—your story could be made into a movie one day!"

She cracked a feeble smile at last. I pushed the record button.

"Ready?" I asked.

"What do you want me to say?" she whined, sounding vaguely annoyed. "I don't even know where to begin."

"It doesn't matter, Mom. Anything you want. Here, why don't you start reminiscing about your early childhood, your adoring parents... their loving marriage...?"

"Yes, not like mine..." she finally relented.

She spoke in a dispassionate whisper for about forty minutes at a slow, halting pace, jumping from one event to another. I kept encouraging her, asking follow-up questions. At last, she asked for a glass of water and, with a grimace, indicated she was tired.

"That was a good start, Mom," I said. "We'll do it again in a day or two, okay?"

She simply shook her head without a word. I was far from imagining, at that moment, that there would never be another time.

**

Here it is. I knew I'd put it here, I cried in the night's silence.

I placed the small recorder on my desk and went back to bed. It was close to three in the morning when I closed my eyes.

The next day, before my first cup of coffee, I turned on the recorder with trembling hands and pushed *play*. I felt the drum roll in my ribcage and the pounding in my head; I hadn't heard her voice in so long, I didn't know what to expect...

Nothing!...

Incredulous, I pushed *play* again; still nothing. I tried again and again, turning over the mini-tape inside, rewinding and fast-forwarding it, but her sound had died along with her. The tape was as blank as my mind. Yet, I was sure I had recorded Mom that day. I had no idea what had happened.

I sat there for a long while in disbelief before I shook myself up. Then it dawned on me that what I really missed was hearing my mother's voice. I already knew everything she had told me that day, and a lot more.

The question before me was how to go about writing the whole thing. The idea seemed so farfetched, a mammoth undertaking. I had attempted to write slices of her story a few times since that day. Each time I had quit after a few lines. It was all too raw; my mind was jumbled and felt like a crumpled piece of paper. I told myself that I didn't have it in me, that it was a task that would never be done. Besides, it took creativity, and that was a quality I did not have. I viewed myself as a practical individual, grounded in reality, with little or no artistic talent.

What if someone else were to write it for me? I wondered.

I went on the internet and googled "ghost writer." In a flash, a list of options appeared on my screen. Immediately, I called a couple of companies with promising-looking websites. My first contact suggested that I write a synopsis of the story I wished to write.

"That way, we can determine the type of writer we need to match you with," she'd said.

That afternoon, I sat down with my laptop and began writing.

I wrote nonstop for hours in a feverish streak, not leaving my seat, defying hunger and thirst, until very late at night, and, when I was done, I knew I had to write the book myself.

The very next day, I immersed myself in a sea of remembrances—diving in with a scene that had always haunted me and moved me to tears: my parents' wedding night. There were less than seventeen years between my mother and me, and I was mature beyond my age, which explained our closeness and why she found it so easy to confide in me very early on. For a very long time, nobody could actually believe we were mother and daughter and not sisters. This intimacy was both a blessing and a burden, for it made her life and problems feel like my own.

Our symbiotic relationship did not end there. Very quickly, her dreams and their fulfillment had become my own life fixation. To a large extent, she had lived vicariously through me, and now it seemed that had not ended with her demise. I became convinced that the overwhelming impulse to tell her life story was my way of finding out and understanding, not only who she was, but more importantly, who *I was*, independently of her. For if her death had torn me apart, it had not freed me from her.

Such was the project that faced me. Her story could not be told without mine. It was no wonder my breakdown coincided with hers. And now, now that she was gone, I felt like a stranger to myself. For years, I had been under the illusion of being in control of my life, a strong and independent woman, a self-starter, doer, and high achiever. Little did I know! In reality, I had no clue who I was or what I wanted for myself.

Nearly all of my fears, all of my desires, had been hers and hence came first. With her collapse, all my attempts at bringing her lasting happiness, my life's primary ambition, had collapsed too. And in that respect, I was a big failure. With her passing, I was a nobody.

For three months, I wrote with ease and focus—albeit not without a jarring ache—over ten chapters, about 150 pages. That summer, however, my two-year lease was up, and my landlord sold the apartment my daughter and I had been living in. It took me close to four months to find another home, move in, and settle out of my boxes. With the holiday season upon me and a young niece's month-long visit from Paris, I had no time to write again.

My New Year resolution for 2008 was the completion of my book. But that was easier said than done; the process had turned laborious and fraught with doubt. Adding to my angst was the issue of money. My savings were fast diminishing, and I began looking for a job, even considered a return to Wall Street after a four-year absence.

Following their 2003 bottom, the markets had again hit a peak in the fall of 2007, sailing high on a sub-prime mortgage orgy and real estate bubble the likes of which had never been seen. The general euphoria caught up with me, and between December 2007 and March 2008 I sent my resume out and went on a couple of interviews.

The prospect of going back to Wall Street did not fill me with joy, though.

"I don't know what it is; it just doesn't feel right to me anymore," I moaned on the phone with my sister. "It's not that I don't want to make money anymore, God knows I do. It's that I don't want to make it *this* way. I honestly have little interest in a career whose sole objective is to make more money for me and others. This inner resistance is nothing short of inexplicable..."

"But the job you're pursuing is not the same as the one you had before. You wouldn't be a financial advisor anymore, right?" asked Nezha.

"Yes, that's right. I'm contemplating this new position where I would serve as a liaison between a fund manager and their institutional clients, explaining the strategy and rationale behind their picks. Listen, it really sounds like an exciting job if I can get it. You know how attracted to research and analysis I've always been. Plus, I've kept completely abreast of the financial markets since I left Merrill."

"I know—you're always watching financial news and reading the business section of the *Times*," she laughed. "I don't know how you can stand it!"

"It's true. That stuff really interests me. The fact is, in discussions with old colleagues, I often find that I know much more than they do in many areas. I simply don't know what my reluctance is about," I mused.

The biggest impediment to the resumption of my professional life, I assumed then, was my unfinished book, a memoir that, in my mind, had come to signify my very belated separation from my mother, and the rebuilding of my shattered self, a re-birth of sorts. This was far from the clichéd mid-life crisis one often hears about.

Out of work and out of sorts, I still needed to figure out what I actually desired out of life. I subsisted in existential limbo and wallowed in swamplands of murky uncertainty. Angst had become my enduring state of being and permeated the air that filled my lungs with every breath.

Professionally, I had achieved financial success, the so-called "American dream" that my mother had dreamed for me. Intellectually, I had come close to achieving the doctorate my father had once foreseen for me. To be sure, I had always believed those were my own desires and ambitions. So why was I still feeling empty and unfulfilled?

The veil over my eyes was soon to be lifted, for on my horizon was the dawn of my awakening. As the light of day follows the darkness of night, it arrived without warning or fanfare, in the form of a mundane telephone call that tore up the quiet of my home and threw me into the radiance of being, transforming my life forever.

1

The Virgin Bride

She was shivering in the dark but not from the cold. It was a warm night, in fact, but she couldn't keep her body from shaking. She had a long, white sleeping gown on and no *seroual*, the traditional underpants she had worn all evening. Her sister and his mother had made sure of that when they took the wedding clothes off her, slowly and delicately, one piece at a time. She had pleaded for them to do it and not the *neggafa* who had dressed her and undressed her all through the night as she changed from one costume to the next, looking exquisite in her colorful and elaborate headdresses and jewelry.

She started crying a little, but Zhor, her sister, scolded her, whispering in her ear to behave herself and not make a fuss. She held a trembling hand out to Lalla, her sweet mother-in-law. Save me! Her eyes were imploring. Lalla gazed for a brief instant at the anguished, frail-looking thirteen-year-old with tears in her clear gray eyes. Ever so lightly, she touched her cheek with the back of her hand, letting her fingers linger.

"It'll be alright, baby, don't worry. It will be okay, I promise," she said softly.

And then they left the room hurriedly, taking the wedding kaftans with them and closing the door behind. She was trapped then and utterly lonely.

The joyful chanting of the women assembled outside grew louder, and he entered the nuptial chamber, dressed in a magnificent white djellaba which oddly made him look even older and wearier than his thirty-three years. She was sitting in the bed, pale and frightened and so small. She appeared to him like a lovely painted doll, a little skinny doll—smaller than he remembered her, he said later. Her dark hair was pulled back, and she still had her festive make-up; rouge on the perfect lips and cheeks, kohl lining the already-black, fiery eyes, hands and feet decorated with henna in intricate designs intended to bring good luck and protect her against evil spirits.

Ironically, she thought, her luck had just run out and she was looking at evil straight in the eyes. But she was not looking at him, she was too afraid to. Her heart was pounding hard in her chest, and she felt nauseous. He turned off the lantern set on the table in the middle of the room. She heard him move in the dark, undressing himself quickly. That's when the quivering began; she couldn't help it. She lowered herself on the bed, crossing her arms on her chest, stiff as a corpse. If only the darkness could swallow her into oblivion.

She felt him crawling in the bed next to her.

"Don't be afraid," he said gently. He didn't touch her at first, and she kept very still, her legs stretched tight, hoping, praying that he would just go to sleep and let her be. She could hear the noises outside, the voices of women and their laughter.

The celebration was still going on; they were going to be serving the traditional *harira* for breakfast soon. For a while, he just lay there next to her, motionless. She could hear him recite a short prayer, and he repeated in a whisper, as if to reassure himself as much as her, "Don't be afraid." He smelled of musk oil and soap and tobacco.

Finally, he seemed to be taking a deep breath and he extended his hand under the sheet, touching her arm. She unconsciously shielded herself from him. Her fear was palpable, her breathing short and fast paced.

He moved closer to her, repeating again, "Don't be afraid... you know we must do this... It's God's will."

He reached for her leg, fumbled a little with her gown, his long shirt. She could feel his hand on her thigh and she let out a sob. No, she thought, I hate you... don't you know? And she tried to coil away from that prowling hand.

He stopped short, as if he had heard the howl in her head, and he sighed. "Saadia, we must do this, they'll be waiting. It *is* God's design."

He grabbed her more firmly, trying to spread her legs apart, and moved his hand up her thigh, reaching upward toward her groin and her soft and warm, hairless femininity.

The day before, her older sister, Fatma, had taken her to the *hammam* and helped her wax herself clean, leaving her smooth as a baby. This was not the first time, to be sure; Fatma had started waxing her ever since she'd discovered pubic hair growth on her young sister's mons a few months before in the *hammam*. It hadn't been pleasant the first time, but she'd gotten somewhat used to it since.

Suddenly she felt him grow harder against her leg and instinctively grabbed his hand and pulled it away from her in sheer revulsion.

"Saadia," he said patiently, "you can't fight me. This has to be done... just relax and it'll be all right."

Raising himself on one elbow, he tried to caress her. He touched her face and wiped the tears streaming down her cheeks. He lowered his head to kiss her softly on the lips but she turned away in disgust, sobbing now, a tight knot in her stomach and what she guessed was his penis pressing against her skin. She knew she had to let him take her... she was told he would, this was the normal course of things, there was no escaping. She closed her eyes and wished to be dead right there, right then.

When she opened those eyes again, it was all over. He had turned on his side, away from her, and gone to sleep, just like that.

She was wide awake and strangely relieved that it was over, feeling the intense burn and soreness in her loins and the wetness between her legs and on the sheet. She didn't dare touch herself, just pulled her gown down, curled her legs up against her chest and wept quietly. She was mourning the innocent child, forsaken by her loved ones into the crypt inside the earth's core, only to be desecrated.

Later that day, the women would be pleased to display the bloodstained sheet and gown in a big round copper tray—proof of her virginity, her sacrifice at the altar of family honor, which would thence be preserved. She had done her daughterly duty. She had endured this unspeakable humiliation as was expected of her, allowed him to pull her legs up, felt his awkward fingers inside her, spreading her and guiding himself within her, and the sudden intense, searing pain as he thrust his way deeper with a small grunt.

She was thankful for the obscurity, that she couldn't see his face. Besides, she had kept her eyes shut, savagely biting her lower lip so as not to scream, her head turned to the side, clenching the sheet in her fists, feeling his weight crushing her in silent, helpless resignation. He was not a big man, thank God, rather thin and slender, not at all imposing, and he was done in minutes. Panting, he had let out a curious groan and then pulled out of her.

"I'm sorry," he had finally mumbled. "It had to be done." And that had been all-pretty fast, really. To her surprise, she had survived her wedding night.

**

These were the post-war years, the early fifties, and Morocco had been divided into three zones since 1912. Most of the Moroccan territory was under the authority of the French protectorate—a euphemism for colonization. A smaller zone, made up of the Northern provinces, was under Spanish control. And then there was Tangiers, at the northwestern tip of Africa, gateway to the Mediterranean, on the shore opposite the Strait of Gibraltar: Tangiers, once Portuguese, then British, and finally "liberated" under a multinational statute that turned it into a free zone and an International port in 1923.

My mother was born in 1939, at the onset of World War II, in a kingdom with a fragmented soul held together by the French shortly before Germany invaded Poland and before France yielded to the Nazi invasion. Slowly but surely, a Moroccan consciousness began to surface. All it needed was a charismatic leader to drive it forward. That emblematic figure materialized in the realm's young sultan, literally on the eve of my mother's wedding, as he was taken away from his home and thrust into the night of exile.

All her life, my mother had repeated, at every opportunity, and to everyone that would listen, that she had been forced into marriage when she was just thirteen to a man twenty years older than her, forever outraged by the revolting immorality and injustice of it. This, in truth, was not all that unusual in those days, and her parents were far from being horrible tyrants. Quite to the contrary, they were devoted and caring, very protective of their children, and she loved them dearly, and never blamed them.

She was the next-to-last child in a family of ten surviving children, four girls and six boys. Her parents had been married for thirty-five years by then and, when her father was diagnosed with lung cancer, it was decided that they had to marry the little one off before his passing. Unlike her sisters, who were already wed and entirely illiterate—to the point of not being able to write their names or dial a phone number—my mother had been attending an elementary school for girls for a few years and could read and write Arabic. She also had a basic knowledge of algebra. She loved reading Egyptian romance novels and spent long hours, after her chores, dreaming of Prince Charming.

Her parents were already well acquainted with her future in-laws, since one of their daughters was happily married to one of their sons. My mother's family was a mirror image of my father's. They also were ten brothers and sisters born of the same mother, and both my grandfathers had been married only once and had all their children with a unique wife. This was very unusual then in Muslim families. My mother was the youngest sister, my father the oldest sibling—and a consummate bachelor.

My dad enjoyed his single life thoroughly. He was well educated and spoke French fluently in addition to his perfect knowledge of classical Arabic. He was a devout Muslim, which did not prevent him from enjoying good wine and poetry and the company of like-minded men in blissful religious festivals and in private. Publicly, however, my father displayed a permanent frown on his face and looked eternally grumpy and stern. Upon his father's passing, he became even more of a grouch as he assumed the role of elder and head of the family. Tellingly, his next of kin all called him *"Bahssidi,"* meaning "grandpa" in Moroccan Arabic.

My mother was familiar with him and his siblings and had been lampooning him behind his back with the complicity of his own sisters during family gatherings and holidays. In fact, my mother was rather happy when she and her mother paid her sister a rare visit. Furthermore, she had a crush on Hassan, my father's youngest brother, a handsome and gentle young man with a smiley face and delicate features. So when she learned she was to wed one of the brothers, she immediately thought of Hassan. That would have been a match made in heaven, a natural one since they were not very far apart in age and he was still unmarried.

Alas, to her great shock and despair, they had decided on the old grump of the family. Apparently, he had to take a wife first to confirm his status within his clan. *But why her?* She could not believe they would choose her for his consort. By what tragic turn of event had they come up with such a horrifying plan?

Two of her older brothers expressed their disagreement and tried to get their father to change his mind, but no one fought very hard for her, for whatever the patriarch decided was to be: as simple as that. She was taken out of school immediately in preparation for her new life. She cried day and night and even contemplated running away a few times, but in the end she could only submit to her destiny.

In the tradition of Morocco, right after the wedding, she went to live in her in-laws' house in the old medina of Meknes, where her sister Zhor was already living with her husband and his siblings and their wives—those who were still without children. Two of my dad's sisters and two of his younger sisters-in-law were about her age, so she was made to feel at home immediately.

Her mother-in-law, Lalla, was a saint of a woman, a soft-spoken lady who never raised her voice or lost her temper and who welcomed her with open arms. The young women all helped Lalla with the household, while the men went to work or school. What made the first years of her marriage bearable for my mother was the fact that she lived in the company of women in the big traditional patriarchal home in the medina, serving all the men of the house their meals and attending to the daily chores.

The house was a typical Moroccan *riyad*, and all the couples lived upstairs, on the second and third floors, in big private chambers with high ceilings, each furnished with a full bed with a commode and armoire in one corner and a sitting area at the opposite corner. Downstairs, Lalla shared her room with her unmarried daughters while the rest of them, the young unwed brothers, slept together in another large room, also on the first floor.

Additionally, there were a couple of large ornate salons reserved, firstly, for entertaining and guest lodging, and, secondly, for daily dining and gathering with the immediate family. All the rooms were furnished with big sofas lined up against the walls and facing the inside patio with a multitude of pillows and cushions. The sofas were used both for sitting and sleeping when needed. The rooms had no windows on the outside, all the light came in from the large, open-squared tiled central courtyard. Hence the life of the women was sheltered from the outside world and hidden from prying eyes.

My mother met my father alone only at night in their private room, often at the urging of her beloved mother-in-law.

"It's time to go to your husbands," she whispered to her sons' brides, reminding them of their primary roles. My mother followed the others with much reluctance and disappeared in her quarters, where she waited in bed to find out if her husband was in the mood for intimacy, which, thankfully, was seldom the case. When that happened, he would roll over her, press his lips on hers in a feeble attempt to kiss her, and do his business quickly and silently, and always in the dark. It was not much different from her wedding night, lacking the physical although not the emotional pain.

She loathed his inept and dispassionate embrace but submitted to it without protest, even facilitating it so that it would end almost as soon as it began. Her marriage took on its full significance only after she became pregnant with me and everything she had known suddenly changed. She was only sixteen.

Until then she had been playing games along with her sisters-in-law on the sun-baked roof top of the *riyad* while taking the dried clothes off the line. They rolled up a sheet into a ball, stuffed it under their dresses, and pretended they were with child, giggling their silly heads off, imitating a pregnant acquaintance's mannerism. But this was the real thing now. As her belly grew bigger, so did her standing. Her girly status changed overnight to that of "mother-to-be." Because two of her older sisters were childless, the entire family had been anxiously waiting for her to become a mother. So there was considerable joy, mixed with relief, at the news.

To her delight, she earned instant respect and admiration and became the object of much care and attention. This event also somewhat tempered the enormous regret brought about by the news of Hassan's upcoming nuptials to a dazzling red-haired, milky-skinned young beauty, issued from a respectable family from the imperial city of Fez, who was soon to take her place in the family. Hence my birth, combined with the latest betrothal, meant that my father had to set up his own house with his young bride and soon-to-be-mother, marking in the process the beginning of a new era of discord in my parents' marriage.

They settled in a house in the Jewish quarter, the *Mellah* of Meknes. Around that time, and during the years that followed the founding of the state of Israel, many Moroccan Jews sold or abandoned their homes in their old neighborhoods throughout the kingdom for the Promised Land. My father rented his house from a man whose son and daughter-in-law had emigrated against his wishes and whose wife, Rachel, later became a close friend and confident to my mother.

It was a small house with no running water or electricity, but it was clean, bright and cheerful, and it had a pleasant patio with a small well in its central courtyard and an orange tree. When the orange blossoms were in full bloom, the whole house was filled with their sweet, musky scent. In that house, on a warm summer day in July 1956, I was born into the hands of a midwife, one of Rachel's acquaintances, assisted by my two adoring and infertile older aunts.

2

The Blessed Child

What a year 1956 was for Morocco—nothing less than the complete unification and independence of the country! Indeed, my father had been living in the midst of massive political transformation before the news of my mother's first pregnancy was even announced. On November 16, 1955, King Mohamed V and his family returned home from their two year exile in Corsica and Madagascar in a delirium of widespread exultation.

Women, being permanently confined to the sheltered universe of their traditional family homes, were entirely ignorant of anything that did not have a direct link to feeding and caring for their loved ones. Consequently, only men had any notion of the world around them, and rare were those who bothered to share the news or otherwise inform their wives and daughters of any development outside their households.

The triumphal return of the king, however, was acknowledged and celebrated by every woman, man, and child in the kingdom. Literally millions poured into the streets of the imperial cities to catch a glimpse at their beloved sovereign during his tour of the nation. My mother, like all the inhabitants of Meknes, would remember for a very long time indeed that extraordinary occasion-but she also had to think about a more pressing matter.

My father was transported by the rapid changes of the political landscape and its actors. He spent long hours after work in the city's French cafés, in oblivious disregard of all else. He had a close circle of friends who shared the same interests and with whom he enjoyed debating the major political parties' agendas and other significant events of the day.

My mother was almost six months pregnant when Morocco was declared free of the Spanish occupation in the north of the country in April of 1956. Shortly thereafter, this critical event was followed by the end of the French protectorate in the rest of the kingdom and by the abrogation of the international status of Tangiers.

My father came home late at night, often inebriated, and left in the morning for his job as a government functionary in the town hall. He also returned home for his lunch and habitual nap in the middle of the day. Overall, he took little interest in the progress of his wife's condition; she was, he knew, attended by Rachel or one of her sisters almost day and night, and there was nothing that was asked of him. Yet he welcomed my birth with an enormous optimism, greeting me as the blessed child of the Independence, born in a free and unified land. The world was full of promise, he felt, and his daughter would have the greatest of destinies.

My two aunts understood very little of what Independence meant or would bring to their daily lives; they were nonetheless elated by my birth. Fatma was the oldest of her ten siblings and twenty years older than my mother. She knew first-hand what infertility could lead to.

My mother hadn't yet been born, when Fatma became her first husband's first wife. When, after a couple of years, she was unable to conceive, he had taken a second wife. Barely a couple of years apart in age, the two young women lived under the same roof. Naturally, each had her own room, but they quickly became best friends. This was not at all unheard of. But these two got along so well that they fell into the unfortunate habit of conspiring against, and ganging up on, their spouse together, plotting to get their way every which way they could. They took turns nagging and annoying him until he could no longer put up with it all. By then, his second bride had become pregnant; the frustrated man took the unprecedented decision to get rid of the two of them by repudiating them both and marrying... the maid.

For the family, this was recalled as a tragic yet irresistibly comical incident. Fatma, of course, felt she had been unjustly and abjectly disowned when she was sent packing by her first husband at nineteen. She had, however, suffered disgrace and derision with dignity and had just about accepted her new fate.

After only a few months, a widowed older gentleman, with grown children, asked for her hand in a second marriage. The union not only restored her pride, it also gave her great happiness and a new appreciation for life. Uncle Mehdi, her new husband, was a kind man with a good sense of humor and a fun-loving streak. He was quickly embraced by the family and remained a much-loved figure throughout his life, long after the passing of my aunt of a cardiac attack some forty years after he took her as a wife.

When I was born, Fatma lived with him in Sidi Kacem, thirty miles west of Meknes, but she was able to take long leaves of absence to help her little sister during the delivery and first difficult postpartum weeks. Uncle Mehdi didn't mind. He took full advantage of such opportunities by paying extended visits to his married daughter and grandchildren who also resided in Meknes.

My second aunt, Zhor, on the other hand, childless too, had been fortunate enough at seventeen to marry my father's brother, Uncle Mokhtar, a laid-back, handsome man with intense green eyes and a lust for life. His family was too honorable to consider repudiation as an acceptable answer to barrenness. Besides, he was knowledgeable enough to know that it could very possibly be coming from him, as turned out to be the case when a medical exam later confirmed it. Thank God for that. My aunt was far too jealous to tolerate living with a second wife. She adored him and lavished him with astonishing care and affection, working tirelessly to provide him with all the comforts she believed he deserved, treating him as the child they could not produce and the companion she could not live without.

Astoundingly, until her death in the summer of 2006, they had never once spent a night apart from each other, never travelled anywhere if they could not do it together, and she could not eat a meal without presenting him with the best morsels first, even when they were the guests of others. My aunt's extreme attachment made her the object of much teasing within the family. But she did not mind in the least, and even if she did, she could not help herself. She literally was unable to enjoy the smallest of pleasures if her husband didn't partake in it. And he, guiltlessly and without embarrassment, enjoyed her adulation all his life.

During the sixty years they were married, he was rumored to have indulged in a few illicit pleasures of the flesh on occasion. Moreover, he was not the hardest working of men. He relied on her, not only for all the household chores, but also for most of the hard work and responsibility involved in running their farm—a small agricultural property she had bought in the sixties, with savings from her former occupation as a seamstress and a loan from one of her brothers. Neither of them was a farmer, and so she learned the job the hard way, overcoming adversity and taking on the vast majority of the workload—and he let her assume it with no apparent remorse.

Their life was a remarkable love story and undermined most arguments against arranged marriages, as most were, for whatever reason, pretty successful as a whole, and a few, very lucky ones, were nothing short of amazing. And so it was that my aunt Zhor never spent a night in our house unless her husband was there, too. Since he was also my dad's brother, their visits turned into family reunions welcomed by both my parents.

Of course, there were also conspicuous failures, as was my third aunt's marriage. My aunt Aisha was too busy with her own family and children to be involved with anything outside her household. Her three sisters had married men of similar backgrounds—of mixed Arab and Berber descent, whose Moorish ancestors had invaded Spain as early as 711 and stayed until the 1500s. Their families had lived in Granada and Cordoba and were predominantly urban dwellers. So when they fled the final Christian re-conquest of Andalucía, which expelled the last remaining Moors of Granada, they naturally settled in the urban centers of Morocco, like Fez, Meknes, Salé, Rabat, and Tetouan, which others before them had made their homes.

Aisha, in contrast, was married to a member of one of the Berber tribes native to Agadir in the far south of Morocco. A successful merchant, this proud Berber had settled up north in Rabat on the other shore of the Bou-Regreg River across from Salé, the original hometown of my grandparents, and had met my grandfather in the course of doing business. The two men were mutually impressed by each other's fortitude and they built a cordial relationship. This naturally led my grandfather to grant him his third daughter's hand in marriage, his rural Berber heritage not disqualifying him in the least.

Nonetheless, there was a cultural difference of sorts between the two milieus, which may have contributed to the divide between the new bride and her taciturn groom. I remember him as a man with an aloof temperament, who did not seem to have much in common with my other uncles. He was handsome but cold and he looked like a man with a secret life. And indeed, he was reported to have had multiple extra-marital affairs until he was too old and too sick to enjoy them.

There is no doubt that my aunt grew to love and respect him deeply, but he caused her much sorrow. He was said to be living under the same roof, even sharing her bed, and yet not say a word to her for weeks at a time. A sweet and mild-tempered woman, she never complained openly of her lot, but the sad smile on her lips, and wounded gaze in her eyes, betrayed her profound unhappiness. The fact that she lost two daughters and a granddaughter in the most horrifying circumstances in later years did nothing to improve her disposition.

Hence, only my childless aunts, Fatma and Zhor, were there to help and assist my mother on multiple occasions during her childbearing years. They were surrogate mothers to her and her progeny and provided needed comfort whenever they could. Nonetheless, it was her faithful Jewish neighbor Rachel who really was there almost daily to lend her a hand and cheer her up. The two women became very close and enjoyed long afternoons into each other's confidence.

At the same time, the relationship between my parents went from bad to worse. My dad's nightly outings and drinking binges intensified and his periodic spiritual escapades were increasingly intolerable to my mom. He was a faithful practicing Muslim, and one of his greatest pleasures at the time was to attend special religious festivals, known as "Moussems," in honor of great saints. One of his very favorites was the Moussem of Moulay Idriss Al Azhar in Zerhoun, a picturesque little town only a few miles from Meknes overlooking the magnificent old ruins of Volubilis, an ancient Roman City.

Zerhoun, also called Moulay Driss, is known as the First Muslim city in North Africa and it kept its character of sacred city to this day. In fact, its access was forbidden to non-Muslims up until 1917. For an entire week at the end of August, millions of pilgrims, coming from all over the country, gather to celebrate the Saint in prayers and festivities. One month after my birth, my father, unable to resist the lure of the Moussem, left for Zerhoun for a few days in defiance of his family's silent disapproval.

Not surprisingly, my parents' financial situation was made the more difficult by his conduct and my mother was not the type to take it quietly. She greeted him with hostility, and the more she did the greater the alienation between them.

On a rare visit home to her parents in Sidi Kacem, she was so obviously dejected that her father felt compelled to reevaluate his decision to keep her married to my dad. He offered to have her return home and he wrote my dad asking him to divorce her, to which my dad replied that he would consent if she would agree to let him keep custody of their baby daughter. My mother was not willing to give me up, even as her father, who was by now ever so sorry to have been the cause of her unhappiness, kept pressing her to do so. This decision, she was not fully conscious then, was going to seal her destiny and the course of her existence and mine.

Indeed, only three months after I was born, my mother was with child for the second time. My little sister Nezha came to the world in August 1957, just as I was beginning to walk around everywhere, babbling ceaselessly and driving my mother insane with my insatiable curiosity and boundless energy. In contrast, my sister was an angelic baby, calm and easygoing; she didn't even talk until she was about three years old, just observed the life around her in silence, probably turned off by her bigger sister's overly active temperament.

Exactly a year after my sister's birth, my brother was conceived, and he was in such a hurry to come to the world that he came much too early. He was a premature baby, born after only twenty-eight weeks of gestation. Too small and too weak to survive on his own outside the womb, he was kept in an incubator for weeks, which forced my mother to spend all her days at the hospital with him. My aunts, and Rachel, took turn caring for her small daughters at home while she was gone day after day.

Like many preemies, my baby brother Abdu suffered multiple health complications, the worst of which was a condition known as respiratory distress syndrome, a potentially life-threatening breathing problem that caused him, throughout his childhood, to endure, among other things, numerous agonizing asthmatic episodes.

I vividly remember for years being awakened in the middle of the night by the terrifying sound of my little brother sitting up in his bed, in total darkness, gasping for air and yet not crying or calling out for help, so accustomed was he to his affliction.

When the French doctor who treated him ordered his release from the hospital, he warned my mother that the boy's health would continue to be very frail. He sternly told her to be vigilant and take him back to the hospital at the first alarming sign of distress. She was relieved her baby had survived and to finally be able to take him home. But his fragile health remained a source of worry during the weeks that followed and the lack of financial means did not permit her to get him the optimal treatment he needed.

Luckily, one of her brothers, Abderrahim, having heard of her grim situation, paid her an unexpected home visit. He found his little nephew in ill health and his sister's living conditions so inadequate that he arranged for the whole family to move to the city's modern neighborhood. Somewhat reluctantly, my father agreed to the move to a new home.

This was a lovely French villa on the hills overlooking the old medina of Meknes, not far from the hospital. Her brother had not only found the house he was also paying the rent; and he did not stop there. He also arranged to pay for Abdu's medical bills, insisting that his nephew be provided with the best health care and treatment available. This was the same brother who later helped their sister Zhor with the down payment on her farm.

After the death of their father, following his long illness in the fall of 1958, Abderrahim, my mother's third older brother, felt compelled to assist his sisters whenever he could. He had taken over his father's warehouses in Sidi Kacem and he was rapidly prospering in various trades. Through hard work, good fortune, and steely determination, he had built an empire that, today, makes him one of the richest men in Morocco. My aunts often told how harshly their father used to discipline him as a teen, beating him with his belt buckle and leaving him confined for days in one of his storerooms as punishment for some wrongdoing.

Early on, he had married Simone, his first wife, a Frenchwoman who gave him four children, and raised them in an entirely European lifestyle. They barely spoke Arabic as children. If that bothered Abderrahim, he never showed it. But then he never really developed significant ties with his siblings either. He was, still is, an aloof man. His deliberate union to a foreigner had only deepened his isolation from a family still strongly bound to its Islamic heritage. He was a complex individual, a man of few words, tall and good looking, with an especially shy nature and a very sensitive personality.

Then as now, he could alternatively show great generosity or utter indifference, sometimes even meanness, and no one really knew what made him tick, save perhaps his wife. He never opened up emotionally to his sisters, though they all had the deepest affection for him, admiring him, even revering him, as if he were a demigod. The one thing that can be said about him with certainty is that he never failed to be there for his family, particularly in moments of great urgency, of sickness and death.

My mother was not only grateful to him, she was jubilant that end of summer 1959 as she entered her new house. She was carrying her five-month-old boy cuddled in her arms. Rachel, who had offered to come along, was holding hands with her two toddlers in tow.

My mother could not believe her eyes. It was the most perfect little house she could have dreamed of. Built by a French teacher and his wife on the hilltops of Bellevue, a well-kept French neighborhood, it had dark-green wooden shutters and French doors opening onto a small lawn bordered by colorful flower beds. The freshly painted white walls that separated the house from its neighbors were covered with yellow, red, and purple bougainvillea, and in the far corner of the garden stood a majestic mimosa tree from which hung a creaky swing.

As she walked up the alley that led from the front gate to the house door, she handed the sleepy little boy to Rachel and pushed open the door. A dark heavyset woman in her late thirties immediately welcomed her, explaining she had been hired as her new maid by her brother. She, and an old gardener with a toothless smile, were finishing cleaning the house and had been expecting her and the children. My mother could barely hear the maid's words, so happy she was to discover her new home.

She opened the doors, one after the other, turning the lights and the water faucets on and off and flushing the toilet all with a wondrous smile on her face. I ran gleefully after her, shrieking with delight, insisting on imitating her in all she did. Meanwhile, my little sister kept holding on to Rachel's dress, intently sucking on her right thumb while she took in the scene around her.

The little villa had only two bedrooms, a larger one for the parents, and a second one big enough for the children. Both rooms shared a single bathroom with a tub, shower, and sink and an adjoining but separate toilet. The living room had a wood-burning fire place and opened directly onto the sunny garden with its flower alleys.

"This is going to be our family room," said my mother in a cheerful voice. Open into the living room was a large rectangular dining room, which my mother immediately anticipated was going to be perfect for her traditional Moroccan sofas instead, making it a nice-sized salon for guests and visitors.

Directly adjacent to the dining room was the large kitchen with its sink and counter top. It was equipped with an old stove and a small refrigerator, slightly rusty, but in working order. A long wooden table and chairs sat along one of the walls. The kitchen led to a sunny paved backyard set with a laundry basin and clotheslines. All these amenities and appliances, she knew, were going to change her life. At long last, she felt welcomed into the "civilized" world.

We had been settled in the new house for no more than a couple of months when my mother discovered to her chagrin that once again she was expecting. She was already exhausted from the rearing of three young children; she could not imagine having yet another one. Rachel had hinted to her of a medical procedure that could help her interrupt her pregnancy, and she immediately agreed to resort to it without informing my father.

The botched operation almost cost her an arm, and in the end it did not succeed in terminating her pregnancy completely. Although she had conceived of twins this time, in the early summer of 1960, she gave birth to only one of them, a scrawny yet healthy little boy, her fourth child. His twin did not survive.

I was four years old when my second brother, Larbi, was born; my sister was three, and my ailing premature brother just sixteen months. My mom had survived a traumatic episode, had put on a lot of weight, and was tired and depressed. The bungled abortion attempt had angered my dad, and the tension between them had only grown worse. She was full of rage and squarely blamed him for not being more careful.

She had tried time and again to get him to practice withdrawal, as Rachel had taught her, but he was not very good at it, not that he tried very hard, she was sure. He did not see things that way. After all, his mother had given birth to thirteen children, ten of whom had survived, and so had *her* mother.

"It's God's will," my father reminded her, "it's up to Him alone to decide how many offspring we're going to have, and who's going to live or die, not you."

His pious arguments infuriated her even more, she hated his religiosity. It was always God who willed it all. Her husband never had anything to do with anything. But she was the one who, within five years, had carried four children, birthed them, breast-fed them all, and nursed them to health. What had he ever done really? He hardly was around at all... what with their dismal financial situation. If it weren't for *her* brother they wouldn't even be able to afford their medical care, or the maid, or even, for that matter, the roof over their head...

That was that... My father had known all along that the move to the new house was going to have consequences. Although appreciative of my uncle's generosity, he was also ambivalent about its deeper significance. It was all crystal clear to him: The move and his brother-in-law's financial support had rendered my mother bolder in her criticism; and her disenchantment grew more pronounced as his behavior remained pretty much unchanged. Her revolt first expressed itself in her resolution to bear no more children. She loved her kids, but four were more than she had bargained for, and she was determined to stop at that no matter what.

The result of her first recourse to an abortion had been an unsightly scar on the inside of her right arm. And the near-loss of a limb should've once and for all put an end to thoughts of terminating any future pregnancy. It did not in the least. She got herself a more competent doctor and resorted to multiple successive abortions as a perfectly acceptable birth control method in her mind until the Pill finally became available in Morocco in the mid-sixties.

That event single-handedly signified a new liberation for my mother as well as for millions of women around the world. She never again was going to be a slave to her body. A little oral contraceptive had empowered her in ways that only she could really appreciate.

For my mother, the move to the new house had made her material existence easier and vastly more pleasant for her and her four children. The new maid, who also was a cook and a nanny, had been an invaluable help. But emotionally, my mother was not much happier.

She had barely turned twenty-two when the sudden death of King Mohamed V in February 26, 1961, a little over five years after his return from exile, threw the whole country into massive mourning. The widespread sentiment not only echoed but also intensified her own outlook on a future full of uncertainty.

3

A Brave New World

The new King, Hassan II, had been designated official heir to the Throne by his father after their return from exile, and in March 1961, he succeeded him without any problem. The peaceful political transition that took place, and the consolidation of executive powers behind the new king, reassured the Moroccan people and ushered in, what was hoped would be, a new era of stability for the country. The grief felt by the population was slowly replaced by a sentiment of expectation. And so was my mother's disposition.

Her brother Abderrahim, expanding his business in Rabat, was in search of dependable managers. He knew my father was a principled man who spoke excellent French and in need of better paying employ. So he offered him a managerial position in his store in Sidi Kacem, where he sold everything from hardware, to small agricultural equipment and tools, to school and office supplies, and other staples.

My mother was delighted by the opportunity. My father was more hesitant, for although he had the need, he did not have the desire, for a different job. He was being asked to leave an undemanding and secure post as a government functionary, an occupation he had held forever and was comfortable with.

And he would have to leave his circle of friends and close-knit family for an unknown town and unfamiliar environment. He was more than ambivalent, he was downright miserable.

But my mother had the last word. She viewed this as her ticket to a new life, a chance to lead a lifestyle similar to the one her brothers had managed for themselves and their families, and she was not willing to listen to any argument to the contrary. The fact that her sister Fatma and her husband were living in the same town was also a big factor. Aunt Fatma was like a second mom to my mother, and then to me, whom she loved dearly and treated as the daughter she'd never had. And so it was that in the mid-summer of 1962 my family packed up and moved to Sidi Kacem.

Sidi Kacem is the township's Moroccan name, after a saint who is buried under a marabout on its outskirts. Founded in 1916, the town was first known as *Petitjean*, after a French army officer who helped "pacify" the country's fierce warring tribes. Its population grew quickly with the influx of both French and Spanish settlers—known as the *colons*—fleeing the massive unemployment caused by the 1929 economic crisis in France and the political oppression under Franco in Spain. It grew further during the exodus of the neighboring French-Algerian *pieds-noirs*, disinclined to return to Metropolitan France after the country's 1962 war of independence.

The Europeans were first attracted to the region—known as the Gharb valley—for its fertile agricultural land. In later years, two other factors contributed to the growth of the town and its booming economy: the new train station and the country's second largest oil refinery. So much so that even after Morocco's independence, hundreds of thousands of Europeans elected to stay put. In fact the French continued to contribute manpower and know-how at every level of the economy, and overall relations with France remained cooperative and friendly.

Hence, in the early 1960s, Sidi Kacem was still a pretty little French town with quaint, tree-lined streets and avenues speckled with welcoming sidewalk cafes, nicely kept houses with enclosed lawns and flower beds, and a wonderful elementary school. This was the perfect place to call home and raise a family.

My eager young mother, and her reluctant husband, arrived with their four children in a town bustling with energy, and my uncle's store was right at the center of the action. It was a large warehouse-like store with high ceilings and large glass windows located on one of the town's busiest streets, right across form a big pharmacy and the best French bakery and ice cream parlor in town. In the back of the store stood the house, separated from it only by a large cemented courtyard.

The house itself was not as charming as the one we had left in Meknes, but it was larger, functional, and equipped with all the modern facilities and appliances we had grown used to. Without a doubt, the best feature of the house was its garden. Although located on the side of the house with no open direct access from the rooms, it had a small summer pavilion at the far end of its main alley and a hedge of young fir and cypress trees bordering the wall that enclosed the property. Best of all, our house was situated at a reasonable walking distance from the primary school my siblings and I were going to be attending during our formative years.

**

It was a beautiful sunny morning in the fall of 1962 when I apprehensively let go of my mother's hand and stepped through the gate of my new school. It was the first day of the new semester, and a multitude of children were already gathered in the large courtyard. A few had joined groups of kids they seemed to know and with whom they were sharing anecdotes and laughter while others, stood idly by awaiting directives.

My mother had helped me get dressed in the new pleated navy skirt and short sleeve white shirt she had bought for me a week earlier. She also made me wear the requisite long sleeved school smock that I thought spoiled the whole thing, since it hid my brand new outfit. But there was no way around it. My mother wanted to follow the school rules exactly as they had been laid out for them when she and my dad had registered me only two weeks before for the new school year.

We had almost been turned down due to the lateness of our application, had it not been for my dad's insistence and legitimate explanations. We had just moved to Sidi Kacem, and the school had been closed for the summer vacation. The principal had finally agreed and I officially accepted. I had no idea what to expect, of course, being the first in the family to attend a French school. My uncle had expressly urged my parents to enroll me in *l'Ecole La Bruyère*, which was part of *la Mission Universitaire et Culturelle Française (MUCF)*. After its independence in 1956, Morocco signed a convention with France to continue providing educational assistance under the aegis of the MUCF because the country sorely lacked teachers and establishments. There simply was no other acceptable alternative in the township, especially for girls.

I could still see my mother lingering outside and looking serious and proper in her brand new European suit— a light gray two-piece outfit cut close to the body, with the skirt reaching just below the knee. Her hair was pulled back in a neat bun and she was holding a small leather purse that

matched her shoes. She actually looked a little too formal next
to the other mothers standing on the sidewalk, but she definitely fit right in.

This was not the first time she had dressed like a European
woman. As soon as we arrived in Sidi Kacem, and to the consternation of my dad, she'd started wearing Western clothes
when she ventured outside the house and in the store. Some
of those were handed down from Abderrahim's wife, among
other things. And when her brother gave her some money on
the side to buy her children new clothes and schoolbooks for
me, she got herself a new suit as well.

I was way too young and too nervous myself that day to
read her emotions. But I can imagine what she might have felt
watching me enter the brave new world of French education
and culture. As she let go of my hand that morning with a
mix of anxiety, trepidation, and hope, she may very well have
wished in her heart that my destiny be forever set on a course
toward a bright new future. She admitted to me, much later,
that she had also vowed to herself that, for as long as she lived,
my education would never be cut short by the altar of matrimony, not that I ever was in any danger of that happening to
me.

I was six years old when I started first grade, or CP, which
stands for *Cours Préparatoire*, and when they called my name,
distorting it in the way Westerners often do when reading
transcribed Arabic names, I knew to follow the kids who had
been called before me.

Mme. Blanche, a plum, jovial woman with very short
curly blond hair, welcomed the children in the classroom with
a broad smile and friendly individual greetings. I was last
in the queue, and I hesitated when she spoke to me. She was

using foreign words that I could not comprehend, though her eyes were telling me it was alright. I just kept looking at her smiley green eyes, at once fascinated, speechless, and petrified.

She gently took my hand in hers and led me to my seat. More than two-thirds of the children in the classroom were Europeans; all seemed to speak French fluently. I did not know a word of it and, in that instant, felt terribly lost and lonely. The whole morning I bravely tried to imitate what the other kids were doing and mostly kept to myself, trying very hard not to burst into tears.

That first morning in school I still remember intensely. I ran into my mom's arms when she finally picked me up for the customary noon-to-two lunch break, and I finally allowed myself to cry. During the walk back home, she held my hand and comforted me as best she could.

"It's all too normal to feel lost the first day, honey," she reassured me, squeezing my hand tight.

But her words did not achieve their purpose. I felt utterly desolate. I was still weeping when I got home and my dad greeted me with a question mark on his face.

"What's wrong, daughter?" he asked.

"I don't understand what they're saying, *baba*. I don't want to go back," I managed between my tears. My dad looked intently at me, leaned over me, and said in a soft deliberate voice:

"Wafa, listen... Listen to me. You will learn, and you will learn very well, and one day you will be as great as Dr. Bint el-Shati."

I don't know why his words, at that very instant, had such an unforgettable effect on me, an effect that struck me deeply and has lingered in my soul, shining like a twinkle at the end of the darkest tunnels of my life.

Later, I discovered who that person was: Dr Aisha Abdul-Rahman, 1913-1998, (pen name Bint el-Shati)—was Egypt's leading female Islamic writer and scholar. She was the author of some forty books on the history and structure of Islamic scripture; literary criticism; a dozen novels and short story anthologies as well as hundreds of research papers and newspaper columns.

Obviously, at that moment of distress, I had not the slightest idea of who that "doctor" could be, or what made her so great, and I really didn't care then. It was not his words so much as his tone, which expressed his profound belief in me and acted like a shot of confidence and certainty in my subconscious mind. Just like that, my tears stopped flowing. I raised my eyes and looked right back at him. He held my wet face in his hands and nodded as if to confirm what he'd just said. Then he planted a small kiss on my forehead, turned on his heels, and left the room.

After that day, I never again let myself fall apart in school. I completed that first year in CP with barely good enough results to enter 2nd grade. And even though I was kept back another year in that grade, I finished it the second time around, ranking at the top of my class, as I did nearly all following grades in elementary school after that.

My father took the time many evenings during my first year to patiently help me learn to read and write the French language, going over all the words I had been introduced to in class. He made me repeat each syllable, working on its pronunciation carefully, and then guided my hand while I scribbled each word on a small black slate board with a piece of white chalk until I mastered it.

That particular time created an indelible bond between my father and me, one that only grew deeper as he began to teach me his faith and strong moral values.

He first told me the biblical stories about Abraham and Moses and Ramses and others, awakening in me a sense of wonder and awe. Then he taught me a couple of prayers and eventually how to use those prayers to pray the way Muslims do, by kneeling down and bending over, putting my forehead to the ground in complete submission to God. At no time did he make me feel compelled to practice a rite. He was just initiating me as a father was supposed to, expecting of course that I would become a good believer and a good Muslim, and above all a loving, moral, and tolerant human being, in his image.

Yet, though my sense of morality, love, justice, and fairness grew strong, my religious conviction never came close to matching his, far from it. I believed in God and I wanted to please my dad, but I only prayed sporadically and on special occasions, not unlike the way my mother practiced the faith, rather casually, with periods of added seriousness during the holy month of Ramadan and other religious holidays.

My mother was going through an awakening of her own. Upon her arrival in Sidi Kacem, she had noticed and applauded the way Western women were free to interact with men outside their homes; how they were educated enough to hold jobs as teachers, doctors, nurses, secretaries, and shopkeepers; how they seemed to be in control of their lives in ways she could never imagine her sisters could control theirs. And so she determined to change the course of her life.

She began going to the store more often under the guise of lending a hand, especially taking over when my dad rested at home during his afternoon naps or when he left for one of his long weekends to Meknes or Moulay Driss. She slowly learned more French words as she struggled to communicate with the European customers; she even started taking a few French lessons. She then signed up for driving lessons, understanding that driving a car would give her new wings and the liberty to come and go as she pleased.

My father did not oppose any of her decisions to acquire new skills, although he never encouraged her either. He must have felt threatened by her increasing independence and self-confidence; at the same time, I suspect he secretly admired her determination during those early years, occasionally even poking fun at her. He loved to relate, for instance, how she'd driven right on top of the sidewalk when she was learning to drive in reverse and how her instructor had told her in a stern tone that they would make sure to remove all the sidewalks in town when she got her permit.

He can still recount that same story today, one of the few he can remember with fondness, and laugh merrily while telling it. Then one day, in October 1965, with a triumphal look on her face, my mother announced that she had just passed her road test and gotten her license.

The next thing she insisted on was that my father buys a better car. He was earning a bigger income and enjoyed free housing, yet he still drove a very old Renault *Dauphine*, so called because it was viewed as "heir" to its commercially profitable predecessor, the Renault 4CV. When it was created in 1956, the *Dauphine* was a major success story for Renault. Princess Grace of Monaco herself was known to be driving one in the early sixties. However, the Dauphine we owned was on its last legs and had already let us down on road trips. So my mother convinced him to get rid of it for a newer, though used, white Citroën DS-21, also known as a *Déesse*, or Goddess, thus called after its punning initials in French.

The new DS signaled a most definite shift in our family standing within the community. Unlike the *Dauphine*, which was a small and economical four-wheeler, the *Déesse* was a classy car with a futuristic, aerodynamic body design, and an innovative technology with a hydro-pneumatic, self-leveling suspension system, putting it far ahead of its time for decades to come. My siblings and I could not get enough of that particular feature, which made the car rise several inches off the ground allowing for the smoothest ride on the roughest roads.

At the wheel of the white Déesse, my mother looked positively glorious. She was in her mid-twenties and stunning with all the radiance and glow of youth; a young brunette Brigitte Bardot. She was watching her diet and had lost weight. She had mastered the art of applying make-up and styling her hair, and she dressed in fashionable and flattering Western clothes.

She would go back to the traditional caftan when dressing up for weddings and other special occasions, and she looked like royalty when she did. For it's a well-known fact in Morocco that no other style of dress can compare to the luxuriousness of the Moroccan caftans, which women of a certain standing wear in great pomp during every festive event. My mother was already totally in the know and the latest styles did not escape her.

My father's love for her grew bigger too, and with it a ferocious, all-consuming jealousy. Her beauty and charm made her stand out and be noticed, but so did her sweetness and genuine caring for others. She was far more approachable and popular than he could ever be. Making matters worse, the first impression people had when meeting my parents was that my mother was his daughter. Also, because the store was owned by her brother, most people addressed him by her maiden name, which never failed to irritate him further.

But it wasn't just her presence in the store that was a constant point of contention. He was not only envious of all the attention she was getting from, and giving to, others; he even grew resentful of his own children, the interest she took in them and the money she spent on their clothing and entertainment. There was endless fighting over the latest outfits she had bought for us and hidden away from him until he saw us wearing them. He complained about the little attention she paid him compared to the dedication she showed us. He couldn't stand that she'd take such pleasure taking us to the town cinema on a Sunday afternoon, or to the ice cream parlor on a school break, or to the beach on a summer vacation. He'd explode in fits of rage:

"Do you think I'm Pharaoh going around spending all that money?" he shouted at her in disgust, and she just shut him off by screaming back at him that he didn't seem to have any problem with his drunken parties and weekend getaways.

In the end, she always did what she had in mind, either ignoring his outbursts or confronting him head on, forever acting like a rebellious child with him. Incredibly, her defiance only made her dearer to him, his swelling helplessness and despair notwithstanding. More than ever, she was intent on following a path that was to lead her out of the course that had been preordained for her by her gender.

4

The Emancipation of Saadia

In the winter of 1965, Uncle Abderrahim asked my mother and Uncle Latif to accompany my grandmother for a cataract operation in Madrid. The procedure was considered more complicated than usual, and her doctor had explained that it would be best to have it done in Europe. The trip was to last almost two months, and Mom had to ask my father for his written authorization to apply for a passport. No woman could then get one without the consent of her spouse, father, or brother. None of her sisters had owned one or travelled abroad. To say that she was very excited with the opportunity to visit a European capital and take a plane for the first time would be an understatement. She was literally beside herself.

Grandma's cataract operation was a success, and my mother returned home from her trip with more than sparkles in her eyes and wonderful gifts for her children. My sister and I got our first dolls ever, and my brothers received a remote-guided plane and an electric train. But my mother had also breathed, in deep gulps, the free air of a completely different society, one that was homogeneous in its Western identity and its budding social liberation.

Her own emancipation was more complex because it was taking place in Morocco, a country where the only freedom possible for a woman required that she immersed herself in a foreign culture and embraced it. It also meant that she had to be constantly fending off the implicit condemnation of all sorts of people around her, from her husband to her more traditional relatives to the strangers she interacted with in the course of her daily routine.

Arab women who adopted Western ways had to learn to live with a disapproving society and ignore the ever-so-pervasive cultural concept of shame, or *"ah'shouma"* as it is called in Moroccan Arabic. My mother instantly recognized the meaning of individual liberty in the streets of Madrid. In her mind, the road ahead was being revealed in ever-clearer focus, even if she did not yet know how long her journey would take or where it would take her.

Unfortunately, my grandmother enjoyed her improved eyesight only briefly. Shortly after the operation, she suffered a major thrombotic stroke that left her almost paralyzed and dependent on others. All four of her daughters took turns to be at her side, attending to her needs for weeks at a time. My mother, whose children were all young, was on call during our school breaks. We would then leave for Rabat, where my grandmother had returned to live after my grandfather passed away. Her daughter Aisha, and five of her sons, were settled there already.

But in spite of the distance, her three other daughters, Zhor, Fatma, and my mother, would not think of dodging their duty no matter how difficult it was for them to manage both their households and be present at their mother's side so far from home and for so long. They each somehow found a way to serve their time as best they could, Mom by bringing along her kids, and my aunts their husbands.

During most of her infirmity and ill-health, my grand-mother was living in a big villa with a wooded garden in one of the most exclusive residential neighborhoods of Rabat, the *Souissi*. She shared the house with one of her sons, Hak and his companion of two years, Jacqueline. My uncle Hak was four years older than my mother and perhaps the most gentle, mild-tempered brother of all. After he attended *l'Ecole Spéciale Militaire de Saint-Cyr* in France, he had returned to live in Rabat and taken his mother in with him.

In 1963, while at a party for the Association of French Students, a friend introduced him to Jacqueline, and from that moment on, they lived together through thick and thin, for better or for worse, until his untimely death twenty-six years later in the summer of 1989, at the age of fifty-three. They never had any children of their own, but they could be counted on to provide love and support to many nieces and nephews, and my siblings and me in particular, on more occasions than I can count.

Jacqueline was a French medical student whose parents had moved from Tunisia to Morocco when she met my uncle. To the chagrin of her parents, she chose to drop out of school and dedicate herself to the love of her life rather than com-plete her studies. She loved my grandmother as if she were her own mother and she took on the tasks of interacting with her doctors and administering her medication, two critical services which none of her uneducated daughters were able to provide.

Hak and Jacqueline occupied a spacious wing of the villa, opening up on a shaded lawn and a lighted pool around which they gave some of the most lavish parties in town. Uncle Hak and his two youngest and closest brothers, Latif and Khalid, were always surrounded by attractive women, mostly European, and every young man in Rabat wanted to be part of their circle of friends. Their parties were well known for their buffets, open bars, jazz and rock music, and dancing. They lasted till daybreak, often ending in the pool.

The highlight of our stays at Grandma's house was the mornings after the parties. My siblings and I would get up early and run to the gathering site before the employees had begun cleaning. Crawling on our hands and knees, we hunted for coins that had fallen off the guests' clothes when they stripped them off to jump in the pool.

Those were often rowdy parties in which my mother did not partake much. But she participated enough to enjoy the free-spirited fun of a Western lifestyle widely different from the traditional conservatism of her upbringing. The young European women themselves were acting out in ways unheard of at earlier times, encouraged by a nascent feminist movement that was taking on a whole new impetus thanks to the dissemination of oral contraceptives and the emerging calls for women's liberation throughout Europe and North America.

During one such early visit to Grandma's side, my mother discovered tennis. It happened one pleasant spring afternoon when her brother Khalid, the baby of the family, asked her to come along while Jacqueline and a nurse stayed with Grandma. She quickly accepted, happy to get out of the house and returned again a few days later.

With curiosity and delight, she watched her brothers and their friends play on the clay courts of a tennis club in Rabat, and before long, had decided that that was something she wanted to try for herself. She borrowed a racquet from Khalid and a pair of shoes from Jacqueline, and took her first lesson. That was all it took for her to be hooked on the game, which became a great passion for the rest of her life—not that she ever excelled in playing it herself, though she took lessons

and practiced for years. She remained an avid tennis fan and
watched the major tournaments on TV until the very end of
her life.

Shortly after that first try, she bought herself a full outfit
and new racquet and she went back home determined to continue her lessons in Sidi Kacem. I don't know this for a fact,
but she may very well have been one of the first Arab women
in Morocco to play tennis at that time. It was all too much for
my poor father, who could not believe his eyes when he saw her
out on the court, shamelessly flaunting one of those short white
tennis dresses women wore in those days.

She literally attracted a crowd of gawking kids—ball boys,
trainers, and club employees—every time she ventured on the
court for a game with a friend or a lesson with a trainer. She
wouldn't give it up in spite of her husband's adamant opposition and their quarrels following every one of her appearances
at the Sports Club of Sidi Kacem. Luckily, it was a private club
attended mostly by European families, so there was no scandal
or outcry in town as my father had feared there would be.

That never even occurred to my mother. She did not understand, or wish to acknowledge, how deeply shocking her behavior
could be perceived by the standards of the society she was born
into. She so completely identified with her brothers' lifestyle that
she'd never stopped to consider the alternative or listen to the
voice of reason or naysayers. This was partly due to her circumstances and ambivalent environment: a country in which two
different worlds increasingly lived side by side, a modern French
society and a traditional Arab Moroccan culture.

Up until independence, the two worlds had co-existed without substantial interaction or overlapping. Following the end
of the Protectorate, however, a growing number of Moroccans,
mostly members of the nascent affluent middle class and bour-

geoisie had begun infringing upon the world of the Europeans. My mother, in the footsteps of her brothers, had chosen that new world without hesitation because of the freedom she felt entitled to. Another explanation for her obliviousness to people's criticism, and perhaps the more important one, was her immaturity and spirit of adventure, two personality traits she never outgrew.

Naturally, my siblings and I were completely on her side and acted like her little foot-soldiers shielding her from our father and his obnoxious character. She was so much more fun, and he was, literally, the Grinch who tried to steal Christmas all the time, forever "staring down from his cave with a sour, Grinchy frown."

And sadly, my father seemed as if he never could have any enjoyment, at least in our company. For my mother knew he had had a lot of good times, before he married her, and still did whenever he could, after he tied the knot. However, she would never acknowledge that he also sought his pleasure in the futile hope of healing his heart from the pain his young wife's hatred caused.

In fairness to her, the reason she would never admit a shred of responsibility in my father's persistent vices was that he had long been a known offender and recidivist. His family knew all along that at, thirty-three—and in those days that was considered old—he had remained a hardened bachelor with no desire to get tied down by a wife. They were aware that his idea of bliss was to spend time with friends, women of little virtue, and plenty of wine, not to mention the occasional hashish pipe—all of which he did even as he considered himself a pious and committed Muslim.

But what might appear as a hypocritical conduct could easily be understood, as my father saw it, in the context of balance and moderation in all things. In other words, love of God did not preclude a little hedonism on Earth. And so my father's period of self-indulgence did not, in his mind at least, negate the true and sincere nature of his religious devotion.

The problem was that, very often, he showed little restraint in his hedonistic pursuits. His mother, and his siblings, had known that about him but kept it hush-hush, never speaking of it in public. They had hoped in earnest that marriage and family would put some sense in him. They had not anticipated that the woman they chose for him would be the wrong one for the job.

All the events of those days: the interaction with store customers, the trip to Spain, the rubbing elbows with carefree party-goers, the tennis lessons, all contributed to my mother's mounting ambitions. Her early successes emboldened her further and led to her decision to enroll in the L'Oreal School of Hair Styling and Coloring in Casablanca, which trained new hairstylists during a ten-week summer program.

It had been only four years since we moved from Meknes to Sidi Kacem, and she had grown into a vastly better informed, knowledgeable, and confident young woman. She'd made many new friends and acquaintances at her tennis club and at the store, and she was keeping au fait of all sorts of events and developments outside her home. Understanding that a hairstylist's career could provide her with greater independence, she soon expressed interest in acquiring the professional expertise.

The L'Oreal School program was only available in Casablanca and required knowledge of French; her mastery of the language was still tentative, to say the least. But those were details, which my mother was not going to let deter her from her objective. She got her sister Fatma to replace her at Grandma's side and packed up all four of us children during the first weekend of the summer vacation of 1966. My father drove us to Casablanca and, after a couple of days, returned to work in Sidi Kacem. We happily stayed behind in Uncle Latif's apartment, a bright, contemporary twelfth-floor flat filled with cool modern furnishings.

My uncle Latif, perhaps the most charismatic and best educated in the family, was the eighth brother of the clan and barely a couple of years older than his sister Saadia. Following the advice of his older brother, Brahim, he had graduated from *l'Ecole Supérieure d'Agronomie de Rennes* in France, an agricultural-science college, with the intention of working with him on his land. When he returned, he chose instead to stay in the city and work with his brother Abderrahim.

His was a booming office-furniture business, which Latif helped re-structure and re-organize, significantly contributing to its growth. He was mostly stationed in Rabat, where the company's headquarters and his brothers were established, but he was setting up a foothold in Casablanca with the intention of expanding into the main economic and financial center of the country. He had also recently met Hélène, who lived in Rabat and was to become his first wife.

All in all it was no surprise that he wasn't using his apartment in Casablanca very much that summer. My mother could not have asked for a better location. In order for her children not to spend the whole day indoors, she had instructed the maid to take us to the beach of AinSebaa, only minutes away from the apartment, for a good part of the week. On other occasions, she was to take us for strolls on the city's main boulevards, with their eye-catching stores, and treat us to a movie matinee or an ice-cream cone.

The Casablanca of the 1960s had little if anything to do with its famous Hollywood depiction during the early days of World War II. The picture that, in the words of a New York Times travel reporter, made "this port city forever recall the black-and-white era of foggy steamships and fedora hats," was long gone. This was a time when the city was full of life and vibrant energy, beaming under the luminous light of its endless blue skies and bright sun, proud of its grand colonial boulevards with their wiry Art Nouveau architecture: the *Boulevard de la Liberté, Boulevard de Marseille,* and the landmark *Boulevard de la Gare* with its charming *Marché Central.*

If you cared to ask the young generation of that era, they would gladly tell of their vivid memories of Casablanca's striking Art Deco buildings, townhouses, department stores and bustling cafés, neo-Moorish palaces and hotels, and famed cinemas, such as the Rialto theater, the Opera, the Lynx and the Empire. This was a city where young people relished their afternoon matinees at the movies—S*partacus, Cleopatra, La Dolce Vita* or *Lawrence of Arabia*—and then gathered around a table at a sidewalk café, smoking cigarettes and dreaming of a world of boundless possibilities. My siblings and I were thrilled to discover the excitement of this big metropolis after the sedate life of our little town.

My mother started her training that Monday. She attended school six days a week and worked on her feet ten straight hours a day, returning home in the evening exhausted but pleased with her effort. Only on Sundays would Mom allow herself a well-deserved rest by joining us on the beach. When her program was over, she had somehow climbed another mountain and managed to graduate with flying colors.

5

The First Kiss

He followed her into the café, gesturing to the waiter with his hand that they'd be right back. He continued after her into the hallway leading to the ladies room. She didn't look back, but she felt his presence behind her. She had no idea where this was going, and she could not control her heart; it was now thumping in her chest like a wild beast. Her head was buzzing, her thoughts foggy and getting foggier.

She put her hand on the doorknob and pushed the door just enough to slip inside. But she couldn't close it behind her. He had already sneaked in right after her. He looked at her with intense, feverish eyes, waiting for her reaction. With his right hand behind his back and without turning around, he locked the door. She was avoiding the eyes, thinking she was going to faint from lack of oxygen. The small bathroom smelled of disinfectant and bleach. The light of day was filtering through a small window with a sanded glass pane. She was standing between the toilet bowl and the white sink on which she was leaning for support.

Without a word he got closer to her, put both hands on her shoulders, pushed her back to the wall and kissed her with his mouth open taking all of her mouth in his with incredible lust and passion. *Oh lord, I am lost*: That was not a thought, rather a realization of helplessness. She threw her head back under the force of his grip and closed her eyes. Spontaneously, she lifted her arms upward to take him in her embrace then his head in her hands and kissed him back with all the desire he had awakened, with her mouth open too, her lips hungrily reaching for his, panting hard, feeling the warmth in her loins and him getting harder against her.

Never in her life had she felt anything like the fire that kiss had suddenly ignited. It went on for what seemed like an eternity; time was standing still.

"I've been dying to do this since the day I first saw you," he whispered under his breath. "You're so beautiful; you've been driving me insane, completely insane."

He squeezed her arm while he was still kissing her lips, biting them lightly. Pulling her hair back with his other hand, he lowered his head to her throat, kissed her neck, licked her earlobe, and went back to her parted lips. It was all very fast paced, very intense, messy, getting out of hand. Then swiftly she felt his hand on her breast as he was pushing the fabric of her sun dress and then pulling her bathing suit strap down her shoulder, his fingers touched her naked breast.

She trembled at his touch, but she couldn't get enough of the taste of his mouth, of the sweetness of his tongue and the softness of his lips. She responded to his kisses with all the passion she could muster, deeply breathing the sun-tanning oil on his skin, and it all felt so staggering and so good, until she sensed his hand reaching down between her legs. She wanted to cry her desire, her longing... Oh, how much she wanted him... she so wanted... but... the sound of children screaming outside—no! She was mad. What was she doing?

A fleeting moment of consciousness flashed across her numbed mind: her four children were waiting on the beach for her... This couldn't be happening.

"Wait! *Stop* it," she heard herself finally say. "I can't do this." It was a sigh more than anything. She tried to push him away from her, tried to collect her thoughts, her senses...

"Shhhhh. Don't say that."

He seemed not to believe her and he went back to kissing her lips.

But it was over; the burning guilt had entered her brain and shattered the magic of the moment. She wanted to shout her pain and frustration.

Instead, she whispered, "You should leave. Please..." She didn't look at him.

"I can't do this. Just... go."

She finally met his eyes, and he looked hurt and incredulous, but he didn't say anything. He straightened his shorts and shirt slowly, still staring at her, brushed back his hair, then he gave her a peck on the cheek, unlocked the door, and left.

"I'm going to check on the kids," he said at last. She quickly locked the door after him, let herself down on the floor, and closed her eyes, trying to gather herself and overcome the deluge of sensations that had just submerged her, her nostrils still full of his scent.

She could not believe what had happened. She had known him for about two months, since he came over one Sunday afternoon and talked to the children on the beach. He introduced himself to her with a seductive smile.

His name was Youssef; he was a lifeguard in the summer, a middle school teacher the rest of the year. He couldn't be older than thirty, probably much less, mid-twenties. He offered to watch over the kids during the week, to teach them how to swim, and she readily accepted. He seemed friendly and looked so handsome, lean, and muscular, his hair lightened by the sun and his teeth bright white in the middle of his sunburnt face. She had felt the attraction between them right away, and she loved seeing him every Sunday when she and the children went to the beach together. He never failed to join them and spent a couple of hours in their company.

She'd enjoyed the ongoing flirtation; it had all seemed safe and innocent somehow, until that moment. She'd asked him where she could find a bathroom, and he'd offered to take her to the nearest café, explaining that it would be a lot cleaner than the public facilities set up on the beach.

Next to him, during the walk to the café, she had felt the rising sexual tension and lost all her poise—had let him follow her, wanted him to follow her. She could not explain it to herself. It had just happened, caught her off guard, and swept her off her feet, erasing any reasoning power she had left. And now she had known her first real kiss, her first lustful encounter, and it was as if she was born again, she had felt... *alive*. She knew her life would never be the same.

**

My two brothers had become fast friends with Youssef the lifeguard, playing ball, burying him under the sand, and learning to body surf the small waves. My sister did not mind him either. *I* did not like him a bit. For no reason at all, I just couldn't stand his jokes, particularly when they were at my expense. The others seemed to like his stupid tricks, though; one of his favorite was to pretend that he liked me so much that he was going to marry me. I was ten already and old enough to know better, but at the mere thought of matrimony,

I would just fall apart and cry my heart out. For years, my family laughed about that joke and my bizarre reaction to it, and for years I could not understand or explain what it was that had provoked my tears and my irrational fear.

Were it not for my mother's intimate confidences much much later, neither my siblings nor I had any recollection of anything of particular interest that last Sunday on the beach. Our summer vacation in Casablanca was fast coming to a close and we were already thinking of school starting in a couple of weeks. That fall, and for the first time, all four of us were going to be attending *l'Ecole La Bruyère* in Sidi Kacem.

My mother's new hair salon was adjacent but separate from my uncle's store. It had its own entrance and window on the street, and, because of its great location and pleasing décor, it immediately attracted a clientele. She had been planning its design over the summer and had my dad inquire into the cost of the equipment, necessary plumbing, and renovations. A meeting with her brother Abderrahim had cleared up all the authorizations and financial hurdles, and nothing seemed to be standing in her way. The opening took place about a month after school started, and it immediately gave my mother, not only new financial leverage, but also a belief in herself that was both exhilarating and empowering.

The school year went by painfully, though. My mother threw herself into her new occupation and neglected her home and children altogether. Her relationship with my dad was worsening as her old dislike of him turned into deep-seated, unrelenting hatred. My father seemed even more bewildered, and found solace only in drinking and crabbiness, which did nothing to improve the tension in the family.

She would not have sexual relations with him, if she could avoid it; no longer willing to put up even with the smallest form of intimacy she used to tolerate from him. Things had changed, going from bad to worse, and he did not know why or what to do about it, except showing his discontent with his unpleasant scowl. He withdrew further into himself, talked less, and looked for his old friends' companionship whenever he could. He travelled back to Meknes frequently, drank heavily, started attending Moussems and religious festivals again, and slowly deserted his responsibilities at the store.

My siblings and I spent more time at Aunt Fatma's house. She was a fabulous cook and enjoyed spoiling us. Her husband, Uncle Mehdi, entertained us by cracking jokes and making fun of her. He would ask her for his doctor-prescribed "dietetic meal" after he had just fully enjoyed the delicious specialty she had prepared for lunch or dinner. At other times, he made hilarious faces for our benefit when she fell asleep in front of the TV and snored loudly with parted lips. He was also able to make our warts disappear within days by lightly spitting on them, first thing in the morning, and then rubbing the saliva into the wart with his finger. We thought he was a magician, at once fascinated and sickened by his wizardry.

The following summer, my grandmother passed away. She was sixty-five. The entire family came together for her funeral in Rabat, including my father's side of the family. Of all her sisters', my mother's bereavement was the most heartbreaking. She was devastated and grieved for days on end. When she returned home at last, she found herself confronted with my dad's professional neglect. She had no choice but to assume his load and cover for him at the store while attending to her salon at the same time. The world slowly seemed to be caving in around her. This went on for almost a year as things gradually came unglued.

The political situation in Morocco at that time had also been showing signs of profound popular discontent. The country was beleaguered by mounting economic problems, uncontrollable demographic growth, a soaring unemployment rate, and a continuous rural exodus into the urban centers. The opposing political parties were uncooperative and irreconcilable, the king unable to form a government of national union as he had wished. After massive political upheaval and rioting in Casablanca in 1965, Hassan II personally assumed full executive and legislative powers under a *State of Exception*, which was to remain in effect until the seventies. This was the beginning of an era that came to be known as the *Years of Lead* (*Les Années de Plomb*), so-called because of the ruthless and cruel political repression that ensued throughout the land.

My family's own years of turmoil began in earnest in 1968. Uncle Abderrahim, who was expanding in Casablanca on a big scale, was no longer interested in keeping his mismanaged Sidi Kacem store, especially after some troubles erupted between him and his partner in that venture. It was decided that the store was to be sold—and, with it, Mom's hair salon.

That's when my mother determined that it was time to move to the big city. That summer, while my father stayed behind to oversee the store closing and assure the smooth transition to the new owners, she rented the first floor of a two-family house in *les Orangers*, a picturesque Rabat neighborhood. By the fall, and with the help of Auntie Jacqueline, she had enrolled my two brothers and my sister at *l'Ecole Lamartine*, a French elementary school nearby; I was accepted in the *Lycée Descartes* in 6th Grade.

For almost a year, the store's ownership transfer was bogged down by partnership and legal issues, and my father travelled back and forth between Sidi Kacem and Rabat, getting desperate about his precarious situation, both professionally and emotionally. He would certainly have preferred that we returned to live in Meknes and for him to look for a job similar to the one he had held in the past. But under no circumstance would my mother even consider that possibility. She was happy to be away from my father, and she started fantasizing about life without him, toying with the idea of leaving him and opening a hair salon in Rabat.

Only in Morocco then, family laws were entirely governed by traditional Islamic Sharia Law, and a woman could not get a divorce unless her husband decided to grant her one or simply repudiate her, neither of which my father had any intention of doing, for he neither believed in divorce, nor did he want to be separated from his wife and children.

Their life together was turning into a tragedy of sorts. As often happens within dysfunctional couples, the more she wanted to run away from him, the more he refused to let her go. Fortuitously for him, two factors worked in his favor. First, my mother's fantasy was still in its infancy and had not yet taken hold in her mind; second, her family put considerable pressure on her to return to her senses, for her children's sake.

Uncle Abderrahim once again came to the rescue, in the summer of 1969, by getting my father a manager's position in an orange grove farm in Bou Maiz, a few miles south of Sidi Kacem. The news was perceived as a death sentence by my mother, who ultimately had no choice but to pack up and return to her husband's side. There was no middle or high school in Sidi Kacem or its province, so while my siblings returned to *l'Ecole La Bruyère* in Sidi Kacem in the fall, I stayed in the boarding school of the Lycée Descartes in Rabat.

The farm in Bou Maiz was beautiful. There were hundreds of hectares of all kinds and varieties of citrus fruit— oranges, clementines, grapefruit, lemons, and limes, planted in long rows and irrigated via a modern system of canals. In the spring, all the trees came alive with sweet-smelling orange flowers that could make one dizzy, so strong was their perfume. We had never drunk so much fresh-squeezed orange juice or eaten more delicious oranges and clementines as when we lived in the midst of those magnificent groves. To this day, I cannot find an orange that tastes as sweet and delectable.

The house, which had been built by French settlers, was as typical as to be found in the heart of Provence. It had a red slate roof, wood-burning fireplaces, shaded verandas, and a big, stone construction that gave it an imposing allure. Adding to its appeal, magnificent, tall cypress trees bordered the long path leading up from the main road to the house. The beauty of our new property somewhat reconciled my mother with her lot, and she appeared, at least on the surface, to have accepted her new circumstances.

She initially occupied herself with gardening and taking care of a vegetable patch near the house. She would also play tennis in the town after she dropped off my siblings in school in the morning. But soon, she again got involved with the daily running of the plantation business, especially when she felt my dad was slacking off and not performing his duties adequately. She'd hop on, and drive, a tractor if there was a shortage of workers, or keep the books if they were falling behind. The quarrelling and infighting resumed anew, and I was glad I was away in school for weeks at a time, coming home only during long school breaks and vacations.

Before I was kept away in boarding school, I was not a particularly sociable and outgoing child. In fact, I was a rather withdrawn and serious girl. My favorite pastime was reading, reading, and reading some more. I read at home, taking my books to the dinner table until my father rebuked me and put a stop to it, and then I ate as fast as I could so that I could return to my story. I read on vacation, staying indoors, until I was pushed outside for fresh air, and then took my fiction with me, too. I read during visits to relatives, whom I barely heard or replied to when they spoke to me until my parents reprimanded for my rudeness. I read during long road trips until I got car sick and threw up by the roadside. I read late into the night until my mother showed up at the door and turned off the light, and then, as soon as she left, crawled under the cover and read with a flashlight. I was so totally absorbed by the fantasy world books opened up for me that I grew up without even knowing it. I cannot remember times when I played with dolls or other little girls, not even my own sister.

Perhaps reality was too raw for me to make sense of and cope with, so I wanted nothing to do with it. I was well aware of my parents' ongoing, all-consuming discord, and as much as I tried hard to keep out of it, it was too hard not to side with my mother. She was closest to me and my siblings, the one to look after us and our well-being, our friend and confidante. At the same time, I was unconsciously bewildered by my betrayal of my father, whom I loved and needed to admire in spite of his off-putting character and cantankerous demeanor.

From birth and during my early years, I had known I was his favorite child. I had never really acknowledged my profound attachment to my father, was not even consciously aware of it. In fact, I had never admitted to it openly for fear of alienating my mother, whom I also wished to protect. As to Mom, she was in many ways far too juvenile and uneducated to realize the damage the rift between her and my father was having on her children, and especially on me. So until I reached my teenage years, books remained my dearest and most reliable refuge.

6

Forbidding Years

Sleeping at last... ending the pain... erasing the present...

My thoughts were slowing down, the pounding in my chest finally quieting. I took a deep breath and closed my eyes, feeling the wet pearls of sweat forming on my upper lip. The room was dark, the air moist and heavy. Faraway thunder began rumbling. It was soon going to rain. I was lying on a mattress on the floor with my clothes on, my dark hair spread on the white pillow, my left cheek still burning. But my fear was now gone.

In my head, the images of that evening were flashing on the blank screen of my mind like one of those black-and-white silent movies playing in slow motion. She had slapped me across the face with incredible violence and with all the fury she couldn't rein in.

"Because of you, I ruined my life. I sacrificed it all for *you* and this is how you repay me!" she spat the words at me like a snake.

I did not know which hurt the most, the blow or the words. But I couldn't stop to think; I screamed back at her, my hand on my burning cheek.

"*You* are destroying *our* life now. You only think of your-self, always... only you... but what about *him*? What about *us*?" I threw my arms wide open, I could still see the tears in my dad's eyes as he left me standing outside the house. "I don't think he deserves such hate, such anger... all the time... every day. Just stop the insults... just stop."

I couldn't speak any more; I was choking on my words, tears streaming down my cheeks, my face distorted with rage and despair. I hated her so much, wanted to hurt her back, have the last word. But I could see in her eyes, she was not going to let me. She was beyond mad at me; she couldn't believe I could be defending my father again, taking his side so blatantly, knowing what I knew.

"Get out of my face, or I'm going to *kill* you, you hear?" she hissed.

She turned around and left me standing there in the middle of the patio, sobbing noisily, defeated; I slowly walked to the small bedroom I occupied with my siblings and was relieved to find it empty. Through my tears, I could see the mattresses lined up directly on the ground with the sheets folded under the pillows. I sat down on the edge of one of them, howling even louder.

Holding my head in my hands, I let my grief pour out of me like air out of a balloon. My head was killing me. Oh God, *why*? *Why* is this happening? I can't *take* this any longer; can't *live* like this anymore... Couldn't she see how much pain I was in? Oooh, my head!

I stood up and walked to the bathroom next door. There was no one there; it was all silent, and I felt forlorn. My siblings were all watching TV in the living room on the other side of the house, trying to stay out of the storm that had once again broken out between Mom and me.

We had been staying, "camping" really, at Uncle Latif's small house in Kenitra for two weeks already amid constant and palpable tension, and they were getting used to our ferocious displays. This had become a common occurrence since I started middle school. We would be bucking heads, usually about Dad, screaming at each other like two shrews in the market square, but it had never gone this far.

My father had found out where we were staying and had showed up to once again persuade his wife to return to her senses. She had refused to let him in, asked me to see him off. Certainly she hadn't hit me in quite a while, and never with such cruelty. Previous episodes of physical mistreatment were mostly part of the way she felt she had to discipline her children—mostly me—for being insolent or disobedient, which I was frequently guilty of. I had just turned fourteen and quite ahead of my years. I was no longer a child and felt more like her equal, if not in age in maturity, I thought.

I stopped in front of the medicine cabinet and glimpsed my distorted, swollen face in the mirror. I looked hideous... I turned the faucet on and let it run for a while; the noise of the water rushing down the spout was soothing. I leaned over and splashed my face with the cool water, blowing my nose loudly. My temples were throbbing, my head aching, murky thoughts jamming my mind. I felt queasy; the ache in my head wouldn't let up.

I pulled open the door of the cabinet and reached for the aspirin bottle, twisted the top off, took a handful of the little white tablets, and put them in my mouth. I reached for the plastic cup packed with toothbrushes on the sink, emptied it all at once, filled it with water and drank it. Then I took another handful of the little white tablets and flushed them down my throat again, and I did it again and again until it was empty. Little hiccups came out of my throat.

I felt bloated and in a daze. I could still see my dad calling me out, the pitiful expression on his face as he implored me to talk to my mother, to convince her to return home. I kept shaking my head as if to say it would be futile... really useless... Mom was too stubborn... never listened to me anyway... all hopeless.

I reached for another bottle full of pills, another pain killer, *Optalidon*, an anti-migraine prescription drug, and went through the same deliberate, methodical gestures until I had swallowed all of its content. It was hard to finish off the pills, and I started choking a bit as if I were going to throw them all up. But I persisted, pushing past my body's reflexes.

I had no real intent or understanding of what I was actually doing at that moment, but I cannot be sure. Somewhere, somehow, like a small bird crossing a cloudy twilight sky, the thought crossed my disturbed, gloomy mind, a fleeting morbid inspiration. I was terrified but hopeful still I would be found in time and rescued just before dying, and then, *then*, my mother would be plagued with guilt and sorrow. This was really my revenge, her punishment; I was going to have the last word after all.

At last, I backed off the sink littered with toothbrushes, caps, and empty aspirin bottle, still clasping the *Optalidon* container in my hand. I had hesitantly returned back to the room and lay down on my back when, suddenly, the house was rocked by the crashing sound of lightning falling nearby. I barely budged. A beam of dazzling light brought the room out of its deep shadow for a brief second. I shivered a little, held my breath.

This is the end, I thought...

And the sky opened up and the rain came down like a torrent, washing away all the sins of the world, wakening the scents of the dried summer earth.

**

That night, Uncle Latif returned home earlier than usual. He was told I was in the bedroom, brooding after another bad fight with Mom. He found me lying in the dark almost unconscious, still holding the Optalidon bottle. Immediately, he called out for Mom, picked me up in his arms and rushed me to the hospital, where the emergency crew pumped my stomach. As I began emerging from my profound torpor, I dreamt I was in a state of crazed sexual arousal, pulling out my tubes and throwing myself at the intern, the nurse, and even my uncle before I ran under the shower to cool off. Only that was not a dream.

My mother told me I had indeed acted outrageously but that my doctor had reassured her that it happened sometimes and not to read anything into it. Coincidentally, my attending intern, Dr. Benhallam, was a cousin of my dad, and he took a particular interest in me, following me closely. This familial connection made it difficult for me to overcome the embarrassment I felt toward him for years afterwards.

Seventy-two hours later, I was sent home.

My botched suicide attempt changed nothing at all. Even worse, that terribly selfish act had failed to earn me the love and attention I was so in need of. When I tried to protest to Mom and put in plain words my pain, she felt she was under attack and compared my situation to her predicament. She believed *she* was the victim, not I, whom she always struggled to provide with a decent life, a good education, and bright prospects. It was the same recurring theme I had heard before, a long-lost argument. It never failed to shut me up and make me swallow my anguish hard, forever deepening my resentment of my mother.

And yet the summer of 1970 had begun as a time full of excitement. My mother had rented a very small, drab-looking "cabanon," (basic wood cottage), in Moulay Bousselham ("Moulay" for short), a little beach town with a sandy ocean beach and a lovely lagoon. Many Europeans from all over the region, from Meknes to Rabat, had built their summer cottages in Moulay and loved to spend their vacation fishing, boating, and playing cards. They held lively tournaments of pétanque and volleyball, and gathered for an anisette drink or dinner at the famous Miramar and Potinière. Year after year, they were joined by an increasing number of privileged French-speaking Moroccans who enjoyed the same things.

The atmosphere was convivial and pretty much everyone knew everyone else. I'd spent the school year away from home in boarding school, in 7th Grade, and so I'd become fairly independent and self-assured. I'd learned to smoke in hiding in the dormitory's bathrooms with a bunch of older girls and I was ready to put my books aside, date boys, and have some fun. My mother had picked up smoking as well, she barely scolded me, but I did not dare smoke in front of my dad.

In the Lycée that year, I'd had a crush on an older French boy, a senior, who never paid me any mind. He had blond hair and blue eyes, and he was the prettiest boy I had ever seen. He turned up at Moulay that summer; although I still was incapable of approaching him—he didn't even see me. Perhaps because of his lack of acknowledgement, I redoubled my effort to be noticed. I spent my days on the beach and participated enthusiastically in the evening activities.

Often at night, my sister and I met other teenagers and young people at the movies and then later in the small town's disco, where we smoked, kissed, and pretended to be cool. My brothers had their own friends and met them for their own play and games. My mother had met a group of friends too, and she partied as hard as any of us, happy to be rid of my dad, who showed up only infrequently.

Until he did, one time, when he arrived unannounced and found no one home.

It is unsettling to me that I had almost no remembrance of that particular day until my sister recently reminded me of exactly what happened—that Dad had had a vicious argument, and not just with Mom, when he showed up in Moulay that evening. He and I confronted each other in our first violent quarrel. I was very angry at him, and was impertinent to the point of contempt.

"Go ahead, hit me. Do it, if you're a man. Only you're *not* a man... you're a wimp." I was daring him with my face, within inches of his. My sister had been shocked by how much disrespect I showed and the episode had stuck in her memory with great clarity. I blamed him for being old-fashioned and sanctimonious, for not understanding any of our needs and aspirations, and for always playing spoiler.

Today, it is clear to me that I also resented him for not standing up for himself, for letting my mother emasculate him and deprive him of his dignity time and time again. I hated his weakness and obvious impotence! All he could ever do was retreat further into his isolation and display bitterness on his face for everyone to see. The clash between him and my mother was even worse that evening. She had been dropped off at our cottage by a young and attractive friend of her younger brothers. When Dad saw them, he literally exploded in anger and jealousy, and my mother answered him back with hatred and derision.

"Don't you *dare* insinuate anything improper, you spineless hypocrite drunk... we're on vacation to enjoy ourselves, no thanks to you. Why do you even bother to show up here anyway?" And so it went, with her words cutting deeper than knives, and my father throwing accusations around, unable to shut her up or control the situation.

Things went out of hand, with Mom breaking dishes and screaming hysterically. Finally, she ran out to the neighbors' house and called her brother Latif to come and take us out of there. We finished the last month of our vacation in Uncle Latif's summer rental in Kenitra, a few miles north of Rabat, awaiting Mother's next step.

Things could not have been easy for her as she tried to find a way to separate from her husband and keep her children. She came and went to and from Rabat, attempting to convince her older brothers to help her find a way out of her miserable marriage. Uncle Latif was fully supportive of her and helped us financially. But her oldest brother, Mohamed, with whom she had the least affinity, was steadfast in his opposition. He thought her conduct was reprehensible, and that her total independence could only lead to more embarrassment for the family. In the course of a heated argument and in front of us all, he slapped her viciously, ordered her to return to her husband and told her to thank God for what she had.

We returned from that visit seething against our uncle. None of us forgave him for a very long time. My sister said to me once that she had felt that slap as much as Mom, physically, as if she had been hit herself, and hated our uncle with all her might. She added that she remembered vividly the feeling of oppression and "imprisonment" we felt when we lived with Dad and completely identified with Mom.

But it was not her brother who compelled Mom to reconsider and go back to Dad one more time. The ordeal of my hospitalization, and my failed suicide attempt, had affected her more than she'd ever admit, not that she ever verbally expressed any guilt or responsibility. On the contrary, she rejected the blame that my father was squarely laying on her. If anything, she blamed him. My reckless act had complicated and undermined her effort, and she was frustrated.

Thus she was forced to return to the Bou-Maiz farm with my brothers for their last year in elementary school in Sidi Kacem. In the fall of 1970, they were entering 5th grade together. My sister was starting 6th grade and hence joined me at the Lycee Descartes' boarding school.

**

Strangely, in the absence of a mother's soothing empathy, I did not seek comfort or companionship in my sister. Just recently, I asked her on the phone if she recalled how she'd felt that summer.

"I was thirteen, for God's sake! I remember every detail," she answered with indignation.

When she finally revealed her thoughts to me, saying how devastated she'd been, she choked up. "I watched them take you away... I was so scared. I stayed awake all night until they came back at the crack of dawn and told me you were going to be fine." She stopped and I heard her cry at the end of the line.

"I'm so sorry!" I said at last.

I wished I could have been there to hold her in my arms and ask for her forgiveness. We were only one year apart in age, but it could have been decades for all I knew. After all those years, it is disconcerting to me to finally concede I had shunned my little sister, discounted her as if she wasn't even there. She had grown from a silent baby to an angelic and timid toddler, then to a talkative and often funny thirteen-year-old. Her relationship to our parents was more harmonious, less traumatic, because she was spared the closeness and involvement they had reserved for their eldest. Not having a sister she could play with, she had also turned to books for her leisure.

Nezha explained that I had always considered myself a grown-up and seen her as a child. Our parents had contributed to this estrangement by allowing me privileges that they denied her and our brothers, like staying up late at night, being allowed to watch TV shows they were not permitted to see, and generally promoting me as the mature child worthy of most of their consideration. I suppose I felt flattered then by my parents' endorsement and my little sister could only pose a threat to my established status in the family. So I did everything I could to put her down every time she made any attempt at getting closer to me.

Once again, as she often had in the past, Nezha seized this opportunity to tell me how incensed I had been when mother dressed us alike, something she liked to do when we were little, how mean I had been when she'd put on an old dress of mine that was passed down to her. She reminded me that I would sometimes give her a piece of clothing only to reclaim it in fits of jealousy when she looked good wearing it. I often belittled and put her down, widening the gap between us and alienating her further.

One other incident that had bruised her soul still stood out clearly in her mind while it remained buried deep under the rubble of my recollection. It took place during a party at home with our boyfriends, relatives, and acquaintances. We were, respectively, eighteen and seventeen. She was dancing to an oriental beat with her arms graciously undulating and her chest thrust forward in a slow and sensual motion, attracting admiration and praise, when I viciously lashed out at her.

"You have no breast to show for it. Leave that to me! In fact, you ought to put your hands in front of your face, since they're your best feature."

I had always made light of it, arguing that was just a bad joke. Finally facing up to the truth, I struggled with the guilt of my atrocious conduct. What kind of a person would do or say things like that? Feebly, I protested that I couldn't have. She swore it was all true. Deep down I knew, of course, she was right.

I feel profound sadness as I write these words and mull over the emotional wreckage in my past. We all want to believe in the inherent kindness of our nature, and the realization that evil can indeed find a place next to the goodness in our heart is profoundly disturbing. The hurt I caused my little sister in those days can never be undone. Ironically, neither can the hurt that I caused myself by rejecting her, condemning myself to loneliness at a time when I was so in need of the love and support of a sister. In the end, justice has somehow prevailed.

7

A Taste of Freedom

Within a year, on July 10, 1971, and again on August 16, 1972, King Hassan II survived two spectacular assassination attempts and credited his miraculous near-death escapes to his "divine protection," or "Baraka," as he called it. Worst of all, both coups had been plotted by two of his closest and most trusted generals.

The first, a random shooting conducted by two-hundred and fifty young cadets from a Middle-Atlas military school, occurred in bright daylight, during the King's lavish forty-second birthday party in his summer palace of Skhirat, a beach resort a few miles south of Rabat. In a bloody two-and-a-half-hour gun battle, the cadets killed ninety-two guests and dignitaries, including the conspiring general, and injured a hundred and thirty-three. The king was unharmed.

The second coup was led by General Oufkir, the kingdom's number two man at the time. Hassan II was returning from a three-week sojourn in France when his plane was attacked in flight by four F-5 Fighter jets. They shot at his aircraft and destroyed two of his plane's three reactors. A few passengers were injured, but the king himself once again escaped unscathed. He succeeded in driving himself away from the airport in a nondescript car after his plane crash-landed.

After being informed that the king had survived the attack, the fighter pilots shelled the airport, killing a few people, and continued shooting at the official motorcade en route to the palace in Rabat. Around midnight, it was reported in an official statement that General Oufkir had committed "suicide" and "shot himself" for his treason, in the presence of the king.

That summer of 1971, only a few days after the first botched coup in Skhirat, my mother dreamt of plotting her own marital "coup" against my father. She had been biding her time until my brothers graduated from elementary school. In her mind, it was unconceivable that she'd stay with her husband after her youngest children had gone off to middle school in Rabat. At long last, the stars aligned in her favor when Dad was abruptly fired from the citrus farm.

"I'm going back to Meknes to look for a government job," he told mom that night in a gloomier than usual tone.

She instantly realized this was the occasion she had been hoping for. She took a deep breath before she answered in a conciliatory voice, "Well, since the children are on vacation, I guess it would probably be better that they and I go to Rabat and spend the summer with my brother Hak."

My father was probably relieved that his wife didn't burst into angry blame and reacted so calmly.

As the summer drew to an end, it became apparent that Dad was prolonging his absence. His search for new employment was taking a lot longer than he had anticipated.

"Assuming he's looking for a job at all," my mother once blurted out in disgust.

In fact, I suspect, she was rather hopeful that he wouldn't find a satisfactory position, and that he'd remain in Meknes. Her yearning for freedom was taking shape and a way out had begun to surface in her mind. She wished to get rid of him at any cost; the question was how.

For the first time, she sought the advice of a lawyer-I am not sure how she came up with the idea, since this was not a customary approach to divorce in Morocco. The attorney informed her of a provision in Sharia law that allowed a married woman to divorce without her husband's consent. She could file on grounds of spousal abandonment of domicile, stipulating that my dad had disappeared and failed to support her and his children after he was sacked. This meant she had to wait for a few more months, praying that my father would not show up but stay away and out of touch.

By the fall, she had enrolled my two brothers in the Lycee Descartes' boarding school with Nezha and me. Then she moved to a small apartment in Salé while awaiting the outcome of her latest course of action. My father did not even have that address, and Mother quietly and anxiously counted the weeks that separated her from victory. She was lucky enough to have the monetary support of her sympathetic younger brothers, who paid for our schooling and living expenses. But she was acutely aware of the need to earn an independent living.

That opportunity presented itself when she found a small, fully equipped hair salon for sale in Rabat, not far from the old ramparts of the ancient Medina. After a mad scramble to find the necessary financing, she got a small loan from a family friend and shortly thereafter opened her new shop.

My father was in the dark about what his wife had in store for him. Amazingly, we did not see him once that entire summer or during the weeks and months that followed. At one point, we heard that he had briefly worked in a farm in the northern region of the Gharb, but that the main house on the farm was too small and insalubrious for our family to live in. And so after only a few months in that job, he made his way back to Meknes and kept a low profile, either out of guilt, or shame, or both. My mother was not asking anything from him, which made it easier for him to drift and hope for better days.

After school started in the fall, we only saw our mother sporadically too, and only during school breaks. She worked long hours, trying to keep afloat, pay back her debt, and make ends meet. But she was not complaining, so hopeful she was she would soon be free at last.

In the early summer of 1972, she moved from Salé to Rabat into what became our home for the next twenty years. The new residence was located in the center of the city, in Place Piétri, a lively neighborhood near the main train station and the quaint old *marché des fleurs*. It was also only minutes away from the beautiful *Cathédrale Saint-Pierre* and the Royal Palace, known as the *Méchouar*, with its contiguous mosque and white minaret.

The two bedroom apartment was right across the Alliance Française, on the fourth floor of a clean and modern walk-up building. Uncle Khalid had first rented it as a bachelor pad before passing it on to Mom. But, while the flat was too large for a single man, it was barely big enough for a family of five and, often, a live-in maid as well.

My siblings and I had to share a medium-sized, square bedroom with a small balcony overlooking low rooftops and the rear facades of neighboring buildings. It was sun-drenched every morning and for most of the day, and had two large built-in closets. The four of us slept in two bunk beds, and we shared, with mother, one large blue-tiled bathroom fitted with a bathtub, a sink and bidet, and a small window allowing in both daylight and fresh air. The toilet itself was in a space adjoining but separate from the bathroom, with its own door and casement. Next to our bedroom, the large airy kitchen opened onto a small laundry veranda with a sink and clotheslines.

On the opposite side of the apartment, mother occupied the master bedroom. Through its west-facing windows poured the golden afternoon sun. Adjacent to it, a fairly spacious, rectangular living room overlooked the street from a narrow covered terrace. In the dark, windowless vestibule, which every room opened onto, a dining room table with six chairs was squeezed in. A round, white low-hanging paper lantern radiated a warm glow in the center of the wooden table, providing the only light. This was far from luxury living and rather cramped, but it provided us with a convivial home where we entertained countless friends and enjoyed some of our greatest memories over the years.

At long last, the attorney notified my mother that she was officially a free woman. One unlikely morning, my father, who was staying here and there at different family and friends' houses, was summoned in front of a judge in Rabat. To compel him to agree to divorce, my mother formally promised to drop all charges and forfeit any subsequent legal action for child support or alimony. My father was deeply humiliated, faced with either granting her a divorce or going to prison. He chose to let her go. After more than a year of absence, he did not even find the courage to pay a visit to his children that day. He took the train right back to Meknes.

She had reached her goal. After almost twenty years in a reviled union, my mother had defeated her husband. As our father vanished from our lives, so with him did everything that was seemingly backward and old-fashioned. We had once and for all chosen our mother's camp, and it was firmly set on the grounds of modernity and French culture.

My father, I imagine, was devastated by the break-up, but he must have been far too exhausted by the relentless battle my mother had waged against him to put up a fight. Years later, he confessed to me that he had never quite understood what happened to him. To him, the shocking rupture was a cause of misery and mourning. He was without a job, without a home and family, homeless and desperately alone, he had no clue what would become of him.

His wife and children had deserted-no, "rejected, him, like a dog," he often liked to say... And yet, what crime had he been found guilty of? What had he done to deserve such hatred from those dearest to him? His bewilderment and despondency naturally led him to search for a modicum of comfort where he always turned to, in his faith.

In his hour of estrangement, my father soon was attracted to mysticism as preached by the Sufi mystics of Northern Morocco, in the region of Tetouan. Before long, he was drawn into the religious brotherhood known as the Tariqa and embodied in a shrine founded two centuries earlier by a descendent of an ancient Sufi clan. In Islam, the Tariqa is the "special way" of mystical Sufis. It adheres to the basic principles of Islam while encouraging its disciples to deepen their personal interaction with God with prayer and meditation. It is more spiritual, inclusive, and gentle and stands in contrast to the Shari'a, Islam's orthodox religious law.

Each Friday, the shrine would hold religious recitals and spiritual concerts in a characteristically Morocco-Andalusian style. There he met the woman he was going to marry within a year of his divorce.

Lalla Badia was everything that my mother never was and could never be. A deeply devout woman, a musician, and singer at the shrine, she was the unmarried daughter of its current leader.

A very gentle, very petite woman—she stood no taller than five feet—with light blue eyes, blondish hair, and a melodious voice, she was about thirty years old and still unmarried. She spoke in a soft voice with the accent of the people of Tetouan, skipping the "r" in a distinctive way, mixing Spanish words into Moroccan dialect. She had a cheerful disposition and was a dutiful and humble wife, cooking and cleaning for her husband and sharing his love of God, the Tariqa, and a modest traditional existence—all of which put her worlds away from my mother's aspirations and way of life.

Only a few weeks after the divorce was finalized, my father was invited to Fes by Uncle Mohamed, who met with him in one of his rug factories and offered him a managerial position. Not surprisingly, my uncle was still staunchly against his young sister's unconventional divorce. She had gone against his wishes, and he was not about to forgive her.

With little introduction, he sternly exclaimed, "You *can* get your wife back, you know," adding authoritatively, "by force, if necessary." He paused and stared at my father, waiting for an answer.

My father looked away, an expression of deep resignation and hurt about him. My uncle leaned over his cluttered desk agitated.

"I can tell you this, her divorce shenanigans are a fraud and unsustainable in a religious appeal," he said angrily.

My father kept silent, frowning, his thick black eyebrows forming a dark cloud over his eyes.

"No," he finally said, staring at his hands. "I no longer wish to compel her to live with me in eternal discord. After almost twenty years in a wretched marriage, it's time for all concerned to move on." He looked up at my uncle, his eyes betraying the beaten man he was. "I thank you for your support, Mohamed, but it's too late now, and it's for the best." He added in a sigh, "It's God's will, and I surrendered to it!"

When he returned to Fes to start in his new job, he was a newly married man. He appeared to have found closure. His union with Lalla Badia had helped him heal his wounds and calm his heart, although, I discovered later, his unrequited love for my mother never completely died away.

My mother never once paused to consider the consequences her divorce would have on her husband. I can still remember that sunny Sunday morning, sitting in my pajamas at the small kitchen table, buttering my toasted slice of French baguette ready to dip it into my bowl of café-au-lait.

"What's going to happen to Dad, now, mom?" I asked, concerned.

She was reaching for a clean cup in the cupboard overhead. She turned her head and glanced at me.

"He can go to hell for all I care," she said between clenched teeth. "He only got what he deserved as far as I'm concerned," she added, pouring the steaming black coffee.

She had her back to me, but from the tone of her voice, I knew better than to pursue the conversation. In my heart, I felt an unfathomable sense of loss and grief, although I could not put the feeling into words. So I pretended to quietly rejoice with her.

My siblings and I were without a doubt relieved that our parents' miserable marriage had finally ended. But we were also, consciously or not, ambivalent about the future, and there was a considerable level of financial and emotional insecurity that persisted in our minds despite our mother's cheerful optimism. At least, there was for me.

My mother had dreamed of her freedom since her wedding night, and it had finally happened. She had successfully liberated herself from the yoke of matrimony, willfully closing that chapter of her life, and was now ready for the next one. For a while, she displayed her official status of "divorcée" as if it were a trophy for everyone to see.

Since we resided in Rabat, my siblings and I were able to live at home and take the bus to school, which presented us with enormous unsupervised freedom. My brothers were twelve and thirteen years old, respectively, Nezha was about to turn fifteen, and I had just celebrated my sixteenth birthday. Our mother felt we were old enough to handle most situations on our own, and she to have a life, too. We had a roof over our heads and all basic necessities, but she had little understanding of our terribly contradictory emotional needs—or indeed even her own.

On the evening of August 16, 1972, one day after we celebrated my sister's fifteenth birthday, we were at home waiting for dinner when, suddenly, like an ominous presage of things to come, the summer sky was torn by the thunderous roar of the four F-5 jet fighters and loud artillery fire at the nearby Royal Palace.

8

The Loss of Innocence

Having escaped two military coups, the Moroccan king was pretty much divorced from his countrymen, isolated, and in constant fear of another rebellion. As never before, suspicious of everyone around him, he clung to absolute power. It would take three long years for Hassan II to finally devise a strategy—an expensive war in the sands of the Sahara that bankrupted the nation's treasury and kept it frozen in time—to once again unite his people and his opposing political parties around him.

Those years were marked by a period of intense confusion for me. I was in a state of limbo and felt terribly lonely. My mother appeared unaware of my inner turmoil, perhaps because of her own personal tumult. Shortly after her divorce, she began dating. At first, I was consumed by jealousy and resentment. Eventually, I got used to the idea of my mother seeing other men. In fact, my siblings and I even liked her first serious boyfriend, a smart and friendly young engineer whose widowed mother expressed alarm at the news of her unmarried son seeing a woman with four children, including two teenage girls. He and my mother bravely resisted his familial pressure, but after only a few months their liaison succumbed and they broke up.

My mother was well aware of the baggage she had to carry with her in any relationship. Four teenagers are a more than taxing load for a thirty-four-year-old, newly divorced woman desperate for true love and a little support. Yet she was too feisty, and she had fought too hard for her freedom, to let that hold her back. She was a gorgeous woman-child, often reckless, her zest for life contagious.

She was sought after and pursued by many suitors. Had she been living in Paris, her conduct would not have raised an eyebrow, but in Rabat she was living on the edge of appropriate behavior and needed to be considerably more discreet. There was too much gossip, too many rumors circulating around, fueled by the narrow-minded, conservative mentality of the Rabatis. Such tittle-tattle and hearsay never failed to make its way to my uncles' ears.

Fearing that their divorced sister's liberated behavior would bring shame and dishonor to the family name, her brother Abderrahim-himself under pressure from his associates and older brothers-bribed her into closing the hair salon that could have made her autonomous. Barely eighteen months after starting her own business, she foolishly agreed to return to the fold of dependency. The truth was that it had never been easy for her to be a hairdresser, and she was already drained by the long hours and back-breaking work.

Financial independence meant considerably more perseverance than my mother was ready to endure, especially at a time when she was beginning to savor her single life. Hence, when Uncle Abderrahim promised to put her on his payroll and deposit a fixed monthly allowance directly into her checking account, she accepted the offer. She sold her shop and no longer worked for a living. But if the stipend gave her a degree of security, it was barely enough to pay for rent and bare necessities.

It was not nearly enough to support the lifestyle she so desired—the hobbies, the car, the clothes—all the material things she needed to appreciate the leisure life, which her free time now allowed her to pursue. As a result, we were always in debt, falling behind on the rent, utilities, grocery bill, car installment, and auto insurance. We were incapable of living within our means. We even run a long monthly tab at the corner grocery store.

The more frivolous the spending my mother indulged in, the more fragile our financial situation became and the more distress I personally felt. Throughout most of my adult life, the monetary question was unlike any other psychological issue in my mind and remained my greatest source of stress. It never failed to plunge me into an emotional quicksand in which every attempt to fight my perceived entrapment sank me even deeper. It suffocated me to the point of actual physical pain, as if the world around me span out of my control, annihilating my vital need for order and security.

So it was that my parents' separation and our uncertain financial situation, combined with my adolescent growing pains, triggered yet another episode of severe depression. The summer of 1972 ended on a horrifying note for me. My mother simply could not comprehend the reasons behind my frequent crying fits and temper displays. A doctor prescribed a period of rest in a clinic, but in Rabat the only place that would accommodate a depressive teenager was the psychiatric hospital.

One late morning my mother, armed with the doctor's note had me admitted to the Hospital Al-Razi. By nightfall, I thought I would indeed go mad if I stayed in that place. It was terrifying to be among severely disturbed patients. I felt powerless, could not believe that my mother had left me there, and for hours frantically implored apathetic attendants to call her back, to no avail. Eventually, after a good dose of tranquilizers, I went to sleep.

When my mother visited me the following day, I ran into her arms in tears and begged her to rescue me.

"Please, Mom, please, get me out of here," I sobbed, "These people are really *crazy*, Mom. I'll die if I stay here. Please don't leave me..."

"Okay, honey, yes, of course, I will take you out of here." She was kissing me, holding me tight. I breathed her scent with relief and, for a brief moment, wished I were a little girl again. She immediately agreed to sign me out and took me back home with a Valium prescription. I shall never forget that harrowing day. I know its scarring memory was still lurking in my psyche years later when I was faced with a different tragedy, in a nightmarish role reversal I could never have fathomed then.

After my failed suicide attempt two years earlier and my ignored cry for help, my short stay in the mental institution did nothing to reconcile me with my mother. I begrudged her perceived carelessness, and my animosity toward her did not diminish. Mine was a grievance that only amplified with time and remained beneath the surface, ready to explode in a torrent of anger and sullenness.

This inner volcano, forever on the verge of erupting, was to haunt my close relationships all my life. Deep down, I did not trust my mother's judgment and I thought her decisions, particularly the financial ones, were flawed and foolish. I knew she was uneducated, and even though she hid that burdensome fact beneath a sophisticated front, she could not overcome many of the barriers that her near-illiteracy subjected her to.

Gradually and willingly, I assumed greater responsibilities until the burden of the world nearly squashed my spirit down. Unconsciously, my mother and I switched places; I took on the role of the serious and trustworthy parental figure that in my eyes she seemed ready to vacate. I was sixteen and felt driven into a portentous adult reality while my mother was drawn to a bright youthful world of indulgence. The question was whether she had robbed me of what was rightfully mine or had I been the one to unwittingly hand it over to her? Either way, I was frantically trying to make sense of the world, as perhaps most teenage girls do, regardless of their circumstances.

I was in tenth or eleventh grade then and fiercely argumentative, questioning of established authority, and developing lofty ideals. Evidently, I had little or no experience myself, but I was convinced I knew the Truth. At the same time, I struggled with violent mood swings, and my mother was invariably the main target of my wrath. Today, I can only imagine how helpless she must have felt and why she appeared to be so unsympathetic when in fact she was at her wits' end and had to leave me be or lose her mind altogether.

My sister's reaction to the same circumstances was entirely different. Where I never broke the rules and worked very hard to stay on top of my academic obligations despite my perpetual angst, Nezha was getting totally disinterested with school. She, a quiet and dispassionate little girl, had turned into a wild and impertinent teenager after our parents' divorce. She had first been thrown out of the Lycée Descartes at the end of ninth grade for failing mathematics and Arabic. Her precarious academic situation was apparently aggravated by her insolence toward her teachers.

Mom then had her enrolled in ninth grade in a reputable all-girls high school that offered a similar curriculum but with even more emphasis on the two classes she had flunked. That did not last long. Nezha dropped out of that school the first year and refused to go back. Recently, she told me that the principal had ordered her to her office and, in no uncertain terms, told her that without math and Arabic she could not hope to go very far.

To which she had replied without missing a beat: "Well, then, I'd better leave right now. That way, I won't waste your time or mine."

She giggled at the thought of that scene.

"Incredible... the nerve and insouciance!" she exclaimed. "I think I felt a sort of superior intelligence. I was above everyone else... I, who was once so reserved and timid," she sounded truly puzzled, "I wonder why suddenly, at that age, my personality changed so completely?"

She paused for a moment and then said very deliberately, "I think it had to do with the divorce, the new lack of restrictions we all felt. Living with dad was like living in a prison." Another pause, before adding intently, "So much fear, so many worries, all that hurt and all at once, freedom..."

I was baffled that my little sister had experienced the same feelings as Mom. To me, the freedom was always double-edged, exhilarating, yes, sometimes, but ultimately frightening, too. And yet when she decided to drop out of school, she had not stopped to consider she could be hurting Mom, causing her a great deal of disappointment.

Nezha had literally turned into a little monster, bold and disobedient. For one thing, she loved to go disco dancing and would just go out several nights a week without permission. She would patiently wait until Mom went to bed. Once she was sure she was asleep, she'd slip out of the apartment and stay out until the wee hours with her adult friends in discos around town.

I was a wimp compared to her, always afraid, always anxious. Most astonishingly, in spite of her wild behavior, Nezha never came back home drunk, or high, or pregnant. She smoked a little but did not drink much and never did any drugs even when surrounded by people who did a lot of them. She did not have sex until much later than me, and only when she fell in love for the first time, and then she took the pill.

One time, she was caught returning home at three or four in the morning. Mom yelled and slapped her hard, mostly because she had feared for her. Nezha just decided to run away from home, leaving Mom devastated. For days, she searched for her desperately, asking friends and acquaintances in vain, until my sister took pity on her and resurfaced.

I could never have done anything even remotely as irresponsible as that. I realize today that I hurt my mother in ways that cut far deeper than my sister did. I had spent most of my life obsessing about my wasted childhood and shattered adolescence. It had been all about *me*, my feelings, my anger, my pain. Suddenly, it became crystal clear to me that I had been blind to my mother's hurt and dismissive of her wasted childhood, shattered adolescence, and broken dreams.

Throughout my youth I never fully appreciated her profound despair while living with Dad, never given a thought to her difficulties with her children, particularly with my sister's acting out and my hostility, never once considered her lonely struggle to keep us safe at all cost. I never reflected, then, on the unfairness of her condition, her dogged battle to survive in a world hostile to her gender, unprepared and unarmed with no education or fortune. I was way too angry, too resentful and totally insensitive to her plight.

The abuse she endured from me, her oldest child, she did not suffer from any other human being, not even my dad, because she loved me unconditionally and she forgave me, always, as only a mother can.

My mother, my sweet tender gentle *maman*—I weep uncontrollably as I write these words and my belated sorrow overwhelms me. Why did it take me so long to recognize my obstinate refutation?

Over the years my sister often reproached me for not being kinder and more compassionate toward our mother.

"You judged and condemned her incessantly," Nezha reminded me time and again, adding, "You sympathized with Dad more eagerly than you ever did with Mom."

And then my sister said something that made it all transparent:

"You showed more compassion for Dad because he seemed weak and you felt he needed your protection. Mom, on the other hand, appeared strong and stubborn, magnificently daring and brave. She could handle your pouncing."

She spoke the words purposely, yet she managed to not sound judgmental.

All the same, her statement felt like a blow in my stomach; I had been fooled by my mother's façade and not looked below the surface, not penetrated the depths of her solitary struggle. In the past, I had just brushed off my sister's accusations, always rejecting her arguments outright.

Denial, I find, is a strong sentiment; it can take over one's lifetime perception and still not be vanquished. Today, I finally understand how, in later years, my self-righteousness might have contributed to her devastating illness and ultimate collapse. Ironically, in my teens, instead of being insubordinate and defiant like my little sister, I behaved more "responsibly" by projecting my angst and fear on my mother—and I steadily tore her down.

9

Wanton Times

Unlike my sister, another way I acted out was to attempt to fill the void left by my father's absence and my mother's perceived indifference by indulging in casual sexual relationships. Although in those days, throughout the Western world, promiscuousness was common behavior. I was attracted to older men, often ones I admired in some ways and hoped to emulate—but also men, whose love, protection, and guidance I yearned for like a lost orphan.

The contradictory messages I was receiving from my environment did nothing to help me control my urges and wait for more meaningful relations. My mother's own conduct was of no help to me; she was older and ready and she was entitled to a fulfilling liaison. I needed to feel loved and was looking to fill the emptiness within. The society I was part of was split between a forbidding traditional convention and a liberal Western code, itself in full transformation. I entered my sexual years with mixed signals and great needs.

My first lover happened to be a neighbor, a handsome artist who had been acknowledging me from afar with a broad grin and a friendly wave. I could see him standing at his window across the rooftops of our neighboring buildings. I finally met him on the street one day, on my way back from school, and he introduced himself with a smile and affable demeanor.

"Hey, you're my lovely neighbor!" he exclaimed with a cheerful tone and a piercing gaze into my eyes. I took the hand he was extending.

"Yes, I recognize you. You work from home?" I asked.

He laughed, "Yes, I am a painter. That's my studio."

"Really?" I was instantly interested, "What kind of painting do you do?"

"Oil on canvas," he said, quickly adding: "Actually, I'm putting in the final touches for a show next week. Would you like to come?"

I was sold. Kamil was indeed a charming and free-spirited up-and-coming artist of medium height, lean, and dark, with intense black eyes. His paintings were compelling and shadowy, a fusion of abstract expressionism and cubism, a wholly intangible evocation of a tortured psyche, which at once fascinated and intrigued me.

I met him a few times at the gallery where he displayed his paintings, then, when the exhibit ended, he asked me to visit his studio. Predictably, when I arrived, he quickly took me in his arms and greeted me with a long kiss. In spite of my slight apprehension, I had expected it, and it felt good. Underneath his untamed appearance, Kamil was kind and sweet... and married, although this fact concerned him not in the least. A self-confessed hippie, he rejected all established social values that could put any restrictions on his belief in universal love and peace.

According to him, so did his French wife. He explained this to me matter-of-factly as he kissed me and battled with my bra.

"This is my first time," I had whispered to him without him asking, "but I'm on the pill."

"Good," he'd let out under his breath.

The contraceptive had been prescribed to me by my mother's gynecologist, to regulate my erratic menstrual cycle, so I was never burdened with the fear of an undesirable pregnancy.

Kamil was not interested in the details at that moment. I felt awkward, self-conscious, and could not stop thinking his wife could walk in on us at any time. He'd told me she was working and would not be home until much later. Nonetheless, laying there against him, on the couch of his studio, surrounded by dozens of paintings propped against the walls, with the smell of paint and solvent infusing the air, I found it hard to relax and take pleasure in the moment.

This first sexual encounter felt like an odd mix of effort and embrace; I was not sure what to make of it. It was a bit too raw and painful to be entirely pleasurable, and it was not at all romantic. I was relieved to be rid of my hymen and pleased that he had been both gentle enough, and patient enough.

Afterwards, he got up, disheveled and stark naked, lit an already-rolled joint, and offered me a hit. I shook my head. I took a cigarette instead, partly covered my exposed body with the towel he had used to cover the couch, and stared at him. The pungent smell of weed invaded my nostrils.

I was fascinated by his ease and lack of shame. He flipped through a clutch of brushes, jammed into a large cup, and picked one. Then he mixed some paint in a small, stained tray before applying it on a canvas in an easel, in front of the window. The shades were pulled all the way up, and the late afternoon sun was streaming right through the glass, highlighting the specks of dust hanging in the air.

I watched him in silence, smoking my cigarette. Standing in glorious nudity with his dark shoulder-length hair, short beard, and slim waist, halfway between the shadows and the light, he looked like a cool picture of Jesus. He took deep hits from his joint, head tilted to the side, contemplating his unfinished work.

I felt out of place and edgy in that strange, untidy space where no set of rules or preconceived notions seemed to apply. I gathered my clothes and asked him where the bathroom was. He turned sideways, grinned at me, and pointed with his paint brush in the direction of the hallway.

"The first door to your right," he mumbled holding the smoke in his throat.

When I came back, all dressed and cleaned up, he had put his jeans back on, zipped them up, keeping the top button undone. A stained rag was hanging out of his front pocket.

"I'm leaving now," I said. He put down his brush and walked toward me.

"Will you come back soon?" he asked.

As he did when I had arrived, he, again, took me in his arms and buried his head in my hair in a warm bear-hug.

"I'd like to see you again," he said affectionately. The hair on his chest felt soft against my cheek.

"I don't know. Maybe."

I enjoyed the comfort of his hold. He kissed me on the lips and looked at me keenly, with the pensive look of one in hashish bliss.

"I'm glad you came today," he murmured.

Strangely, I, too, was happy; I couldn't have hoped for a more casual defloration. It was perfect as far as I was concerned. I thought about it often, and always fondly. It felt honest. No big words or promises or pretenses. We were merely attracted to each other, expressed it, and moved on, period, no strings attached and no remorse.

Still, I needed to share that momentous event with someone, so I told my sister, who, in the course of a heated dispute, immediately broke the news to our mother. It landed me a memorable slap on the face; perhaps my mother felt she had to do something about my new condition. I can't really say; we never spoke of it again.

The only other time I had sex with Kamil was during a birthday party he and his wife were giving in their flat. She had welcomed me as if she knew me, which I thought was a bit odd. By the end of the night, almost everyone was gone and I was thinking of taking my leave as well. I'd had a little too much to drink and was blissfully tipsy when he dragged me to their bedroom and began to make love to me in the semi-darkness. I thought that was creepy but did not find it in me to push him away.

Within a few moments, I felt the presence of someone else in the bed with us. I didn't know how it happened, but his wife had apparently joined us, and before I realized what was going on, I felt her touching me, intimately, slowly at first and then with resolve. I started to protest feebly but swiftly felt my loins overwhelmed by the most elating sensation I'd ever experienced. A giant tidal wave was rolling over me, rising and falling, over and over. I entered a tunnel of ecstasy, my breathing accelerating, my heart beating frantically. She would not let go of me,

"Yes, yes, that's it," she whispered in my ear, breathing hard herself. All at once, the growing fever engulfed me, a volcano erupting and crashing over with astounding fury, and I let out a cry, which she silenced with a hungry kiss, her hand lingering on me. For a few minutes, my body twitched and quivered until she turned away and I lay there, limp and unresponsive, thinking I'd lost consciousness. It was all bewildering, incomprehensible. I was sure I had died, and that was why I was shedding tears, a sort of release weeping.

My hosts busied themselves with each other now. I finally gathered the strength to run out of there, my legs still wobbly, ashamed, and confused. Later, I realized I had just experienced my very first orgasm, but had also been used as someone's birthday present. For a while, the feeling dallied with embarrassment in my mind. I never saw them again and never told anyone. Secretly, I confess, I had been initiated to a new wonderful world of self-gratification.

My subsequent lovers were as different as they were colorful, and endearing, each in their own way. There was my eleventh-grade French teacher, whom I found not particularly good looking. He was small of stature, blondish with bright blue eyes and a very deep and sexy voice. He was highly intelligent, sharp, and witty. If his looks were not what had attracted me to him, I was captivated by his irreverent wit above all. I was also under the spell of his voice and particularly his laughter, a deep, mocking laugh that lit up a cheerful twinkle in his eyes. A hardened bachelor and chain smoker, he lived alone in a small apartment littered with books, papers, and half-full ashtrays, where the odor of cigarette permeated the walls and the sparse furniture.

I loved French literature, and he made it even more exhilarating for me. His class was my favorite because of the lively debates he encouraged and moderated. Our relationship started innocently enough, with long after-class conversations on Voltaire and Sartre around coffee and cigarettes, often with other students, sometimes in his place.

Eventually, we ended up in bed, and that actually was what prompted the demise of our affair. Sex was rather pathetic. He seemed as inexperienced as I was, and I was clueless about what the problem could be. Our attraction was more intellectual than physical and should have remained that way.

Years later, I learned he was in Paris, living with an old classmate of mine. Said was one of my best high school friends. Pretty and effeminate, he was joyful and fun-loving. We had some great moments together but never ever brought up his sexual orientation. He playfully dated girls and acted the heterosexual part even though it was apparent to all who knew him that it was blatantly deceptive.

When I heard of his ongoing romance with our old French teacher, it all made sense to me. My teacher's inadequacy during our intimate moments was explained, Said's sexual preference confirmed. Sadly, Said died of AIDS in the early years of the epidemic that spread throughout Europe and North America. I never again had the chance to get back in touch with him or my unfortunate teacher.

I was introduced to David at a party attended by all of Rabat's rich and beautiful people, and from the way he looked at me, I immediately thought him a womanizer. His seductive smile, perfect tan, and sweet talk were all red flags. But I was too young, easily flattered, and I let him seduce me without much resistance. A successful Jewish business man, highly attentive to his appearance, he was a charming, attractive dandy, and not much of an intellectual. He was in his mid-thirties and thought himself a paragon of elegance and style. He drove a brand new German car and had a pad in the center of town, where he enjoyed his extra-marital affairs discreetly. I happened to be one of them.

At first, I was surprised by the location of his little love-nest. Then he explained to me that there was so much business and pedestrian traffic in that neighborhood that no one could really tell who was coming or going. It was like hiding in plain sight. He picked me up from home as he would any business associate. The first couple of times at least, he opened the car door for me like a gentleman. But David was married, and he was known in town, meaning we could not be seen together on a date anywhere in public.

Our relationship almost immediately turned into a sordid sex act and little else. We had no real conversations and nothing in common besides those precisely timed encounters. Quickly, the bare sex turned stale and I couldn't help but feel like the heroine of a cheap novel. I grew frustrated and supremely bored with him and soon ended the affair.

When I met Jean, the beautiful and stylish son of an African ambassador, I was looking for something more exciting, if not more fulfilling. A very tall and athletic, sexy young black man who moved on the dance floor like a born performer, he was beyond good-looking—he was stunning. When he danced, he exuded sexuality and, true to his persona, he made love like a God. I was not in love with him but with his looks, his shiny, ebony skin, statuesque body, and soft thick lips. He introduced me to the soulful music of Marvin Gaye and other Motown legends such as Smokey Robinson, Otis Redding, and Aretha Franklin. Despite his youth, he had an aura of worldliness and sophistication about him that fascinated me. Because of him, I would forever associate Barry White's sensual music, deep baritone, and explicit lyrics with slow and sultry lovemaking. But he had just graduated from high school and was about to attend college in France, which quickly put an end to our relationship.

By the mid-summer of 1974, I had enough self-confidence and experience to feel somewhat in control of my destiny. In retrospect, my early relationships, all put together, were a mix of profiles I admired, wishing perhaps they would rub off on me. It's enough to say that neither my mother, nor I, had yet experienced a truly loving, giving relationship. It turned out those were just around the corner, waiting for us.

10

Sex and Betrayal

Since early childhood, summertime had always been synonymous with sun, surf and sand for my family. The summer of 1974 was also a time when, Mom, my sister and I spent many Friday and Saturday nights in discos or parties as the best of friends. Such a friendship between mother and daughters seemed special at the time, and even endearing, had it not been for the fact that it indicated the beginning of a profound and, I realized later, questionable transformation in our relationship.

My early promiscuity had an unforeseen effect; it turned my attention, away from my mother, who until then had been the center of my universe, to men. And that shift resulted in turn into a growing harmony between my mother and me. No longer was she the object of all my frustration.

Having escaped the deep level of conflict I experienced, my sister did not perceive such events as intensely as I did. As far as I was concerned, my mother becoming my friend signaled the end of her parental authority. Such authority could have provided not only structure, but also sanctuary, to a teenage daughter in the throes of conflicting emotions and moods.

Neither Mom, nor I, was remotely aware then of the enormous implications of such a change in our attachment.

It was around that time that she met Berto. He was the owner of one of the very first well-equipped gyms in town. She had wanted to learn more about it, and Berto had shown her around. The chemistry between them was instantaneous. A handsome man of average stature, he had once been a body-building champion, and photographs of him posing with trophies were posted on the walls of his office. He was thinner than in his pictures but still athletic, and looking even better. His curly black hair and straight, narrow nose gave him the distinguishing look of Michelangelo's David. Best of all, he was funny and had an engaging personality. My siblings and I enjoyed his company and adopted him with open arms.

My mother loved his lean, toned body, and she was infatuated with his looks. Never before had she felt anything as passionate as she did with this man. He initiated her to gym workouts, including weight-training, jogging, good diet, and nutrition. He was slightly younger than she, was married, but had no children; he was separated from his wife-who had, in fact, left him to go live in Paris in pursuit of a career. He was neither an intellectual nor a spiritual soul; happily neither was Mom. It was mostly his charm and warmth that made him well-liked by everyone who knew him.

What Berto introduced in my mother's life was infinite care and affection, love and tenderness, laughter and joy, and so it was no surprise at all she quickly fell in love with him. After having experienced the dread and gloom of marital life with my father for two decades, she was delighting in the fathomless pleasures of reciprocated love. In the eyes of her beloved, her true self emerged, and she became something other than mother or wife; she became a woman. The power of his love had freed her from her lifelong shackles.

"Strong" is far too weak an epithet to accurately describe their physical attraction. It was an ardent rapture. They were enthralled with one another. And sex meant the total communion of their bodies and minds. It's impossible for me to forget how happy and fulfilled my mother was in those days. She floated on a white cotton cloud, her eyes sparkling, her face glowing, her yearning as a woman finally vindicated.

I remember well catching them in the middle of the afternoon, absorbed, behind closed doors, in their uninhibited sexual frolic. I recall smiling to myself, feeling uncomfortable for being there, hearing them laughing like two kids engaged in carefree, intimate games, oblivious to the world outside.

This picture of bliss was not unblemished. Their liaison had to be kept as discreet as possible, because she was a Muslim and he a Jew. And even though both were Moroccan, their religions made it impossible for them to be together openly and even less likely to formally commit to each other. That created a host of problems for them, many of which came from his father.

The Jewish patriarch was very strongly opposed to his only son's affair, not only because my mother was Muslim, but also because she was a divorcée with four children, and he was officially still married. From the outset, their liaison was doomed. Yet despite the insuperable odds against them, their union lasted close to six years. Long after it was over, my mother remembered it as one of the most fulfilling times of her life.

The night I first met Paul, Berto was taking my mother to dinner and had asked me along. We went to the *Jefferson*, a popular restaurant that doubled as a disco. Paul, who owned the place with Jeff, an acquaintance of Berto's, immediately rushed over to greet us and take us to our table. The place was still quiet, with only a few diners sipping their cocktails. The club did not get loud until later, when it turned into a nightclub.

I was not immediately attracted to Paul, not because he was not a good-looking man—he was! Tall and thin with wide shoulders, he had smiley blue eyes and a handsome face, but he was balding prematurely, and quite visibly, on the top of his head, and that turned me off initially. I was only eighteen, after all. He did attempt to hide it with that silly hair sweep balding men seem to favor, thinking perhaps no one would notice.

Of course, it doesn't seem fair that a thirty-four-year-old man would have to contend with such a random, often traumatic, occurrence. Paul was about the same age as my mother and older than Berto. But age was not the issue; I was almost exclusively attracted to older men. In retrospect, it is odd that it did not raise any red flags in my mother's mind either. But then why should it? At eighteen, she's already had two children and the sight of an older man with a much younger woman was, and still is in many places, an acceptable fact of life.

That night Paul was pleasant and thoughtful. Throughout our dinner he hovered over us, attending to our wishes, suggesting special wine and dishes, and never ceasing to devour me with his eyes. When my mother and Berto got up to dance, Paul came and sat next to me.

"Would you like something else to drink?" he asked, lighting my cigarette.

"No, thanks, I'm fine," I said. "Everything was delicious."

He smiled. "You're beautiful, you know that?" He kept his eyes locked into mine. "Are you seeing someone?"

His blunt question took me by surprise. I shook my head. I was beginning to feel his attraction.

He wanted to know everything about me, asked all sorts of questions while barely answering mine. I did manage to learn that he was divorced and had a young son, who lived with his ex-wife. He also owned, with his younger brother, an interior design shop in Place Piétri, a few blocks from our apartment. As the night progressed, he had to turn his attention to his business, but before he excused himself, he asked me for my phone number and handed me his card.

After a couple of weeks, we became lovers, and before long I was spending so much time with him that I was practically living with him. In late August, he took me on my first trip abroad, to Spain's Costa-del-Sol. We drove to Marbella and Puerto Banus. The marina that would later become the hall-mark of the small town was still under construction. I was in heaven.

For the first time since I started dating, and almost a decade after my mother's first trip to Madrid, I took in the exquisite whiff of unbridled individual freedom. I was free to share a hotel room with Paul, hold his hand, and let him kiss me if I so desired. I was free to wear a low-cut dress and show off my suntanned skin.

Some of which I could still do in Morocco's big cities in the mid-seventies, but always with the intimate awareness that I was a Muslim girl living in an Arab country. I was mixing with Frenchmen and playing by the rules of a minority foreign culture in a traditional society. As a modern French-educated young female, I had always known there were things I simply could not do. It was easier for a Muslim man, with a similar education and upbringing, because his gender allowed him to marry a Christian, or a Jew, while a Muslim woman could not.

As a result, I was always careful not to ruffle too many feathers, plagued with the self-consciousness of a social outcast adopting liberal conduct at my own risk and peril. At the most unexpected times, I could be the object of a disapproving stare or demeaning slur, or even humiliated by a perfect stranger by being denied the rental of a hotel room with a non-Muslim, or even simply be arrested by the police.

In Spain, I did not have to be concerned with prying, condemnatory looks from men in the street and everything around me felt exciting and open-minded. By the time we returned home, I was completely in love with Paul, and I felt secure and happy. His charming little villa in the Souissi became our love nest. When I was there, he paid me particular attention, bringing me breakfast in bed and preparing delicious home cooked dinners. He was considerate and sweet, and went out of his way to create a loving environment for me.

In September, school started. The class *de terminale*, or twelfth grade, is, without a doubt, the most demanding year of high school, and every senior in a French lycée dreads it to this day. I had picked Economics as a major and I knew I had a heavy workload ahead of me. In June, students have to take the *baccalauréat* (also known as the *Bac*), which is made up of a series of comprehensive exams over the course of a few days. Failure in one discipline can mean failure of the entire grade. From the onset of the year, neither my head nor my heart was focused on school. Nonetheless, I undertook to do my best.

In mid-January 1975, Paul left on a long business trip in Paris looking ahead for business opportunities with an eye to leaving Morocco in a year's time, perhaps in anticipation of my own departure for college in France. I felt down and dejected without him, and my objective was to study hard to finish my senior year and pass the exam. I was determined to wait for

Paul and write him often. As fate had it, that was counting without Michel, who was about to storm into my life—unexpected and uninvited.

**

I was sitting on the rug of the living room, my legs folded under me, hunched over the coffee table. My school books scattered in front of me, I had started composing a letter to Paul, instead of studying. At that moment, my sister walked in with three strangers. Michel was among them. I was mildly exasperated by the intrusion, and my first impression of him was one of vague displeasure.

Dark-skinned, with a sharp nose and piercing hazel eyes, Michel had a full head of light-brown hair, a wide, cocky smile that displayed perfect white teeth, and a contagious, cascading laugh. Arrogant and charismatic, Michel was a gypsy-half-blood, who had honed his skills in the school of hard knocks, on the streets of Toulouse, and he spoke with the strong drawl of the region. Something about him betrayed his rough edges, the fact that, at thirty-two, he was a survivor, a sort of rebel, and an experienced hawker.

Above all, Michel was a born seducer; when he put his gaze on me, I was reduced to hapless prey. It felt like there was nothing I could do to save myself from his claws. I looked scruffy and plain, my hair dirty and pulled back, lounging in sweat pants and old shirt, and far from looking my best. And yet, at that very instant, Michel saw something he liked and decided he wanted. Unimpressed, I wished he would leave so that I could get back to my letter and linger in my melancholy. Instead he continued to joke, laugh loudly, and take up center stage late into the evening. My brothers were subjugated, my sister conquered. Michel was really there to sign her up as a new hire.

Nezha was interested in the book-retailing position proposed by Michel because it held the promise of better earnings, even though there was no base salary offer, only a flat commission. This kind of direct book selling was difficult since it involved a lot of prospecting and cold calling on potential clients at their homes and offices. The books, all French, were mostly compilations or expensive leather-bound sets, such as the Jacques Cousteau Collection and the Great French Literary Classics. The targeted clientele was necessarily well-to-do and French-educated. On the positive side, it did not involve being trapped in an office all day and offered the possibility of extensive overseas travel.

Shortly after I first met him, Michel showed up again at my doorstep, but he was not there to see my sister. He asked me out for a drive and coffee, which sounded more appealing to me than studying, so I followed him. He took me to his car, a bright red Porsche Targa with a removable roof. Although I was impressed by the sleek machine, the car actually evoked something in my mind about its owner that I am sure was the opposite of what he wished to convey. It was screaming, *I am a bragging show-off, a bad boy, and an immature pleasure seeking playboy,* in other words, not exactly the type of man I wished to be associated with. Besides, I was in love with someone else, and the thought of cheating on him was repugnant to me.

But then something happened to my better judgment that I am still trying to make sense of today. Michel was patient and persistent in his courtship on our first date. The afternoon turned into evening, the coffee into dinner, the couple of cigarettes into a full pack, and the casual meeting into a late night in an ocean-side hotel. He told me of his travels to magical lands, his passion for foreign customs and people, his love of freedom and open coexistence.

He did not believe in fidelity and commitment or, for that matter, in marriage and children, or any of the conventional ideals that I valued. He lived by the pleasure principle, in the moment, with no encumbrance or guilt. And he knew how to be convincing. The doubts and arguments of an eighteen-year-old, no matter how astute, were no match for his persuasive talents. The more I tried to resist him, the more charm and seduction he deployed, always with wit and humor.

After he seduced me, and I hesitantly surrendered my body, Michel began his subtle subjugation of my heart by inviting me along, with a couple of reps, for a long weekend trip to the south of Morocco. During the day, we travelled south to Marrakech and beyond. At night, we explored the far-off sensual terrain of our bodies. We went farther than Zagora, to the golden sand dunes of Tinfout, surrounded by high desert mountains, on the edge of the Sahara. After the sun had set, we met in the intimacy of our hotel room and immersed ourselves in the depths of uninhibited passion. It was my first trip to the far reaches of my own country. It was also my initiation to the guilty pleasures of illicit love. Michel had set out to show me the beauty of my land. In so doing, my infatuation with him grew, and so did my insidious entanglement with the deceit and betrayal of Paul.

Upon my return I found Paul's first note to me, a small 3"x5" card sent more than two weeks after his departure.

Amour, he wrote in a rather succinct way,

A word to tell you how much I miss you. As promised I'll be brief. Quite a few contacts... I am in good spirit... I'll call you to explain in details. I hope you're working hard. I love you. A bientôt, Paul.

I looked at the little card, wondering why he couldn't find fifteen minutes to compose a real letter. He had never promised to be brief. I suppose he meant he had warned me. I wrote him back eight pages, complaining a little, but it was only to mitigate the news I was about to deliver. This was my first letter to him, and already it shrieked of duplicity.

I want to tell you how much I miss you too and how lonely I feel... I love you as much if not more than before...

I saw a lot of people lately. I didn't go looking for them; they came to my house while I was working, one afternoon. Since I don't know the south of Moroccan, I took advantage of the opportunity to go with them for a weekend. We went south of Zagora, to the dunes of Tinfout in the Sahara...

I signed up for the baccalauréat. I applied today and I paid the registration fee. Fortunately you left me a little money... Speaking of which, honey, this situation is no longer possible between us. It is insufferable to me to think that you have been supporting me for a few months already and that it's likely to continue... Luckily I think I found a great job for the summer...

He replied quickly, apparently none too happy with my revelations and focusing on one thing only, my "weekend in Zagora." "Who were the people you left with?" and he immediately asked that I give him all the details of my trip along with "the first and last name, age, and profession of every person" I had traveled with. But then, thinking he was perhaps too harsh with me, he asked whether I could take a few days off and join him in Paris, since I had a free round-trip ticket. He was referring to a free First Class air fare I had won in a Miss Morocco pageant over the Christmas break.

I quickly jumped at the opportunity, skirted my academic responsibilities again, and was off to Paris.

11

More Lies

It was my first flight ever, and in first class no less. I was served a delicious meal and free-flowing champagne, though it was not potent enough to drown my escalating guilt. Two issues were foremost on my mind: the first was my cumbersome secret. Would I be able to continue concealing my brazen infidelity? Second was Paul's revelation only a week earlier that he had been getting ready for hair prosthesis, a procedure that would permanently hide his baldness.

Be prepared to meet a new man... since I really don't look the same, he had written me.

I had no idea what to expect and, judging from my own nervousness, could only imagine the level of *his* anxiety. What was he going to look like with a hairpiece attached to his skull? I wondered.

It was early afternoon, and the sun was shining brightly, that late February when the aircraft touched the ground and shook me out of my reverie. I got off the plane a little inebriated, an inane smile on my face and my cheeks on fire, ready to discover the City of Lights.

But first I was about to meet the "new" Paul... I walked slowly, taking deep breaths. I tried to regain my composure while keeping in step with the flow of passengers. First, the police... The young officer behind the glass pane took my passport. He asked me where I was staying while stamping my document and giving it back to me.

"Have a nice stay," he said nonchalantly. I nodded, hoping for the same.

I was expecting to see Paul in front of me at any moment. But not quite yet: I had to retrieve my luggage, then go through customs—more dazed walking and finally people gathering just ahead of me greeted by their loved ones. My heart was now beating faster, my head pounding a little. I should stop thinking and relax, I kept urging myself. And then I saw him.

Damn... It looks so bad, so very obvious, I thought.

It looked exactly like what I had feared, a toupee placed where his bald spot once was. Combed to the right and parted on the left side, the dividing line of the part showed no skin at all giving away what it was supposed to hide. It was long enough to cover his ears, his long fashionable sideburns, and the back of his neck. He did not have a long neck to begin with, but now, it seemed his head sat directly on his shoulders in the most unbecoming fashion. I smiled bravely back at him, well aware that his eyes were two glaring question marks. He took me in his arms.

"You had a good flight?" asked Paul with a cheerful tone.

I felt weird being held so closely in public. But I wasn't in Morocco anymore, I reminded myself. Suddenly, I had mixed feelings about him, about us. The whole thing was so bizarre. He stepped back, pulling away from me with his hands still on my shoulders.

"So, what do you think, huh?"

Slowly, he turned his head left then right; he sounded so happy, eyeing me from the corner of his eyes, so proud of himself. I knew I had to lie; there was no way I could tell him how I felt. Was that thing not affixed forever, literally stitched to his head? I laughed nervously.

"Wow, it's *incredible*. It's really—" *quick, what was the proper word?* I was trying to think fast— "*nice!*" I said finally. I was aware that did not sound too "nice." Thankfully, he helped me out,

"It takes some getting used to, I know," he offered.

His eyes were smiling at me now with that familiar twinkle I loved so much. I kissed him and took his hand in mine, not wishing to say anymore.

In the end, I did manage to have a wonderful time in Paris, even forgot Paul's silly prosthesis. The glorious French capital made yet another lifelong conquest and enthusiast of me. I felt at home with the language, the culture, the food, and going back home was the hardest thing I had to do. When Paul saw me off at the airport, holding me tight for a goodbye, neither he nor I could ever have imagined that we would never see each other again.

**

I landed in Rabat under a heavy rain, which only worsened the feeling that I was literally returning to confinement. Going back to the grind of a *terminale* year evoked panic attacks in me, studying for the *Baccalauréat* even more. I knew I had not prepared nearly enough for the exam. Time had been running out on me fast. I was doomed to fail. I had far too many absences, and there were too many gaps in my scholastic requirements. I was just denying reality, only pretending I was still in a position to do well enough to pass.

Deep down I knew it was not going to happen, but I couldn't admit it to myself, let alone divulge it to anyone else. For the first time in my life, I had flunked an entire academic year and I felt as removed from student life as I could possibly be. I had entered an entirely different universe and I needed a way out. I was just waiting for a pretext to call it quits and save face.

Michel presented me with the excuse I was hoping for. He reappeared in my world as soon as I got back from Paris. He had no idea I had gone to meet my previous, and still very present, boyfriend. I had mentioned, when I first met him, that I was seeing someone. But then, when I started seeing him regularly, he assumed it must not have been very important, and hence, for him at least, the case was closed. Only it was not, not for me, which really meant I was unfaithful to both men in earnest, a situation about which I was in total denial.

It was springtime in Morocco, the best time of year for Michel to be extending book prospecting to Marrakech and the great south with his entire team. Traveling to the most remote parts of the country, well beyond the urban areas, was his way "to combine necessary tasks with pleasurable ones," as he put it. Morocco had always been one of his favorite destinations.

"Come along with us," he proposed with his usual alluring, everything-is-possible magnetism. "You can learn the business, make some money and at the same time get to know your beautiful country."

The offer was far too tempting to turn down. My academic battle was already lost, and the amorous war in my heart unsustainable. Yet when my body soon again yielded to Michel's ardent demonstrations, my reason valiantly tried to stand adamant. For over two weeks, I followed Michel in his adventure, thinking this was only temporary folly. How could it be otherwise? He was not a man with whom a young woman could build a family. I was keenly aware of that.

I wanted to believe that I was still Paul's girl and that I would soon return to my sanity. On the other hand, and for the first time, I learned the skill of bookselling, earning in the process my own commissions and receiving my very first paycheck—all of which came as a revelation to me then, and opened a new world of possibilities.

Toward the end of March, Paul was still in Paris and had no idea what I was up to-until I got a short express-mail letter where he laid down his doubts, anger and frustration with scathing sarcasm.

Fourteen days without any news from you is absolutely abnormal. I had your brother on the phone and by manipulating him {...} I learned that it was all a big party for you now. Erfoud last week (I didn't know that, in that region, books sold so well) and Marrakech this week {...} I realize how much of an idiot I have been with you. In any case, I don't begrudge you; I'm the only ass here.

His letter made me feel dreadful. I thought of myself as a monster of insensitivity, a ghastly, horrible slut. I was sure he was hurting badly; I could feel his pain and puzzlement at my behavior. It had been just a little over three weeks since I left him in Paris, after what had seemed like an idyllic romance.

Worst of all, I could not even explain my behavior to him because I myself had no idea what I was doing. I had abandoned all pretense at controlling events around me, simply grateful he wasn't there to confront me face to face. That night, I cried in shame and baffled remorse. My reason was completely muddled, and I had no one to confide in or ask for advice; doing so would have been tantamount to admitting my disarray, mostly revealing my true self, and the very nature I was steadfastly hiding underneath a self-assured veneer.

Besides, whom could I really open my heart to? My mother was self-absorbed by her own sense of rebirth, that magical unearthing of love, lust, and sex that one stumbles upon for the first time. She was also unaware of the drama that I was going through because I appeared grown-up, more mature, and happier.

Moreover, she and I had just begun enjoying what I think of now as a sort of nascent peace, an imaginary amity. Today, I cannot even call it friendship, though that's exactly what we thought it was then. Friendship implies intimate confidence and the sharing of secrets between peers. Not that mother-daughter relations cannot be friendly, obviously they can, but not at such at an early age, and only within defined boundaries.

Now, I believe a parent must insist on, and a teenager must show, fundamental respect at all times. A mother should not hesitate to step in and impose strict limits and purposeful guidance when necessary, which a peer cannot. In reality, my mother did not know any better, and, as a consequence, I failed to show her any real deference. From her perspective, there was reason to rejoice. There were no more sour arguments between us. I apparently was no longer in the throes of depression, although something else was fermenting beneath the surface, of which my mother was oblivious. In the end, her own beguiling love affair and my misleading poise combined to dupe us both.

Perhaps because she had been married so young and had her children at about the same age as I was then, she felt I was capable of assuming responsibilities on my own. Today I feel her permissiveness was an abdication of her parental obligations rather than an appreciation of my trustworthi-

ness and maturity. Furthermore, the belief that if you trust
your children they will do the right thing is quite errone-
ous in my view, because they are not in a position to know
what the right thing is, especially when events become too
confounding.

In my case, warning signs were everywhere, apparent to
all who were willing to take notice. The impulsive surrender
of my mother's maternal duties during my teen years contributed to my making the wrong choices when my life became
entangled. Instead of striving to surmount the academic and
emotional obstacles I encountered, I simply evaded them, hoping they would get resolved somehow.

When I saw Michel again, I was aware he was probably
going to tell me he was leaving soon. I was toying with the
idea of telling him about Paul but could not come up with the
proper words. Instead, he promptly rescued me from a morti-
fying confession.

"This is going to sound crazy," he began, after our love-
making. "I want you to come with me." He spoke quickly as
he reached for his cigarettes on the night table.

I was lying in bed, next to him, sweating in the cool moist-
ness of his hotel room, caressing his back with my hand, feeling its wetness. I had been thinking of his looming departure
and of Paul's imminent return, not knowing what to make of
either, not wishing to let Michel go or to face up to Paul just
yet. I doubted that my life could get back on its old track, or
that I wanted it to. I was just biding my time, waiting to see
where another day would take me.

Michel turned back toward me, with a second cigarette
for me. He smiled with his lips closed, squinting, as he
exhaled the cigarette smoke out of his nose, before declaring,

"I love you! I can't possibly leave without you." He pulled me against him and laughed lightly.

Ordinarily self-assured, he was always awkward in romantic moments. But his eyes were dead serious. I knew he meant it.

"I love you too. And I don't want you to leave me here, either," I blurted out without a second thought.

I was relieved he had decided for me. The thought that my mother could object did not even occur to me. This was the answer to all my problems, I thought, the end of the mayhem that my life had turned into. Oh, there was no question I was smitten with him. And it wasn't just sexual craving. The lure and excitement of the adventure ahead got the better of me as well.

By then, I had demonstrated to him and myself that I could sell books and earn money too. I had a natural talent for salesmanship and Michel had trained me very well. Plus, there were all those fascinating countries he wanted to show me and I was dying to discover.

As I expected, my mother did not seem to object...or did she? I don't recall whether she tried to change my mind at all. It is actually very possible that she attempted to make me reconsider. Watching me drop out of high school in the middle of my senior year, when she'd always been so proud of my academic achievements, must have been disheartening to her.

In all fairness to her, I knew full well that she was easily fooled, and I often took advantage of that fact. She was quickly overwhelmed by me because, in all our interactions, I never failed to shut her down with my knowledge and vehemence. And even if she did voice her disagreement or apprehension, I simply didn't listen. Furthermore, my sister had already started her own overseas travel by going on a six-week trip to Algeria with some musician friends.

By the time Paul returned to Morocco, a few days later, I had already left the country with Michel.

12

Running Away

We drove through Spain all the way to Toulouse, on a road trip that took three days and two nights. Michel let me drive his Porsche, rooftop down, the music of Jethro Tull's *Aqualung* blasting out of the powerful speakers, the wind in my hair, blowing my worries away. I had left everything I had ever known behind, not without regrets for all the pain I had caused the first man who really cared for me.

In France, Michel and I stayed a few days in a stately villa owned by two business associates in Pechabou, a small village seven miles from Toulouse. Built on the outskirts of the old village, the grand ivy-covered mansion boasted more than half a dozen rooms that served as a sort of free and impromptu bed-and-breakfast to all the reps who stopped by on their way to and from different parts of the globe. Three double French doors opened from the large salons onto a paved veranda, which in turn led to a big tousled garden.

There, an old dried-up fountain covered with pigeon droppings stoically endured its continual defacement. Tall sycamore trees bordering the garden conferred a sense of former glory on the property. Under the bright sky of the Midi-Pyrenees region, the beautiful old villa insisted on holding its head high, disheveled because no one stayed there long enough to care for it, yet still resolutely swollen with pride.

In its state of apparent anarchy the house perfectly matched its bohemian occupants. A cheery irreverent camaraderie, and a carefree attitude, infused everything and everyone all the time. I was not at all used to such easy, blithe living. Nobody took offense if you slept in their bed, couples changed often, privacy was unheard of, and it was not a shock to anyone to find someone in the kitchen preparing a cup of coffee in their birthday suit.

My jumbled mind might have been appeased by the non-judgmental disposition of those around me, had it not been for my own rigid, ambiguous principles. I was disorientated and felt painfully normal, almost old-school. The house in Pechabou was not an actual hippie colony, but it was not far off. These were venturesome young people who loved to travel but also wanted to make money and own fast cars. Universal love and pot-smoking did not necessarily exclude materialistic pursuits in their minds.

The queen bee of the community was the main owner of the house himself, a forty-something, good-looking bisexual with graying temples, tight jeans, and cowboy boots. Jacques was the embodiment of laid back, make-believe fantasy. Married once and divorced, with no children, he had lived through the rebellious sixties penniless and free. He now wished to triumph over the seventies with the same freedom, only with vastly more money and a lot more sex. If he could only stop time! In his head, he was a twenty-something still, hip and cool. He slept with women half his age, pledging neither love nor fidelity, and drove a shiny white Porsche Carrera and a racy red Lamborghini.

Most unsettling to me was Michel's unanticipated atti-tude. No longer was I the exclusive center of his attention. He seemed perfectly comfortable in the casual promiscuity of the Pechabou villa. Clearly, from the anecdotes he and others were fond of telling, he had long been a master of the incessant game of luring and seducing young, beautiful women for one-night stands. My presence was not exactly conducive to such diversion, I was convinced of that, though he frequently set out to mollify me.

"I can't believe these chicks, always walking about half-naked, sleeping around with whomever, indiscriminately," I exclaimed in disgust one morning when I returned from the bathroom and slipped back into bed next to Michel.

It was already midday, and the sun was high up in the sky. It was not unusual for us to get up at such hours. We were often staying up late into the night with scores of strangers, acquaintances, friends, and associates.

"Come on, baby, don't be such a prude," he muttered in my ear teasing. "At least you know you're the only one I really care about."

He knew what to say, what I wanted to hear.

Then he added half-jokingly, "Hey, how about we play together sometime?"

His clear insinuation was not at all amusing to me. "Are you crazy or what?" I snapped, pulling away.

I faintly recognized the knot of angst building just below my solar plexus, and I was fighting hard not to let it overcome me.

I barely heard him murmur with a chuckle, "You don't know, you might just like it."

"Stop it! It's stupid, and I don't want to hear of it." I had raised my voice and jumped out of bed, reaching for my robe.

"Look, relax, okay? It's just a game, an inconsequential and harmless game," he said calmly, a smile still playing on his lips.

But I knew all too well his persuasive talents. I didn't believe or trust him, when it came to sex. I was trembling with the now familiar, helpless, rage that jealousy awakened in me.

"Relax, baby, I'm just fooling with you." He knew not to insist further. He pushed the sheets away and got out of bed.

"I'm going to take a shower," he said, and left the room.

That was easier said than done for me, and, of course, when mixed with my bemused state of mind, very disturbing. I had no intention of partaking in the orgiastic mood around me. I was mightily jealous and, from then on, became suspicious of every girl I met.

Thankfully, we remained in Toulouse and its region just long enough for Michel to show me around his hometown. *La Ville Rose,* as it is called—thanks to its older, rose-red bricked buildings—is famous for its grand plaza, charming pedestrian streets lined with alluring stores, its Garonne River, and the many canals that crisscross the town. Toulouse is also reputed for its museums, art galleries, and some of the most impressive churches in Europe, though we visited only a couple. The historical and cultural attractions of his home town were of somewhat lesser interest to Michel than to me, and I did not know enough then to venture out on my own.

On the other hand, he did introduce me, quite extensively, to the rich cuisine of the region. Old family restaurants and picturesque cafes were preferred meeting places for Jacques and him. There, they invited dozens of people, both veteran sales reps and potential hires, to mingle and share delicious food and wine in a relaxed atmosphere. They spent countless hours relating travel anecdotes and fantastic adventures in exotic lands. They appeared in expensive sports cars, attractive girls in tow, and they did not leave until they had charmed their audience and collected their contacts.

I did not really understand it then, but now I appreciate how successful this carefully staged recruiting effort was. When Jacques, and his partner, Jean-Pierre, first founded their book distribution business in Toulouse, they did it with little money and a lot of savvy. They signed lucrative contracts with various publishers on all overseas-sold books. The more they sold, the greater the commissions.

At first, they did most of the traveling and selling themselves, with their girlfriends and next of kin. Soon, they realized they needed to have hundreds of salespeople, in as many countries as possible, to be profitable. That's where Michel came in. He was a skilled salesman and a charismatic recruiter and, very quickly, became indispensable to the growth of the company.

As the business operations grew, and the need to shelter higher profits became more pressing, they added warehouses and administrative offices in Geneva, in the heart of the old city, and new headquarters in the tiny sixty-two-square-mile principality of Lichtenstein. At the same time, they offered Michel a minority stake in the firm. Recruiting had become the engine of their growing business model, thus the necessity of a plentiful and endless supply of reps, a sales force compensated solely with a fixed twenty-percent commission with no travel expenses or other benefits.

The trick was to convince droves of young people to leave their homes, travel overseas to sell books, and finance it all out of their own pockets. For that, Michel and his partners turned their lifestyles into advertising billboards for the dream life, a world of fun, adventure, and success. That's how I fell for, and unwittingly participated in, an incessant promotion campaign designed for hiring new recruits. And even though there was really nothing sordid or unethical beneath it all, I can now make sense of my inner resistance to that unrelenting sense of excessive and forced joie de vivre.

The time to leave Toulouse and head for the Geneva offices finally came. Michel's presence was required to report on his trip to Morocco and to start preparing the next expeditions. It was a lengthy transition for me. My only occupation was to follow Michel and wait for our next trip to begin so that I could be working again. With all the free time on my hands, I couldn't help but dwell on the sad mess I had left in Morocco.

The news I was getting from my mother and sister was that Paul had been devastated by my departure. My family had been trying hard to assuage his pain, explaining that I could not resist a great opportunity for work and travel, and that I would soon be back.

My lingering guilt and remoteness from Michel's entourage partly explained, without excusing, my desire to maintain a relationship with Paul from afar. Emotional insecurity was another reason for me to keep an anchor in the sea of free-spirited living I had plunged into. Thus began anew my familiar pattern of a twisted double life, simultaneously avowing love for two men.

From Geneva, I called Paul to explain why I had left so abruptly. I had barely uttered a few words when he let his anger explode.

"Listen to me, *please*, listen," I begged.

He hung up on me instead. I did not call him back; I couldn't really talk anyway. There were too many people around me. I took a pen and paper and scribbled a note to him. But instead of coming clean once and for all, I ran from the truth and again reverted to the crudest of lies.

How must I tell you that your anger is unjustified and unfair? You're right, I haven't been entirely honest with you {...} I left with a man, it's true, but it's not a sordid sex tale as you think it is...

My employment contract is being prepared; I'll send you a copy right away {...} I don't despair to be back with you. Because I love you whatever you may think.

Was this misleading letter my way of getting back at Michel? Was I seeking revenge for the jealousy blind-siding me? But why punish Paul? I will never know.

Michel and I stayed in Geneva for over a month. During that time, I called Paul at every chance I got and wrote him several more letters, all on the same theme, swearing my endless love, my fidelity to him, and begging him to wait for my return. All along I was living an actual love relationship with another man who knew nothing of my duplicity.

At the end of May, Michel and I left Geneva and returned to Toulouse on our way to Montreal. My last letter to Paul, sent from Quebec City, was dated June 17, 1975.

Today, as I stare at all those epistles on my lap, I can't stop my hands from shaking and my heart from sinking. One after the other, I opened and read through them, in shame and sorrow. Paul had returned all my letters to my mother in a final act of closure. His action stood in noble contrast to my endless delirium of lies and cowardice.

Curiously, were it not for the reappearance of those letters, I would never have imagined myself capable of such unforgivable behavior. I had totally obliterated that episode of my life from my recollection and always prided myself in my honesty and moral virtue. I had forgotten all about the skeletons in my closet, and pulling them out signified the purging of my soul.

13

Travel and Self-Discovery

Back in Toulouse, after a three-week trip to Canada, I found myself dealing with Michel's philandering yet again. After one too many fights, I took a plane home, vowing never to see him again. Despite his loving reassurances, I was getting weary of my constant suspicion. More than ever, I felt as if I wasn't living my life. But that was counting without Michel's tenacity. Within hours of my landing in Morocco, he was at my doorstep. He had taken the earliest flight he could find after learning of my departure.

"So you thought you could just leave me, just like that?" he asked me with his trademark smile and singing twang.

I couldn't believe he was indeed standing right there, in front of me. I was flattered by his impetuous reaction. But I had no desire to go back to Toulouse and be waiting around for him, victim of my own distrust and consuming angst.

"There is no way I can live this way, Michel. It's killing me," I said without inviting him in.

He pushed the door open, dropped his bag on the floor, his jacket on the back of a chair in the dark vestibule, and took me in his arms.

"But we're not going to stay there indefinitely..." he protested gently.

"Listen, I cannot imagine what kind of a future we could have together. We're too different. That's all."

My head was now resting on his shoulder. I was aware of the deep apprehension inside me as I uttered these words. I had no idea what else I could be doing anyway, or what my fear meant. I was more confused than ever about my options. I pulled back hesitantly and looked at him with tears behind my eyes, my heart aching, knowing I loved him still and was torn inside at the thought of never seeing him again.

"Look, I have to take a team on tour anyway. We'll go to the Middle East and Africa. I promise." He pulled me closer against him, adding in a whisper, "I can't let you go. I don't want to lose you."

I wanted to believe him. I had no design of my own or any goal I wanted to pursue beyond what he had to offer me. I certainly was not ready to return to high school or go back living in a cramped apartment with my siblings. It was much easier to go back with Michel. Besides, when we were travelling I felt safer with him than when we were in Toulouse.

We left France the second half of August 1975. My sister and her boyfriend, whom she had just met in Morocco that summer, had been persuaded by Michel to join us. Coincidentally, he too was from Toulouse, and his name was also Michel. We quickly resorted to calling him by his last name, Riva, to distinguish between them. Nezha had gone back to France with him, on vacation presumably, and was staying with his family. A tall and handsome twenty-two-year-old, with a cheery nature, Riva was deeply in love with her. It took him only a few minutes to make up his mind, drop his job as a Peugeot mechanic, and join our team on our upcoming journey. As it turned out, his skills did come in handy multiple times during our trip.

Michel bought a beat-up white Renault 16 with a hatchback and a spacious enough interior to accommodate the driver and three additional passengers with luggage. We all had very little financial means but Michel had reassured us we would be making money throughout our travels. We were going to sell books wherever we found French speakers and keep all cash deposits as advances on our commissions.

It turned out to be a once-in-a-lifetime adventure. Two teenage girls and six young men started off with three old cars and slept many a night in gas stations, on roadsides, in crummy hotels, and in people's homes, in far-off Christian missions, and in the middle of the jungle only to be awakened by tiny incredulous rainforest Pygmies. We ate what the natives ate and drank mostly tap water. But we also discovered lands of legend and history, people of diverse cultures, colors, and creeds, sites of ancient civilizations and untouched wilderness, and when after almost a year we finally found our way back home, we were grown, enriched, wiser and forever transformed.

That is not to say that such a transformation happened to me graciously. Throughout our journey, I often found it hard to cope with the difficult circumstances and had frequent arguments with Michel. He was supremely at ease in any and all situations, no matter how incongruous or uncomfortable.

"It's like feeding jelly to pigs," he would remark mordantly in my direction time and again.

His sense of humor, positive attitude, and hunger for life never ceased to amaze me. His funny side, in particular, was most attractive, though, at the time, I did not always appreciate those qualities to the fullest. It was only later that I actually laughed off the dreariness related to the lack of basic comfort and acknowledged the extraordinary journey of discovery I had been fortunate to experience, at such an early age, thanks to Michel.

The long road-trip took us down the breathtaking Yugoslavian coast—today known as Slovania and Croatia—through Northern Greece to ambivalent Turkey, the country that knows not where it really belongs, Europe or Asia, and where we spent three weeks before heading for Iran still under the Shah's rule. After a fruitful two-month stay in Iran, we headed for Iraq and left it in a hurry. Under repressive Baath Party rule, the country felt most unwelcoming; then quickly onto Jordan, and Egypt before we made it to Djibouti, our port of entrance to East Africa. We had the most profitable two-month business results in that tiny enclave before push-ing through Ethiopia to Addis Ababa and back southeast to Kenya, then Uganda under Idi Amin Dada to Rwanda, long before the genocide that ripped it apart.

After a month in Burundi, the fourteen-days-thousand-mile-long journey through Eastern Zaire—today known as Congo—during the rainy season, on dirt roads and across bridgeless rivers, led us to Central Africa and finally Cameroon, where our last car broke down and refused to go any farther. We had visited seventeen countries in all from the end of August 1975 to the end of June 1976, a little over ten months. We sold an astonishing amount of books, as much as sixty-thousand dollars' worth on a good month, an accomplishment which made the expedition a lucrative adventure.

But, my return to Europe meant going back into the back-ground, waiting around, and following Michel from Toulouse, to Geneva, to Andorra. My sister and her boyfriend decided to settle in Morocco where they rented an apartment and continued to make a living selling books. I only worked sporadically, performing administrative tasks in Geneva; otherwise I was still without a goal, often in fear of Michel's philandering, made the more seemingly inevitable by his occupation as a recruiter.

In Andorra, Michel's partners owned a quaint hotel, called the Kandahar, located at the bottom of the slopes of the Pas-de-la-Casa ski station in the Pyrenees. I was so useless I did not even learn to ski until the last weeks of my four-months stay there. We travelled infrequently, and only for short supervisory visits, to resident teams in Africa and overseas french territories. Every three or four months, I returned to Morocco to visit my family.

On one such visit, in April 1978, my brother Abdu was almost killed in a devastating car accident, on the road from Rabat to Casablanca, where he was then attending school. His girlfriend was driving and died instantly when she hit an oncoming truck head-on. Their two friends, riding on the back seat, escaped safely, but Abdu suffered extensive head trauma and broken limbs. He went into a coma that lasted days and underwent innumerable hours of surgery. His injuries were so severe, he was told he would never be able to walk again and sent home.

After I had lived so aimlessly, away from my family for so long, I instinctively felt responsible for his care and, without being asked, assumed the position of primary caregiver. For the following few weeks, I became his personal nurse, attending to him in every way, changing his bandages, cleaning him, feeding him, and interacting with his doctor.

It soon became evident that he was in need of more advanced surgical procedures, and I set out to find a facility in France. His surgeon referred me to the reputable *Hôpital Raymond Poincaré*, in Garches, on the outskirts of Paris. I had my brother admitted in the summer of 1978. For an entire year he endured many complicated operations and long hours of rehabilitation but, in the end, he was able to stand and walk on crutches.

My brother's accident deeply affected me and gave me a new sense of purpose. Life felt more precious to me, my family more important. I could no longer wait around, hoping for someone to help me make something worthwhile of my existence. It became crystal clear to me that I had to take my future into my own hands. So right after my return from Paris where I left my brother in the hospital, I decided it was time for me to finish high school and take the dreaded Baccalauréat exam. I returned to Morocco and enrolled in a correspondence course for the *terminale* year.

For the duration of that academic year, I focused almost exclusively on my studies, working only part-time selling books in Rabat and Casablanca. By that time, Michel had begun to fade in the background. We had effectively split up without ever voicing it overtly. To my surprise, and despite a subdued anxiety, I felt a whole new level of enthusiasm and motivation, but also a renewed sense of confidence in myself. I was single, and I was focused.

I did meet a kind, young, and attractive Moroccan architect who graciously offered to help me with my math lessons, and we briefly had an affair. I knew a relationship was only going to complicate things. It was a little sad; he really was a special man, and although he never declared his love, I knew he had real feelings for me. From my point of view, it was a matter of timing and of not wishing to remain in Morocco for too long.

In the spring of 1979, my mother, sister, and I drove from Rabat to Paris to visit Abdu in his Garches hospital. It was the first time that the three of us had gone on a long road trip to Europe by ourselves. I had money in the bank and felt comfortable paying most of our travel expenses, including food and lodging.

There was an intoxicating feeling of independence and self-assurance in the air despite, or perhaps because of, the absence of a male presence. Michel had let me keep a cute, "super-mini" Renault 5, color *aubergine*, with an Andorra plate which I used everywhere during those couple of years. The little R5 greatly contributed to my budding emancipation.

**

The trip started promisingly enough amid lively conversations until we reached the Rif Mountains and the twisted and, at that time of year, deserted road that separated Larache from Tetouan and the Port of Ceuta, the Spanish enclave on the Mediterranean coast of Morocco. We had planned to take the ferry-boat across the Strait of Gibraltar, from Ceuta to Algeciras, before nightfall. I had taken that trip many times with Michel in the past few years, and I was supremely confident. Perhaps a little too confident!

As the sun descended behind the mountains, shedding dark shadows on the green slopes, we passed a lonesome gas station on the roadside.

"Let's fill up the tank and be on the safe side," suggested my mother.

I glanced at the gauge; it indicated enough fuel.

"No, I still have gas, and we have to hurry to make the last ferry," I replied with poise.

As we approached Tetouan, the car unexpectedly slowed down, hiccupped, and silently gave out its last breath. The three of us looked at each other in dismay.

"What did I tell you, huh?" Mom started, "We ran out of gas!"

"Oh, my God!" Nezha exclaimed from the back seat.

"I can't believe it, Mom! The gauge was clearly showing plenty of gas to get us there and then some. I swear I don't understand." I was stunned.

Darkness had fallen fast. The small crescent moon peeking from behind a cloud was too feeble to lighten up the cold mountains. A heavy, ominous stillness surrounded us. We were three attractive women, alone, and scared, on a desolate Rif Mountain road, in the middle of "hashish country." And drug traffickers were not the only danger. We were easy, defenseless prey for any small-time bandits.

"Okay, don't worry. We'll be fine!" I said quickly. "I'm going to hitch-hike to the next station. You two stay here and wait for me. Lock yourselves up inside the car."

I tried hard to keep an even tone of voice, not let my fright show. I was not about to panic so easily, especially when my mother and little sister were counting on me.

I got out of the car.

"Okay, Mom, get behind the wheel, Nezha and I are going to push you on the dirt shoulder," I said assertively.

Within seconds, a car appeared around the curve. I signaled the driver to stop. The old man in a brownish djellaba and white turban came out of his seat, an expression of surprise on his face. He kept shaking his head, speechless, as I told him our predicament.

"The next gas station is not too far," he finally said. "I can take you there and you can find someone to drive you back to your car." He shrugged his shoulders as if to say, this is all I can do for you.

It was pitch black by then. The thought of leaving Mom and Nezha alone in rough country gave me cold sweats.

At the station, I quickly filled up an empty plastic container with gasoline, borrowed a small hose, and singled out a truck driver who was paying the young attendant.

"Excuse me..." I scrutinized his wrinkled, sun-baked face, soft eyes, and graying mustache, and felt I could trust him. "I need a ride back to my car a couple of kilometers down on your way. Can you drop me off? I'll pay you," I offered hesitantly.

He looked at my container and hose and shook his head smiling.

"Run out of gas, huh?" He chortled revealing his brown teeth. "Sure, let's go." He pushed his ski hat back on his head and took the container from my hand. "You don't have to pay me," he mumbled starting his engine.

"Not too fast, please," I urged him as I anxiously, stared at the indistinct roadside. And then I noticed a small vehicle with blinkers on and flashing headlights coming straight at us.

"Here they are!... stop, stop right here, please."

"Thank God you saw us," said Mom, sticking her head out the window. "We were afraid you'd miss us."

I jumped out of the truck and thanked the driver. He insisted on lending us a hand and set out to transfer the gasoline from the container to the car himself. I was grateful to him. I couldn't imagine having to draw the fuel with my mouth into the hose without swallowing a mouthful.

"Just after you left, a car stopped and gave us a bit of gasoline that they pumped out of their tank with a tube," Nezha explained smiling.

"Great!" I sighted with relief. "These people are all really nice. The trucker refused cash." Then it dawned on me. "I guess we missed the last ferry. We'll have to spend the night in a hotel in Ceuta," I said.

No one cared at that point. We had passed our first test of the road.

After a good dinner and a comfortable night's sleep, we caught the early morning ferry to Algeciras and headed up north on the way to Marbella, Malaga, and Barcelona. We had just hit the first highway when my mother again suggested that we fill up the tank. Again, I looked at the gauge and reassured her that we would have enough to the next gas station. Thankfully, it was bright sunshine in a cloudless blue sky when, as we approached the next station, the car sputtered and stopped dead in its track yet again, this time just a few yards away from the gas pumps.

"No way!" I said incredulous.

"You're so obstinate, a real mule," sighed Mom in reprimand.

"The gauge is not working," I heard Nezha grumbling in my back. "Didn't you get that last night?"

"Okay, okay, okay... my mistake, my bad. Let's not bicker," I said lightheartedly. "The station is right here. You two just get out and push me to the pump."

"Next time, I'm driving," said Mom as she stepped out of the car.

"Why don't *you* push?" Nezha retorted.

"Because I am the boss, that's why!" I said, laughing hard this time.

"You both stay in the car, I'm pushing," said Mom with fierce determination.

Both my sister and I stared at her and together burst into laughter. We were still laughing when we noticed the gas attendant staring at us in disbelief, then grinning widely as he shouted something in Spanish in our direction, and walked over to help push the car to the pump. Needless to say, we never again run out of gas.

In France, we spent our first night in Toulouse, where we paid a short visit to Larbi, then a freshman at the *Université de Toulouse*. He was lonely and homesick. We found him living in a tiny studio in an apartment building occupied mostly by prostitutes. They were all pretty friendly, according to him. We took him out to dinner and to *Superman: the Movie*. I wanted to leave the next day, but Mom would not set off until she made sure she did Larbi's laundry and cleaned up his place.

Eventually, we started off for Paris, driving four hundred and fifty miles in one day, stopping only for food and gas. We arrived in Paris at around 7:00PM and checked in a small hotel in the heart of the 6th arrondissement, between Boulevards St Germain and St Michel. We were dead tired. Still, we were so excited to be in Paris that my sister and I decided to drive around the city by night, even catch a movie on the Champs Elysees if possible. Mom chose to call it a night.

We were waiting for the light to turn at the corner of rue Dauphine when suddenly a group of loud youngsters surrounded our car and one of them yanked my door wide open.

"Where are you two babes going? Wanna give us a ride?"

He snickered stupidly, showing his crooked teeth, and gestured at his friends as if to demonstrate his boldness.

"What's the matter with you, dim-wit?" I yelled, startled. "Are you crazy? Let go of the door now!"

Thinking fast I tried to drive off. But pedestrians were still crossing the street in front of the car, so I just stood there ready to hit back if he touched me. I heard Nezha shouting at them to quit their stupid games. Some gawkers stopped and briefly observed the scene, wondering what the commotion was about. After a few minutes of hesitation, the thugs finally wandered off.

"Shit, can you believe this?" I looked at my sister, visibly startled. "From now on, we better keep our doors locked," I said.

She touched my hand gently and smiled.

"Yes," she said, "But let's not get too upset because of these jerks. Let's have fun!"

We had a particularly good time in Paris. Most importantly, Abdu was in good spirit and on his way to recovery. To his delight, we took him, first in a wheelchair then on crutches, for short releases out of the hospital. One of his favorite expeditions was a late evening to the Lido for an unforgettable dinner and show. With his forehead still bearing large fresh scars and bizarre-looking hardware sticking out of his pants, he was quite a sight indeed. The long metal pins and nails protruding out of his thighs and legs held his fractured bones firmly in place. Even though the poor fellow looked like a young Frankenstein, he wouldn't stop cracking jokes at his own expense, and beaming so happy he was to enjoy some fun time.

He had survived countless operations, battled frightening infections, persisted through agonizing hours of physical therapy, and endured sleepless nights, confined to a depressing hospital wing far away from home for an entire year. Yet the experience had somehow made him a different person, a compassionate, eminently friendly young man, enormously popular with hospital staff and fellow patients alike. Mom, Nezha, and I returned to Rabat relieved and optimistic about his condition and future prospects.

14

The Way to America

In mid-June 1979, I passed my high school exam, the dreaded *Bac*, with flying colors at long last. That summer, my sister and I planned to drive to Paris again and bring Abdu back home. Only when I signed him out of the hospital, I decided we had to celebrate both his recovery and my belated graduation. What better way to do that than by visiting Italy again for a couple of weeks? Since our first time in Venice in 1975, I had wished to go back and also explore further south, to Florence, and Rome. My sister and her boyfriend decided to come along as well.

The following summer and fall I went back to work selling books in Rabat and Casablanca with the idea of making some money before enrolling to university in France the next year. Only as fate will have it, a different path was awaiting me.

"How would you like to go to New York, Tokyo and Hong Kong with me next week, Wafa?" announced Moulay one evening in late November 1979.

Taken aback, I took the drink he was handing me before quipping: "Are you kidding me? God, I'd love to!" I looked him straight in the eyes, and sighed. "But I don't think I can afford it, unfortunately!"

"I know that, that's why I'm inviting you all expenses paid," he retorted casually.

"Wow, how about me?" interjected his friend Jackie as she extinguished her cigarette in the ashtray on the coffee table.

"You're welcome as well, of course," replied Moulay.

"I wish I didn't have to work," said Jackie. She pointed at me. "But you can. You're a sales rep, free to work when you please, right?"

I nodded, eyes sparkling. "Moulay, come on, be serious now. It'll cost a fortune, I can't possibly..." I began.

"I'm dead serious," Moulay answered. "I have to go to New York for business, but I've wanted to visit Tokyo and Hong Kong for a long time and never got a chance. I have a little time off, and I'd like to take advantage of my trip to America. So what do you think?" he insisted.

I hesitated.

Moulay was a longtime family friend. I liked him very much and often met at his place, around the corner from our apartment, after work with other friends. His offer was very tempting though I was a little concerned about his ulterior motives, being well aware of his awkward attraction to me.

"Look, you don't need to worry," he promptly reassured me. "I enjoy your company and I really don't like to travel alone. Consider it your graduation gift, okay?" he winked.

His frank speak did not really surprise me. Moulay was an intelligent and generous man. He had sensed my lack of romantic interest in him for some time and accepted my friendship without resentment, not seeing it as rejection and definitely not shunning me from his life.

In the end, our journey further underscored his kindness, and I enjoyed his company without a trace of guilt. Not only was he a big-hearted person, he was also a real gentleman and a fun-loving companion with an enormous appetite for life, food, and drink. A plump man with dark skin and a jovial face, he laughed easily and wholeheartedly. He spoke fluent English and made friends effortlessly. In every city we visited he made sure to book two separate hotel rooms and never once tried to renege on our friendly arrangement.

For almost a month, we spent time together sightseeing, shopping, dining, visiting his many friends and business associates, and attending local entertainment venues. Later, he often escorted me back to our hotel only to go back out, alone or with another friend, to a gentlemen's club to indulge in more earthly pleasures and often excessive drinking. On such occasions, he would not reemerge until late morning. Luckily, I never was an early riser.

Landing in New York City for the first time was an eye-popping experience. We stayed at the cavernous Hilton hotel on the Avenue of the Americas. My first steps into the shaded canyons of midtown Manhattan blew me away. I was dizzy with the sheer scale of it all: buildings, avenues, streets, cars, food portions, and people; it was a world unlike any I had seen before. I was thunderstruck, transported by the heightened pace, boundless energy, baffling diversity, infinite ambition, fearless vision, and voracious material appetite, and couldn't help feeling small, foreign, awkward, and totally awed.

There was but one cloud in that bright firmament of wonderment. Throughout our visit, my impressions were tainted by the frustration caused by my ignorance of the English language. I had to rely on Moulay to translate for me, explain to me, and speak for me. Suddenly, all my previous travel experience amounted to little or nothing, obliterated by sensory overload and my inability to understand the written or spoken message, and thus communicate freely.

I nonetheless marveled at the extravagance of the holiday season in New York City, the dazzle of Broadway shows, the fabled Radio City Christmas Spectacular, even the release of Francis Ford Coppola's formidable *Apocalypse Now*. I absorbed it all with astonishment, delighting in the sights and sounds, if not the deeper meanings that only familiarity with culture and language can provide. Later on, Tokyo and Hong Kong were further fascinating discoveries but none came close to the sheer fascination I felt in Manhattan.

I returned home in the new year with one idea in mind—learn English—and without delay. Uncle Hak offered to pay for my school and lodging, and I set out to enroll in an intensive English course for foreign students at the International House of London, a language school on Piccadilly, directly across Green Park and a short walk away from Hyde Park, Buckingham Palace, and Piccadilly Circus. My first accommodation, however, booked from Rabat, was not as pleasant as I had hoped.

I took off from Casablanca on a Sunday in early February 1980, and landed at Heathrow three hours later under a heavy sky and fast-falling darkness. I stepped out of the airport and hailed a London cab, armed with the address of the family providing me with housing. I remember it took a while driving down the poorly lit streets in an unwelcoming drizzle. I finally washed up on the outskirts of town far from Central London in what appeared to be a working-class neighborhood of dull attached houses without grace.

The cab driver immediately drove away leaving me standing nervously on the curve with my suitcase. I knocked on the door and was welcomed by a smiling red-faced lady in a tired house dress. She and her husband offered me tea and biscuits at the kitchen table and valiantly tried to make conversation. Their effort, made all the more difficult by their heavy cockney accent, was commendable but futile; I could not comprehend a word they said.

"Sorry, I don't understand. I don't speak English," I kept apologizing repeating the few words I knew.

Actually, I was also famished and disappointed. I had expected something a little more "charming" and perhaps, too, a warm dinner. They showed me my tiny room upstairs, and I decided then that I would not bother unpack. I went to bed with an empty stomach and a firm determination to move out the next day.

I woke up very early in the morning and somehow managed to get the directions to the train station for the commute to my school. Everything around me appeared, and felt, cold, grey, and damp—very much like the weather that day. I feverishly planned my next move. My first order of the day was to attend my school's evaluation tests, scheduled for 9:30AM that Monday.

Immediately after lunch, I went searching for a new place to live. A friend in Morocco had given me a few addresses where he had stayed when studying in London. First on the list was a house within walking distance of the school.

Located on Chapel Street, a little street between Grosvenor Place and Belgrave Square, one of the most magnificent 19th-century squares in London, the house was owned by an old German woman who rented rooms to international students. Little did I know then that the Westminster neighborhood was none other than Belgravia, famous for its grand, white-stucco mansions, homes to many embassies. What a difference from where I had landed the night before! I instantly wanted to live there. It was picture perfect!

When I knocked at Mrs. Furse's door, I was praying she'd have a room for me. The short and grumpy, elderly woman who opened the door spoke various languages, including French. After inquiring who had referred me, she led me to a spacious, sparsely-furnished room with two scruffy single beds, an old desk, a chair, and a chest.

"You're lucky, I have a vacancy. You'll have to share with another young woman, if you're interested," she said in heavily-accented French. "She's Algerian and doesn't speak much English herself."

She entered the room, pointing to one of the beds.

Evidently the room, which featured an unused fireplace, had either been a study or sitting room in its heyday. It was musty and comfortless, but had high ceilings and old-world appeal.

"I'll take it," I said quickly.

I was relieved she had space for me and unconcerned by the drabness of the place. She shook her head and walked past me to show me the rest of the house. The entire first floor was dark and in serious need of repair, quite a contrast to the sparkling white grandeur of its neighborhood.

"I have half-a-dozen students from all over the world living in the house right now," Mrs. Furse said, closing the door behind me. She paused and took a good look at me. Her grayish, frizzy hair was loosely tied back; her thick unibrow and thin lips conferred a severe appearance to her person.

"Oh, really?" I smiled circumspectly.

I was intimidated by her and mindful not to say or do anything that could get in the way of my renting a room. She pointed to the black phone hanging under the staircase in the corner of the hallway.

"The telephone is only to receive calls."

Climbing the creaky stairs to the first floor, she added "Heat and hot water are on for two hours in the early morning and in the evening."

She stopped at the top of the stairs and opened the door of the single bathroom. I barely glanced at a large white bathtub and free-standing sink—all seemed fairly clean—and nodded.

"Breakfast is included in the rent, and it's served between 7:00 and 8:00AM—no later!—in the kitchen."

The fast, well-rehearsed presentation was drawing to an end. She clearly managed her house with an iron hand.

I agreed to everything she stipulated, paid her the requested £20, and that very afternoon, returned to the suburb to fetch my luggage. I had paid a week's rent for my housing but I did not care in the least. I was out of there and enchanted with my good fortune.

I stayed in London for six frenzied months, taking five hours of English a day, five days a week, and enrolled in the Polytechnic of Central London for an additional two-hour Arabic class, three nights a week. And as if that was not enough, I also signed up for a weekly, two-hour jazz-dance class in Covent Garden.

Determined to catch up on my artistic education, I dipped into my savings and spent every minute of my free time immersing myself into London's rich cultural life. New York had been my initiation, whetting my appetite for art. London offered the same wealth of inspiring, high-quality events. I even put my fast-improving English to the test by sitting through Arthur Miller's masterpiece, *Death of a Salesman,* at the National Theatre.

After almost three months on my own in London, Uncle Hak announced that my brother Larbi, who was failing miserably in Toulouse, would join me to learn English. In mid-April, I moved to a large, furnished room on Draycott Place, in Chelsea, a couple of blocks from King's Road. The studio-type accommodation had all the charm of a hospital suite, equipped with two beds, an open kitchenette, and a coin-activated black-and-white television set. At least the bathroom was on the same floor.

Larbi descended on London at the end of the month and immediately felt at ease in the bustling city, happily tagging along to the cultural events I was sampling. I made many friends in London, but sadly lost sight of them within a few years. That sojourn was positive on so many levels, though. Most of all it was a turning point, the affirmation of my new life and future outlook. I was prepared for bigger and better things. My optimism had reached new heights.

At about the same time, my sister, who had broken up with her boyfriend, went to Florida to visit Hamid, a friend of ours studying in Gainesville. Soon, she met Michelle, a French-Canadian and University of Florida student. Michelle spoke French in a delightful Quebec accent with all its peculiar colloquialisms. The daughter of a rich Montreal businessman, she drove a sleek white two-passenger Camaro with a sky-blue stripe painted on its sides, and lived in a big house with Diane, Hamid's girlfriend. She and Nezha got along so well, she invited my sister to stay with them. For the following three months, she introduced her to the famed party life of the local student community.

Nezha loved every minute of her visit and returned home with, literally, tears in her eyes and the crushing desire to return as soon as possible. When she wrote me in London, I was applying to college in Paris and had not given any thought to the States; my memories of New York had faded away. Nezha kept insisting that Florida was where I ought to be looking for college because of the fun, glorious weather, and conviviality of the American people.

At the beginning of August, Larbi and I returned to Rabat without a clear idea of what to do next. I was still considering college in France when Nezha asked Hamid to meet us at Uncle Hak's to tell the family about college in Florida.

**

Exactly six weeks later, on a Saturday night, September 6th, 1980, my three siblings and I landed in Gainesville and anxiously waited for Hamid to pick us up at the airport.

"Do you see him anywhere?" asked Nezha.

"Nope," I said, "He may be a little late." I looked around one more time. "Do we even have a phone number for him or an address?" I inquired.

"I bet he forgot about us," joked Larbi.

"No way!" I said indignantly.

"Knowing him, it wouldn't surprise me!" Abdu chuckled.

Nezha nodded and feverishly searched her bag for a phone number.

"Here it is." She pulled a small piece of paper out of her handbag.

After several failed attempts to reach our friend from a payphone, we stood there in a row, an air of disbelief about us and our luggage piled in front of us. It was getting late, and the small airport was emptying quickly.

"He's not showing up," Nezha muttered, voicing what was slowly dawning on us all. "He forgot about us, I'm sure!"

"Okay, since we don't even have his address, let's go to a small hotel for the night," I decided, taking things in my own hands.

We got the last taxi available to drive us to a motel near campus, where we booked a single room with two full beds and, after a quick shower, went to sleep, exhausted by the five-hour jetlag and close to twenty-hour trip.

Early on Sunday morning, while awaiting his turn in the bathroom, Larbi turned the television on. He tried changing stations but was astounded to discover that channel after channel was showing the same brand of fervent Christian televangelists preaching to their flocks with dramatic theatricality.

The spectacle left us speechless. Of all the things we'd heard about the United States, that over-the–top religiosity was not one of them. Suddenly, it felt like we had been duped.

Dismayed, I turned to Nezha.

"What the hell is this?" I asked her. "Did you know about these fanatics?"

"No, I didn't. I never saw this when I was here," she replied. "But, then, I never watched TV either."

Later on that day over a gargantuan brunch of pancakes, eggs, and hash browns, Hamid ruefully confessed that he had indeed forgotten all about our arrival.

"I'm sorry. At least you slept fine, right?" He smiled with his usual nonchalance.

"Still, it was unnerving to not see you at the airport," I complained feebly.

"Hey, man, what are those Christian fanatics on TV?" interrupted Larbi in an effort to change conversation. Hamid, after all, was offering to put us up for a few days until we moved to our own place.

"Oh, yeah, the Christian televangelists... They're a staple of the Sunday TV lineup. That's all part of the American paradox; a country where liberalism and ultra-conservatism, even fanaticism, exist side by side." He laughed and began telling us a few anecdotes about the miracles some of the priests routinely performed.

Since we had arrived in Florida with student visas and the academic year had already started, we all enrolled in different levels of English as a Second Language (ESL) classes. In January, I decided to attend the local community college rather than wait for the following fall, as my siblings were doing, then transfer to the University of Florida. In one calendar year, I completed an associate's degree while on the Dean's List.

In the fall of 1981 about thirteen months after our arrival in Gainesville, on Halloween night, I met Robbie.

15

Robbie

The face of an angel, I thought.

High cheekbones framing a flawlessly straight nose; arched eyebrows drawing attention to deep, dark-blue eyes; full lips begging to be kissed; silky brown hair, parted off the middle that fell gently on the forehead highlighting a pale complexion: He was beautiful. The instant my eyes met his, I felt an electric shock, a gut-jerking, heart-pounding pull, an irresistible magnetism.

A slim, six-foot-two, twenty-two year old, Robbie looked like he'd just stepped off the cover of GQ. My mind went blank, and a fever mounted in me that I could hardly control. Adding a sexy elegance to his demeanor, he spoke softly with a refined English accent—though I can't remember a word he said at that moment. I was utterly incapable of thinking. I left him talking to my brother and cousin and ran to the kitchen after Cynthia, grabbed her arm.

"Oh, my God," I exclaimed, staring at her intently, "Who *is* this guy?"

My friend chuckled, delighted with the stir she was pleased to have caused.

"That's Robbie, the guy I've wanted you to meet for so long." She spoke slowly, arranging little cheese hors d'oeuvres on a platter.

"God, he's absolutely gorgeous!"

"Yeah, I know, and a great lover, too," she added with a wink.

"Really? Wow, Cynthia, I've got to have him."

I hesitated for a short second. I, of course, knew Cynthia was married, though I did not know anything about her marriage and never cared enough to ask. She had been dating Hamid when she went on summer vacation to Paris, then Morocco, with him. There she had met me, my brothers, and cousins.

A cute brunette, she exuded confidence. She was smart as a whip and engaging, and she had no second thought about introducing her husband to her male-friends.

"Not tonight, Wafa. Tonight he's with me. You can have him tomorrow!" she said with a composed face, "My husband is in the Bahamas, playing golf, and I am all alone and horny."

"Oh come on, Cynthia...you're not serious, right?" I pleaded.

"Sure I am." She looked up from her crackers. "Surely, you can wait a *little* longer, can't you?" She smiled with a calm detachment.

"No, um, um, I can't, really I can't. I don't know what's got into me. I'm telling you, it's like a train just hit me."

I was following her back into the living room, switching to French so as not to be understood. Cynthia turned her head to me, still holding her tray.

"*Il parle le français!*" she said under her breath.

"Here you are," interjected Larbi in my direction. "We've gotta go, Wafa."

"No, wait, I just got some hors-d'oeuvres," said Cynthia, "What's the rush?"

She put down her platter.

"We're meeting some friends and going to a Halloween party," said Tahar while giving her a kiss on the cheek.

"You did a great job with the make-up," Robbie said as he shook my hand.

I had just spent hours drawing intricate and vibrant designs on the faces of Larbi and Tahar, and both looked striking. I myself was dressed up as a gypsy, wearing heavy, elaborate make up and flashy jewelry adorning my neck, ears, and wrists. My long curly black hair was partly hidden under a colorful scarf and my shoulders covered with a long fringe shawl. At that moment, I felt out of place and unattractive. Neither Cynthia nor Robbie was in costume.

What is he thinking of me? I wondered.

My second Halloween night in Gainesville fell on a Saturday in 1981, a cool, clear, crisp night full of the promise of carnival-like titillation, a new experience for me. What *was* Halloween, anyway? During a trip to Mexico with Michel many years before, one November first, I had witnessed the festivity of *El Dia de Los Muertos*, the Day of the Dead. I had been astounded by the people's joyous celebration and the open display of skulls and paraphernalia traditionally associated with death and the afterlife. Far from being gruesome, the Mexicans were happily remembering their beloved departed. By comparison, in France on the same day, *La Toussaint*-All Saint's Day-is a solemn national holiday, a kind of French family Memorial Day, where people bring flowers to the graves of their loved ones.

Halloween, I was told, was of Celtic origin. It was believed by the ancient Gaels that, on October 31, the worlds of the living and the deceased briefly merge, and the dead come back to bring mayhem to the living world. It was in an attempt to appease those souls that costumes and masks were worn and treats sought under the threat of trickery.

When Cynthia called me at home to ask that we come by for a drink, I had first turned her down explaining we were getting ready for our first Halloween party. The year before, we had just arrived in Gainesville and the whole concept of dressing up and going wild had seemed childish and off-putting to me. This time, the boys had convinced me to join them. Suddenly, I didn't want to go anywhere else. All I wanted was right there in front of me, and I couldn't get it just yet. Nonetheless, I forced myself to go out as planned and wait, as Cynthia had insisted.

In the early afternoon the next day, right after they woke up, I asked Larbi and Tahar to call Robbie and invite him over. It turned out he didn't have a car, so they drove over to his place with my old, beat-up, two-door Oldsmobile Cutlass.

Almost three hours later, they had yet to show up. I tried to occupy myself as best I could, doing my homework and biting my nails. I called Cynthia and asked her for Robbie's phone number. When he answered, he sounded calm and collected.

"Hello?" said Larbi casually after taking the phone from his hand. Apparently the world had not caught up with my feverishness and was quite indifferent.

"What the hell are you doing?" I asked impatiently, "You were supposed to come back home with him."

"Oh, we're just talking," said Larbi unflappably. "I guess we forgot the time."

"You can say that again," I snapped. "I've been waiting for you for *hours* already."

"Sorry," said Larbi, "We'll try to be there soon."

"Well, I'm going to a movie with Cynthia at seven. I hope you'll be home by the time I get back." I needed to quiet my nerves.

"Oh, yes, sure. What are you going to see?" asked my brother.

"Ingmar Bergman's *Smiles of a Summer Night.* It's a 1955 black-and-white movie. Do you wanna join us?" I asked without really meaning it. Sure, I was anxious to see Robbie again but not in a movie theater.

"I don't think so," said Larbi. "We'll see you afterwards, alright?"

"Larbi, wait. What do you think of Robbie?" I tried to steady my tone of voice.

"Oh, he's a great guy. Very smart, travelled a lot. We've been talking non-stop." He giggled in the way he did when put on the spot.

"Okay, then. And, Larbi, don't forget, you're supposed to bring him back home with you," I again insisted.

When Cynthia dropped me off that night, I noticed my Oldsmobile parked in front of the house and suddenly I could hear my heart pounding and feel my stomach tightening. I covered the few steps to my door, agitated, and pushed it open. The three of them were sitting in the living room, still engaged in animated conversation and smoking cigarettes. My mind barely registered all three looked high from smoking weed all afternoon.

That night, Robbie opened up to me spontaneously. He admitted, in the course of our conversation, that he had been pot-smoking since junior-high and that he really wished to stop, adding that he needed someone like me to help him. His honesty and directness immediately seduced me.

He was half-English, half-American, had lived in a few places in Latin and Central America, Africa, and the Persian Gulf. His British father, a high-level executive working for an American oil company, had been divorced and separated from his first wife and child when he met Robbie's mother in California and married her. They had three children together; Robbie, the eldest, had been born in Venezuela.

At age nine, Robbie had left home—then in Kuwait—to attend an all-boys boarding school in Kent. A few years later, he was enrolled in a Central Florida boarding school, where the rules were far more permissive than in England. That's where, at thirteen, he had become a habitual pot-smoker. Money had never been an issue; his parents had always been generous with his allowances.

He was smoking menthol cigarettes as he spoke, squinting to keep away the smoke. I noticed his bitten-off finger-nails while I listened to him, fascinated, with no other thought than to hold him in my arms and lose myself in the dark ocean of his eyes. I was smitten, unmindful to everything else.

Very late into the night, I discreetly urged my brother and cousin to excuse themselves and leave me alone with Robbie.

"Hey, listen guys, I have to go to bed. I have an early class tomorrow morning," said Larbi as he stood up.

"Actually, so do I," Tahar exclaimed.

"But I need a ride home." Robbie looked bemused.

"Don't worry, I'll drive you home. I don't have class till the afternoon," I offered in a casual tone. "You'll have to show me the way, though. I am not yet completely familiar with Gainesville," I said as we walked to the car.

"I live in a trailer about fifteen minutes from here."

"What's a trailer?" I asked

He laughed. "Oh, it's a large mobile home, but this one is connected to the town utilities," he explained, amused. "I've been renting it for the past few months because it has a-how should I say?-special bohemian feel to it," he added.

I was not really hearing him anymore and did not ask any other questions. The road, bordered by thick, shadowy trees, was deserted, the night pitch black. The ambiguity of the moment made it hard for me to reflect. I was trembling inside, trying hard to keep my hands steady on the wheel.

The car stopped smoothly on the dirt road. He gave me a goodnight peck on the cheek and got out of the car. I felt my heart drop in my chest. I watched him take a few steps in the direction of his door, hesitate, amble back and around to the driver's side. I rolled my window down, eyes locked on his.

Slowly, he leaned over and turned the car key off before holding my face and kissing my lips sweetly, then eagerly. I felt his arms reach down, grab me by the waist, and pull me out of the car through the open window without even attempting to open the door. He carried me in his arms up the steps of his mobile home to the bedroom, laid me down on soft satin sheets, and made love to me with passion and tenderness.

Our bodies dissolved into one; our souls sang to the gods in heaven. Our cries, tears, sighing, moaning, sweaty skin, and balmy scents, mixed and fused in a state of perfect bliss, in ecstasy. Time and place were suspended; across the universe, nothing else existed but the two of us, reborn into one.

For the first time, without the slightest bit of guilt, I missed class the next day.

I woke up around two in the afternoon to the sound of chirping birds and the smell of fresh coffee and warm toast. I was starving and bewildered when he entered the room carrying a tray.

"Hungry?" he asked with a smile.

"Oh, yes, ravenous in fact!" I sat up and reached for my crumpled tea-shirt on the floor. He was already dressed in a pair of blue jeans and white cotton sweater.

"I hope you like herb and cheese omelets." He placed the tray in front of me and leaned forward to give me a kiss. Then he sat on the edge of the bed, buttered my toast, and watched me take a bite with a loving gaze.

"Mmm, delicious," I sighed. "You're not eating?"

"Already did, actually. I was too hungry to wait for you." He got up and opened the blinds. "Do you like classical music?" He asked and, before I could answer, went into the living room.

Within minutes, the sound of a Chopin sonata filled the air and he returned with a cup of coffee and a cigarette in his hand.

"I can't believe I missed class today," I said with a grin. "First time it happens! Mmm this is delicious. You're a good cook."

I poured a little milk in my coffee.

"I hope you don't feel too guilty," he said.

He sat next to me and gently brushed the hair off my face.

"Nope, not at all," I shook my head. "It was well worth it."

The thought of the night washed over me. I could still feel him in me.

"I'd love a warm shower after this," I pushed the tray off my lap and leaned to give him a kiss. "Thank you, that hit the spot," I said.

"I can run you a bath if you prefer. Would you like that?" Robbie offered.

I nodded, an ecstatic look on my face, delighted with the attention. Magically, everything he did reinforced my fascination.

He was a dream-come-true Prince Charming—at once cultured, refined, sensitive, passionate, gorgeous, yet humble and sweet.

I slipped back between the smooth satin sheets. I had never met a man who had satin sheets, I'd noticed briefly the night before when my skin felt the silky texture. But then I had never met a man so at ease with his sensuality, so in tune with his partner's needs and loving of the female body.

"Your bath is ready now," the sound of his voice tore me out of my erotic thoughts. He took my hand and I followed him.

The sight of the lit candles and the steaming bubbles made me squeal with pleasure. I took off my t-shirt, stepped into the fragrant bath and sank my body into the warm caress of the water. He stayed to wash me and gently massaged my neck and shoulders, re-awakening insatiable lust and sending us back into the thralls of love. Our burning passion was as impetuous and powerful as a tropical storm, and just as overwhelming. We sensed, hungered, and mirrored the same furious need for love and there was no room for anything or anyone else in our world.

In that complete and utter surrender to each other, we spent the following days, he, taking me to class and returning to pick me up, and I, counting the minutes that separated me from him and the moment of abandon and sweet embrace that I knew would soon follow. The extent of our mutual attraction acknowledged no ends or limits, and for a short while, we lived a blissful existence.

Within weeks, we were living together.

16

Sour Love

"Please, please go, Robbie, please go away."

I was sobbing hysterically, sitting on the cold bathroom floor, my knees pressed against my chest. I kept staring at the door, fearing it would break. My face was ravaged with tears, my hair messy, my heart pounding.

Suddenly, I heard the wood crack and splinter. He threw himself at me. I raised my arms in front of my face.

"No, please," I begged him, "Please stop." I felt nauseous, sick with fear.

"No, I want *you* to stop," he said. "You started this, you wanted to make me feel like shit again, you *cunt*."

He grabbed my arm, pulling me up. That trash word again, a word I loathed and which, for some reason, sounded dirtier and more hurtful than any other he used to demean me. The first time I'd heard it, it came out of his mouth. I didn't even know what it meant, just that it sounded filthy, terribly offensive. I felt full of hate towards him, hate and fear. I tried to pull away from his grasp.

"Let go of me, you fucking asshole, *let me go, you hear?*"

He kept pulling me, dragging me with both hands, deaf to my pleas.

"This is what you wanted, isn't it, you bitch, pushing all my buttons. This is what you were looking for."

"I want you to leave me alone... now... stop it..." I screamed at the top of my lungs. "I hate you! *Don't touch me!*"

I was seething with rage. And, suddenly, he turned, grabbed me by the hair, and smacked my mouth and nose.

"Shut the fuck up, you bitch! You'll have to listen to me now."

I was struggling with his hand as he suffocated me, threw me on the bed and sat on top of me, pushing me down with the full weight of his body. I tried to fight him off with all my might, gasping for air, tears running down my cheeks, meeting his hands. I could still make out his distorted face, the spittle gathering at the corner of his mouth.

He's a beast, I thought. How could I love such a monster?

"See what *you* make me do?" he let out between his teeth, panting noisily, not letting go of me. "I could kill you right now, see? Happy now?"

I felt dizzy, my chest burning, my strength deserting me... *He is going to kill me this time, for sure...* Fear engulfed me as I turned limp.

Abruptly, he released his grip, laid down on his back next to me, still holding me with one arm on my chest.

"All I wanted was for you to come to me and tell me you love me," he said meekly.

I couldn't believe my ears; the same improbable argument. He hurt me because I did not show him enough love! How could I possibly love him when he physically abused me, when every fiber of my being was repulsed by him? Why was it so difficult for him to understand? He really saw it as *my* way to escalate the violence between us, *my* inability to show him affection in a convincing way. He thought it was easy, quite simple. I was sure he was out of his mind, a deranged psychopath, in those moments, and I viewed myself as a pathetic fraud of a woman, who stayed with him in spite of his sadistic streak. He turned toward me again, buried his face in my hair.

"I love you so much, baby, but you drive me crazy," he whispered in my ear. "Please forgive me, I don't want to hurt you-I know I'm a jerk, a rapist... But all I want is for you to love me."

He kissed my neck, pulled closer to me. I remained stiff and unresponsive, scared to make a move, my swollen face still feeling the sting of his fingers. A deathlike blur had swallowed a chunk of my heart. I couldn't begin to measure the depth of my despair.

The first time that had happened I'd found a hand-written statement he had left for me to read. He had the most unattractive, and least readable, handwriting of anyone I knew—all in tightly skewed capital letters and poor punctuation. Today, as in the past, I find it hard to decipher. In his agitated mind, Robbie seemed to have glimpses of clarity and stretches of delusion as he wrote:

We had sunny days, we had dark days, but we loved each other with an intensity I've never before experienced and always wanted. But we played games with each other. Crazy isn't it, two who love but hate at the same time {...} I told her I was tired of this cruel game we both played, I wanted to stop. She couldn't stop; she said I hurt her so much; she wanted to hurt me even more.

I hoped that eventually she would be reasonable and recognize her gamesmanship; I hoped she would see that we both wanted love; I hoped she would stop, forgive, forget, and come to my side. But she didn't. I woke up the next day; the first thing I sensed was that she was not there. The bitch was still tormenting me, still punishing me, and still begging me to stop her from going on.

I went to her bed and I told her to stop, I slipped inside and held her. I was angry, I had wanted to stop, all I had wanted was to feel her affection, but all I did was to punish her brutally. I told her she was evil because she couldn't stop - she was as evil as me because she couldn't stop punishing. I begged her for affection, I begged her to stop me from punishing her, but she was adamant. I hit her, reflexively, I never figured anger and affection were linked so spontaneously. I hit her and I knew then there was no return. I hated her because there was no return.

I begged her pardon, I wanted forgiveness but I knew none was due. I grabbed her, I shook her, I hated her, I abused the only one I loved because she wouldn't and needn't love me. I was forcing her to hold me, but it was a bag of potatoes, a corpse that I held, there was no response—only fear, hate and regret. I couldn't force her to love me, I couldn't beg her for love and yet I couldn't remain unloved.

The rapist's paradox: how can he expect to be loved and understood when he violates another by force? How can he make the assumption he is loved in the first place? – And how can he impose himself on the life of one he loves, without force? What does anyone do, let alone the rapist, when he is rejected? The rapist tries to extract affection violently {...} Wafa, I rapist, am desperate, I lover, accept your conditions. I lover cannot expect your love, I rapist demands it {...} I feel sorry for them both, I understand them both, I love them both, I forgive them both {...}

What did he mean? I kept wondering in vain. And yet his tortured logic did somehow convince me that he loved me enough, his frustration was justification enough, for his abuse. I did not then pause and reflect on the ramifications of his message. I just put it away as soon as the storm passed; not realizing it contained the seeds of years of agony. Today, as I read and re-read it, I'm still hoping to understand the hidden meaning behind his behavior and my decision to stay with him despite it all those years.

In January 1982, I transferred from Gainesville's Santa Fe Community College to the University of Florida, and continued my fast-paced accumulation of college credits in order to graduate as soon as possible. By the summer of that year, my siblings and I became the unwitting victims of Uncle Hak's unpredictable fortune. As his business went from boom to bust, he went broke, and stopped sending us money.

My mother was getting depressed by the day, and I had slowly but surely used up every penny I still had of my savings on tuition and expenses. We were also faced with the meteoric, fifty-percent appreciation of the US dollar that started in November 1980, at the exact time we arrived in America, and went on till 1985.

In August 1982, I wrote a letter to my rich uncles, begging them to help us pay our outstanding school fees. I never received direct acknowledgement for my request but my mother got a little monetary assistance that barely made a difference. She was continually borrowing money from family and friends to send us in America.

After only a few months of living with Robbie, on October 2, 1982, I moved out, following another horrifying fight, and went to live with a kind old lady who rented me a room in her house in a wooded neighborhood of Gainesville, not far from campus. Gina's peaceful presence helped me cope with my heavy heart and study load. At the same time, my relationship with Robbie went through multiple phases of silence, heartbreak, arguments, and passion.

On his twenty-third birthday, in December 1982, he left Gainesville for Houston, Texas, where his parents, taking a break from their lengthy overseas assignments, had recently bought a house. He had failed to graduate as he planned and he still had to turn in a research paper.

In reality, he could have graduated by simply resubmitting the paper, *Exegesis of the Philosophy of Love*, which had earned him high praise from his teacher. But she had proceeded to add his paper so good that it could be used as an honors thesis with only minor adjustments. Instead, Robbie decided to turn it into his magnum opus, a grand honors dissertation on love as both an expression of religious fervor and human emotion. Sadly, the masterwork turned into a quagmire and eventually led to a final incomplete grade for his course and a failure to earn his bachelor's degree altogether.

From January to September 1983, in his parents' house in Houston, Robbie tried to finish his paper. But after months of research and reading the likes of St. Augustine, Rosenzweig, Kierkegaard, and Buber, he turned again to Plato and other Greek philosophers, and never saw the end of it. The depth and complexity of the subject matter became so overwhelming that he retreated into endless procrastination made worse by heavy pot-smoking.

During that time, and in spite of the pain of separation, I focused on the completion of my bachelor degree and, in April 1983, graduated with honors and an election to Phi Beta Kappa, a distinction I didn't fully comprehend then. Robbie and I decided that I would visit him at his parents' house in Houston for a couple of weeks before going to Morocco for the summer.

For the first time in my life, I knew exactly where I was heading after that. I had received a surprising phone call from

New York University's dean of graduate studies, when I least expected it.

"Wafa, it's for you," Gina had said, handing me the phone.

"Who is it?" I'd asked, looking up from my book.

She'd given me a quizzical look that made me smile. I loved that woman with all my heart. A spunky seventy-four-year-old with short, white hair cut in monk fashion, and intelligent blue eyes, she spent her time volunteering at her church and tending to her garden and home. The rest of the time, she spent reading in a comfortable armchair in her living room, pausing every once in a while and admiring the red cardinals helping themselves at her inviting birdfeeder. We enjoyed watching the *McNeil-Lehrer News Hour* and other educational PBS shows. We talked about many things and she, without ever interfering and much compassion, listened to my personal drama.

"Hello, is this Wafa?" the voice, on the other end, had asked.

"Hi. Yes, yes, it is."

"I'm Martin Schain, dean of the Graduate School of Arts and Science at NYU

. We received your application," he went on. "How serious are you about NYU?" he asked me point blank.

"Well..." I hadn't thought about that.

NYU was, in fact, at the bottom of the list of universities I'd applied to. I had already received acceptance letters from Georgetown and Harvard, and even been personally interviewed by a gentleman sent by the School of Advanced International Studies at John Hopkins. The problem was always the same, they would love to have me in their schools, but they couldn't offer any financial help the first year on account of my foreign student status.

The interviewer from John Hopkins had kept insisting that it would be no problem finding me an assistantship the second year. So could I find a way to pay for my first year? No, I couldn't, at all. It was not a matter of choice. I was seriously beginning to lose all hope of attending graduate school, when a New York friend suggested that I try NYU.

"They have a large entitlement program," he'd said, "and a very diverse student body."

So I had sent them a last-minute application.

"To tell you the truth, Mr...."

"Schain," he said. "Martin Schain."

"Sorry, yes, Mr. Schain. To tell you the truth, I've been accepted by all the schools I applied to. The thing is I can't afford any of them at this point. So it's all about financing for me right now," I explained.

"Oh, not to worry," he quickly replied. "You are at the top of our list for a fellowship that will cover your entire tuition."

I held my breath. "You know I'm a foreign student, right? I couldn't even work outside the school," I'd said.

"Well, here it is. You will also be getting a monthly stipend to help you with your living expenses and books."

He had paused waiting for my reaction.

"Wow, really? And... how much would that be?" I'd asked.

"I can't tell you that over the phone. But I can assure you, it's very generous. So, what do you think?"

"What do I think? I think it's great, very generous of you really... I'm speechless... Yes, of course, I'd love to attend NYU," I'd said, elated: The impossible had happened.

He had gone on asking me all sorts of questions about my travel overseas, work experience, and complimented me on my academic achievements.

"You will be getting a formal acceptance letter and more information in the mail within the next few weeks. I'm looking forward to meeting you soon personally," he had said.

I'd hung up and shouted in Gina's direction, "Guess what? I'm going to New York! That was the dean of NYU. They're paying for *everything*. Can you believe it?" I'd said overjoyed.

"Well, I think no one is more deserving than you," she had replied with her customary poise, and she returned to her book.

**

The sun was already shining brightly in the Texas sky on that balmy morning of May. The bedroom shades were still shut, and I slept peacefully.

I had arrived in Houston a week earlier and was planning to stay another two weeks. After five long, tormented months of separation from Robbie, I was anxious to renew our initial commitment to each other. He, on the other hand, was visibly happy to be living at home after so many years away at school. His mother's love and admiration were constant, unconditional, and she showed him total devotion. His relationship to his father was more complex. Robbie felt he was always falling short and, throughout his life, strived to earn paternal respect.

"Hey, baby, wake up, we have to get ready," Robbie called out softly. He jumped out of bed and headed for the bathroom.

I am a notoriously late sleeper, and early mornings are just not my thing. The clock on the night table read 7:35AM.

"It's too early," I mumbled in a sleepy voice, turned over, and went right back to sleep.

Robbie was already in the shower. When he came back, towel dry and ready to dress, I had not budged.

"Come on, Wafa, we agreed last night that we'd explore Houston today. There's a lot to do and see," Robbie insisted, pulling up his jeans.

He walked to the window and opened the shades, letting the sun stream right in.

"No, please, Robbie. It's too *early*," I protested, shielding my eyes. "We don't have to go so early. I'm tired. I'm on vacation, remember?" I pulled the sheet over my head, attempted to ignore him.

He was fully dressed by then.

"Come on let's *go*, Wafa. You can sleep later," he persisted. He pulled the sheet away and shook my shoulder.

"Stop it, Robbie, I want to sleep a little longer. We can go later, it's not end of the world," I replied vehemently and pulled the sheet back over my half-naked body.

Swiftly, his mood changed. In frustrated rage, he kicked me hard with his foot.

"You selfish, fucking bitch," he grunted in disgust.

Shocked, I sat up on the bed and rubbed my leg where he'd kicked me. I looked at him dismayed, completely awake then, trembling, and now outraged.

I yelled back at him. "What the hell is wrong with you, you fucking asshole? I don't want to go anywhere with you now, that's for sure."

I began crying. Furious, he angrily pulled at my sheet again and threw it away.

"Screw you," he said and stormed out the door.

Drawn by the commotion, his mother entered the room and tried to console me.

"What's going on in here, what's all the screaming about?" she asked plaintively. She picked up the sheet on the floor and handed it to me.

"He *kicked* me, out of the *blue*," I said between my tears.

"Oh, honey, I'm sure he didn't mean to hurt you," She began in her soft-spoken way. "You should try to understand, Wafa, he was just really eager to show you around." She sat on the bed and reached for my hand.

She and Jack had welcomed me and made me feel at home immediately, happy to meet their eldest son's exotic girlfriend. I looked at her beautiful face, smelling the scent of patchouli that accompanied her, her silver-gray hair pulled back in a graceful French bun, her gray-blue eyes filled with concern, and I hoped, for a minute, she would understand the extent of my consternation.

"But... but he *hit* me because I wouldn't get out of bed at his command," I protested.

"I'm so sorry, honey. That's not right, I know. But, you see, he was so disappointed. He'd put so much effort planning your day together."

From her expression, I could tell she would take his side no matter what I said. Silent tears kept flowing down my cheeks. I pulled my hand out of hers.

17

Wretched Marriage

After I left Houston, I spent a good part of my three summer months in Morocco, working as an interpreter for a team of American agricultural consultants from California. The Americans were overseeing the implementation of the latest irrigation techniques for the king's large farms in the region of Oujda in the northeast of Morocco. I was in desperate need for money for my big move to New York City. With my summer earnings and small gifts from family and friends, I gathered close to three thousand dollars.

On August 27, 1983, I arrived in New York, alone, and stayed at a friend's while looking for an apartment in the vicinity of New York University for Robbie and me. Incredibly, I was dead set on starting my new life with him, despite everything. Manhattan was still unfamiliar and I wanted to stay within walking distance of my classes in Washington Square. I eventually settled on a charming apartment on Ninth Street and University Place.

A fifth-floor walkup in an old brownstone, the small flat faced south and got plenty of sunlight, as well as stifling heat in the summer, from a built-in skylight window in the living room. The kitchen was the size of a closet with worn-out appliances, the bathroom was antiquated, and the bedroom could barely hold a full-size bed and an armoire, but it was affordable. My NYU stipend was enough to pay the rent. I had already spent nearly all the cash from Morocco on the down payment, first month's rent, a new bed, utilities and only the most basic household necessities.

The moving-in day, the bed's delivery, and Robbie's arrival all were scheduled for September 3rd. He had rented a U-Haul truck, packed it with his college furniture, and driven from Houston with his mother. She was flying from JFK Airport to the United Arab Emirates to join her husband in their next assignment in the Persian Gulf.

Back in May, Robbie had admitted that he was terrified by the big city; I had no idea how much. He had not finished his paper, and his eight-month stay in Texas had not gotten him any closer to his graduation goal. And since he had wasted most of his time getting high—neither studying nor working—his father had refused to give him one more cent. He was meeting me in New York flat broke.

In his father's defense, I must add that a few years earlier, he had offered him a generous sum of money with the choice of starting a business or pursuing a college degree, all expenses paid. Robbie had elected to attend college and now that it was over and he had failed to graduate, his father felt it was no longer his concern. Unbeknownst to me, then, as his parents were leaving the country for their overseas job, I was willingly inheriting their biggest family problem.

I started school mid-September and naturally relied on Robbie to look for a job to feed us. I paid the rent and believed it was only fair for him to contribute his share, especially since I was a full time student. My expectation fell short. After he

arrived in New York, and for the following two weeks, Robbie's
first order of business was to paint the apartment, starting with
the bedroom. I would come home and find him still slogging
on the little room's walls. He wanted it to be perfect. After
much arguing, we decided not to paint the rest of the apartment. Our small, joint bank account, opened with my last three
hundred dollars, was fast vanishing. I'd always been freakishly
insecure about money, but this was worse than I had bargained
for. Needless to say, we were in a constant tug of war.

"Why don't you look for a part-time job, too?" Robbie
asked me one evening. He was lying across the full length of
his old, trailer-days sofa, watching TV, waiting for dinner.

"I already pay the rent, don't I?" I retorted. "Besides, I am a
foreign student, and it's not exactly easy to find work illegally."

I glanced at him from the small kitchen, an eye on the
bubbling pasta sauce.

"As it is, I'm already concerned about our housing. I'm
afraid one of these days someone is going to ask me to produce
proof of our 'marriage,' and then we'll be in even more trouble."

NYU had allowed me to lease one of their rent-subsidized
apartments on the assumption that I was a "married" graduate
student who could not be accommodated in a regular dorm
setting. I had completed the official housing application with
that stipulation.

"Well, then, perhaps we should get married."

He'd said it calmly, with a weird detachment, puffed on
his menthol cigarette, and grinned, waiting for my answer.

"What on earth are you talking about? We can't even
afford a burger and a movie. How can we get married now?"

The thought was both scary and exhilarating, and it triggered a fretful throbbing in my ribcage.

"Why not? It'd just be a formality—we'll get a real ceremony later when things are better."

He stood up and walked toward me.

"That would solve a few problems, wouldn't it?"

He leaned his tall frame over my back and held me from
behind, his cheek touching mine.

"Do you remember the first time we met, at Cynthia's?" he
whispered.

"I sure do."

I smiled at the titillating memory.

"Well, that same night, when I got home, I called a friend
and told him I had just met the woman I was going to marry."

He kissed my neck, holding me tighter against him.

"You did? Really?" I turned around and looked up at his
exquisite features.

"Okay then, let's do it," I murmured.

And so it was that, on October 3, 1983, on a crisp fall morning, without pomp or ceremony, Robbie and I were married in
New York City. We had only one witness, Carlos, a Colombian
friend of Robbie's, whom, for no particular reason other than
he used to get high with him, I didn't like very much. Not a
single member of our families was present, no invitations were
sent, no honeymoon trip booked, no party planned. No one
came, no one was invited, no one was even told until after the
fact. They were all too far away, we allowed by way of justification, and we somehow knew this was no celebration.

In the impersonal and bland-looking City Clerk's office,
downtown, we stood side by side, at once uneasy and solemn,
hearing, without listening to, the man who was marrying
us. We had bought a pair of unadorned, identical gold rings
for fifty dollars each from a store on West 47th Street, and we

were both dressed in plain two-piece suits. The overwhelming impression I retain from that day is still present in my memory: I couldn't repress an undeniable sense of qualm and foreboding.

That same morning we had had a fresh argument about his procrastination and persistent unemployment, and, for days, while awaiting the requisite blood tests, my intuition nudged at my conscious mind. I just kept shutting it down. The only souvenir I had from that momentous event was a photograph of the two of us standing in the park outside city hall. We made a very attractive couple, no doubt, but the smiles on our faces were not exactly blissful. Eventually, even that single photograph, which I had put in a frame and displayed in our apartment, was destroyed during one of our dreadful confrontations.

Fully six weeks after his mother dropped him off at my doorstep, Robbie found his first job at Novo Arts, a hip art gallery located merely two blocks away. He was hired by Marlaina and Linda Deppe, the two attractive owners, to assist with anything and everything. He made about a hundred and ten dollars a week, and he spent almost a third of that on weed.

In December, both my sister and mother came to visit us in New York. Nezha stayed at a friend's nearby, and Mom moved in with us. Life in Morocco had become unbearable for her. She had broken up with Berto, the love of her life, and she was deeply alienated from her society. She had visited us on a couple of occasions in Florida and had fallen in love with America and the American Dream. I believe she had already, albeit tacitly, made up her mind that this was the home she had always longed for. In many ways, the trip to New York signified a point of no return for her. She never explicitly announced her decision to stay; she just did.

There was no room to accommodate her comfortably or with any degree of privacy. We bought a full-size inflatable bed that we dressed every night in the middle of the living room, and for a few weeks we alternated sleeping in the small bedroom and living room with her. The question of affording her an independent living in America became an urgent matter for us all.

Strolling in the West Village one mild winter weekend, my sister and I noticed a new restaurant on Bleecker Street called "Marrakesh West." Intrigued, we climbed up the few stairs to the entrance and found the owners in the midst of renovation for the big opening. We were greeted by two welcoming young Israelis, whose mother, born and raised in Morocco, had instilled a particular fondness for Moroccan cuisine and culture. We became fast friends, and they soon offered a full-time waiter's job to Robbie.

Until he lost his gallery job four months after he started, his ego had remained resistant to the idea of waiting on tables. But after enough of my nagging, Robbie reluctantly agreed to become a waiter in the restaurant on Bleecker. It must have felt like the end of a dream to him. Time was running out fast on the completion of his paper, and the goal of graduating college was ever more distant.

I honestly had no desire to see him give up on his graduation and his pursuit of a fulfilling career, and I would have accepted any sacrifice had I seen even a glimmer of desire and intent in his eyes. Only, when he was not waiting on tables, he was vegetating in front of TV for hours on end, making no contribution to our domestic chores, least of all his research paper. His eyes were bloodshot and empty, filled only with the haze of weed.

Exactly two weeks after Robbie became a waiter, I, too, started waitressing on weekends. Over the summer, I worked even harder, four to five dinner shifts at the Marrakesh West and a few lunch shifts at a new midtown restaurant and catering business called Between-the-Bread. After only three months, Robbie quit on bad terms with our Israeli employers and briefly worked at two other places before being hired as a bartender and catering captain at Between-the-Bread. He stayed employed there for the next six-and-a-half years.

My mother, who was a fabulous cook, also got her first job in America at the Marrakesh West. At home, she was well known, among family and friends, for her delicious Moroccan dishes. Very quickly, and to the great delight of the Marrakech West's owners, she introduced some of her best specialties to the restaurant's patrons. She and Rina, the matriarch and chef, got along very well, but it was my mother's talent that infused the restaurant's menu with its subtle flavors and touch of sophistication. Soon, her famous *bastella*—a filo pie stuffed with chicken meat, eggs, almonds and exotic spices—her delicate *tajins*, and her variations on the popular Moroccan couscous became main staples. Shortly after that, my mother began dreaming of her own business. Her cuisine was highly appreciated, and she began catering small functions out of our tiny kitchen on Ninth Street.

The next step was to find her an apartment of her own. Her first home was on the second floor of a two-family house in Long Island City, on the other side of the East River. A dull and nondescript neighborhood, the area was predominantly inhabited by Greeks and, increasingly, Middle-Easterners. Her apartment had a good-size kitchen and two small bedrooms, one of them overlooking the overhung subway track. Every few minutes throughout the day and night, the N train sent the house shaking and rumbling. But it was spotless, and the Greek landlady, who lived below, was friendly and helpful to Mom. From there, she was able to make a living and even plan for her own restaurant.

After she settled in Queens, and because our landlord had fulfilled his contract with NYU, Robbie and I were forced to move out. We rented a renovated two-bedroom on Bank Street, in the West Village, that was even smaller than the one we had just left. The new apartment was so tiny; we could barely fit in a queen-size bed in the master bedroom and a desk and single bed in the second room. The kitchen opened onto a minuscule living room fitted with only a single window facing a wall. Our dining room table had to be folded, when not in use, to allow us to use the couch and chair.

I completed my first year at NYU with straight A's and was extended another full fellowship and stipend for the following year. Despite our easing financial situation, Robbie and I were still teetering between heaven and hell. But never, no matter how bad the abuse and pain could I ever imagine separating from him. To this day, I cannot account for my obstinate attachment to him.

"I just can't imagine life without him," I would pitiably repeat when my mother questioned me after every pathetic episode.

What sustained me, I imagine, were those rare moments of absolute bliss when we lost ourselves in each other's arms with aching passion. In our times of grace, there was a sort of indescribable elation in the way our very souls seemed to dissolve into one another, interrupted only by our devastating "descents into hell," as Robbie put it in one of his many notes to me. Like me, he was clearly torn and bemused by the clashing emotions that made up our reality.

My darling,

The events of yesterday have had as shattering an effect upon me as with you. I am so sorry to have hurt you, both with the offal of my mouth and with my brutally suffocating hands.

Throughout the night I have been perplexed as to why our blissful rapport of the last weeks was so suddenly and ferociously wrestled from us. Perhaps the depths of our disparaging violence is measured precisely by the altitude of our elation. The more we cling together like desperate souls in our intimate duo-solitude, the more sudden and pronounced the slightest fall from grace. A small fall from such heights is like a plummeting descent into hell. To have the cloak of your ever so vivificating love snatched, for even a brief second, from around me is like being snatched from the womb and being plunged into the chill of the darkest wasteland to be left unto death.

I know there shall be again times of the utmost satisfaction between us, times of such heightened, blissful security; and again times of shattering descent. But how protect ourselves from the ravages of bleak alienation if not by mutual effort to reassure, forgive and warm again the heart that will again carry aloft our fragile spirits.

I have no illusion about this: with you, and only you, have I attained and enjoyed grace and with you have I vowed unto death to strain ever again toward the sublime, peaceful excellence of genuine marriage.

All my love, darling – Robbie"

Mixed with his apology and regret was the essence of his message, his need to share responsibility in the violence, to minimize the gravity of his physical abuse with the expression of his own injury at my hands. Oh, there were more letters, each growing more pedantic and obtuse in its rationale, each finding comfort and justification for "our" actions. I always struggled to make sense of them to find the reasoning behind the pomposity of their verbiage.

The very complexity of the message implicitly solidified in my mind the intellectual superiority of my lover and reinforced my awe of his intellect. Perhaps I was not really worthy of his love; perhaps I did in fact deserve his "punishment," as he put it. My deep-seated feeling of doubt and self-loathing at once concealed from my awareness and manifested in the belief that I was just as responsible for his violence, would keep me chained to him for years to come.

Our positions as waiters reached their peak when I landed a position at the fashionable Café des Artistes, on the Upper West Side. But the lure of increased income came at a great cost to my academic accomplishments. I was awarded another fellowship from the US government just as I completed my master's degree. So I decided to pursue a doctorate. At the Café des Artistes, I was making more money than ever. I was accumulating the more lucrative, highly sought-after dinner-shifts when I submitted my dissertation topic and defended my proposal, but I was getting increasingly tired and side-tracked.

The more hours I took on, the more resentful I became and the more critical I was of Robbie. I often arrived home at two in the morning, after a long fifteen-hour double shift on a Saturday, only to find Robbie lying on the couch watching TV. My feet would be aching, only to be faced with a pile of dirty laundry on Sunday morning before I rushed to my dinner shift. I missed Thanksgiving dinner and New Year's Eve with my family because the earnings would have been too great to pass up.

However, I made a lot of money, and I secretly saved enough cash to pay a substantial down payment on our first apartment less than two years later. When I received a one-year Guggenheim Foundation Research Award to continue my research on "International Terrorism" and help the director of the program, I was ecstatic. I thought then I would be in a better position to finish my PhD dissertation. For four months I managed the impossible—research at the foundation and waitressing.

Three months after we moved to our new home in New Jersey in mid-April 1988, I quit my job at the Café des Artistes presumably to focus on my dissertation and foundation work. Instead, I became pregnant.

18

Baby in a Storm

The pregnancy was not an accident. I had carefully prepared for it, even discussed my intention with my doctor a few weeks earlier.

"Have you ever been pregnant?" he'd asked me.

"No, I've been on the pill forever," I'd told him.

"Then I suggest you stop and try not to get pregnant immediately. Use any kind of non-hormonal contraceptive for about three months, then let it happen," he'd advised.

The objective was to cleanse my system and let it return to its natural rhythm. I'd thought that was a good precaution.

"Do you think it would be difficult for me to conceive?" I'd asked him nervously.

"I don't see why. You're only thirty-one, you're in good health. No, it should be fine." He'd smiled. "Just don't worry about it, okay? After all, you're exactly in the right place, if need be." He had winked at me and stood up to see me off.

Dr. Johnson, a tall Scandinavian-American with curly hair and blue eyes, was my mother's gynecologist. She'd been referred to him when her pre-menopausal symptoms got out of hand, a couple of years earlier, and I had accompanied her to most of her visits since. He was a well-known Ob-Gyn, infertility specialist, and best-selling author on women's health.

I had stopped taking the pill and, without a second thought, winged the question of contraception altogether. I conceived within a month. I was astonished at how quickly it happened. What in the world was I thinking? A baby, at that moment? A wobbly marriage, a very incomplete and listless doctoral research, and an unstable financial situation—those were the stark facts of my life, as I knew them, not exactly the most desirable environment for a baby.

"You know, I really think my biological clock began ticking louder, and my body just tricked my mind," I explained to my sister when I announced the news to her. She laughed.

"Really? But aren't you happy about it?" she asked.

"I *am* happy, of course, but it really doesn't make sense that I'd get pregnant at a time like this."

What I didn't know, then, was that once again I'd found a radical way to escape the unbearable stress caused by yet another academic challenge. The burden of completing my Ph.D. was met by that fear of failure that had already plagued me when confronted with the *Baccalauréat*. And again I was blind-sided by my angst. As I had in the past, I was running away at a defining moment in my life. Again, I chose to take the seemingly easier way out, the path most travelled, and disguised my fear in a way that could never be viewed by others as a lack of judgment on my part.

On the surface, Robbie and I had been married for five years and had just bought our first apartment in a doorman building—a lovely one-bedroom with a large terrace, sitting on the Hudson Palisades in West New York. It faced mid-

town Manhattan, was filled with Eastern sun and boasted one
of the most magnificent views imaginable, nothing less than
the unfolding city skyline from the Verrazano Bridge to the
George Washington Bridge.

Robbie had been at his job for four years, I had a terrific
one-year paying foundation internship, and, it was readily
assumed, I would finish my doctoral thesis after the baby was
born. One of my counselors' assistants concurred. "You'll be
able to do all your writing when the baby is napping," she'd
said. How I wished that were true!

In reality, I had been running on empty for a very long
time. I was burnt-out by eight years of full-time study and
hard physical work waiting on tables, and my marriage was
anything but idyllic. True, most of our relatives and friends
clearly thought Robbie and I had a good relationship going
and were far from suspecting the rot at its core. We were such
a sophisticated, attractive couple. Robbie was well liked, and
not just for his looks, polished manners, and worldliness.

Unlike many globetrotters, who roam the earth with their
cameras, from resorts to retreats, his love of travel did not simply scratch the surface. He showed real empathy and interest in
people, especially the poor and downtrodden of our planet. He
valued their mores and strived to understand their cultures. It
seemed he could converse for hours, engrossed in his interlocutors' stories, with sincere compassion.

In short, Robbie had an uncanny knack for appearing flawless to all those who knew him outwardly, including his own
parents. But perfect he was not. Beneath the shiny veneer were
hidden blemishes: an addictive personality, a perfectionist pro-
crastinator with a violent streak and a foul mouth, prone to
incomprehensible wrath, and in need of constant validation.
It took years before I had the courage to expose his physical

abuse to my loved ones, and even then I am not sure they really believed me until much later.

My pregnancy had its ups and downs, with the first trimester and the last month being particularly difficult. My body turned into a single-minded gestational laboratory responding to no other exigency than catering to the growing fetus in my womb. I had my share of morning sickness, but the most maddening problem was my somnolence. I had been sleep-deficient for so long I'd become used to it; I usually just pushed through my daily drowsiness.

All of a sudden, I had no say in the matter. I would get out of bed in the morning to head for work only to find myself nodding in strange places. At the foundation, my desk was set up in a corner of a quiet and spacious windowless conference room, so I fell asleep on my computer keyboard, for hours, rarely being disturbed by anyone; or perhaps no one wished to nudge me up. I once found myself snoozing on the steps of the emergency staircase. NYU's Bobst Library was a perfect dormitory for my sleepy body when I ventured there for additional research. No place was too uncomfortable for a doze-off, no bookstore or movie theater, and, most certainly, no bus or train, causing me to often miss my stop. It seemed I just napped right through my first few weeks.

Thankfully, things seemed to settle a bit during my second trimester, and I enjoyed a bit more energy. My attention shifted to food, and I fell prey to cravings, with sushi at the top of the list. At that time, doctors were not yet preoccupied with the dangers of seafood to pregnant women, so I just indulged in sushi four to five times a week, often alone, never feeling I'd had enough.

On the whole, however, my pregnancy progressed without any major concern—except I was pretty sure I was induced into labor about two weeks before my official due date, without the open acknowledgement of my physician. How do I know that? Simply because he had asked me to come for a visit at the hospital after I called him about some light contractions. During the course of the examination, he announced that my cervix was dilated a few centimeters. And then I felt it, a distinct and sharp sensation, a quick poke to my membranes. I did not say anything—I wasn't sure of what had happened exactly.

He sent me back home and, within twenty-four hours, my water broke. I was admitted to Lennox Hill around six in the evening on Easter Sunday, hooked to a hormonal IV pump to augment my contractions, and left to wait. After seven hours of labor-the last three excruciating-I delivered my baby at 1:30 AM on Monday. Robbie cut the umbilical cord with a trembling hand.

**

"Don't do it, it's unbearable! Those were the first words you uttered when I called you," said my sister later that day, when she and Mom visited me. "Was it that terrible?" she asked with a smirk.

"Of course it was," said Mom by way of reprimand. "But she didn't mean that, she was in pain."

The two of them were fussing around me; I could see there were flowers in a couple of vases. I was still in a haze, aching all over, and could not sit up properly.

"I look like crap, don't I?" I moaned. "I hardly slept at all. I'm exhausted. I didn't know how to soothe the baby—they gave her a little water." I closed my eyes. "Isn't she beautiful, though?" I smiled feebly. "Can you please get me a mirror and fix me up a bit?" I asked looking at my sister.

Mom kissed my forehead and caressed my head lovingly.

"Don't worry about it. No one else is visiting you today," she murmured. Nezha took a hair brush out of the drawer on the other side of the bed and leaned over me.

"You know... I have to tell you-I'm sure my doctor induced me earlier than necessary," I said. Finding it painful to sit up straight, I bent my head forward instead.

"Really?" Nezha was pulling my hair away from my face and tying it in the back of my head.

"What?" Mom had come back from the bathroom with my make-up bag. My sister repeated what I'd said.

"What do you mean?" asked Mom. "Did he give you any drugs? Did he say anything?"

"No, he didn't. But I felt he did something to me during my last visit on Friday. Now I know he ruptured my amniotic sac."

I took the face lotion from Mom's hand.

"Why would he do that? How can you be sure?" asked my sister.

"When I got to the hospital, I overheard the nurses complaining about the very high number of deliveries they had that weekend. 'Johnson did it again,' one of them was saying. 'He must have all his deliveries done before the week starts—he doesn't like his office hours disrupted,' another one replied. They didn't sound very happy. I'm telling you I was induced. I knew it," I added in frustration.

"What are you going to do about it?" Mom held my hand.

"Nothing. What can I do? The baby was due in about twelve days, it's not unusual. She's healthy, and I am okay. It just bothers me that he didn't even discuss it with me, you know?"

**

Naming our newborn was easy. Robbie and I had already settled on *Sophia* months before. It meant 'wisdom' and sounded beautiful in every language, and both of us deemed 'philosophy,' the Greek word for the love and pursuit of wisdom, to be our higher calling. So naming our baby daughter *Sophia* was only fitting. Our choice of a boy's name had not been as definite.

Sophia was born bald—that is without hair, but also intrepid and strong-willed. I decided to feed her breast-milk only, convinced that formula would not provide her with all the essential nutrients she needed. I breastfed her from the moment she was born and for an entire year without fail. If I was not going to be around for any period of time, I just pumped my milk, no matter how painful, and stored it in the freezer.

My entire purpose was to mother the little miracle that had materialized in my life and brought me a level of love and joy unlike any I had ever imagined. Gone were all considerations for any other obligation. I had completed my internship at the Guggenheim Foundation and was free to devote myself to motherhood with passion and dedication.

Robbie seemed happy and proud. Perhaps the baby would be able to reconcile our differences and help us grow into mature and responsible parents, I hoped. He had taken a week off, and there were moments of great care and tenderness after I returned home from the hospital. For the first time, he was the sole breadwinner and I thought that, in and of itself, would change the destructive dynamic of our relationship for the better.

Sadly, whoever believes that a new baby can heal an ailing marriage has no clue about the strains of sleepless nights and their effect on exhausted parents, especially those who have to contend with the distressing cries of a colicky newborn. Never in my life had I ever felt so crushed with fatigue. When she was napping, which she did only after long spells of heart-breaking howling, I could hardly keep up with my personal hygiene and most basic household chores. I was permanently sleep-deprived and cranky.

I had no help at home except on the few occasions when my mother, or my sister, who worked with Norma Kamali in Manhattan at the time, paid me a visit. My breasts were engorged and sore, my nipples raw and swollen, I could only sit on an inflated plastic bagel, and the rest of my body was still bloated and achy.

Alas, only a few days after Sophia and I returned home, Robbie's demons resurfaced again.

It must have been around three or four in the morning, when Sophia, whose crib occupied a corner of our bedroom, woke up again, wailing on the top of her lungs. I had been feeding her every two or three hours and had just fallen into a deep slumber.

"Robbie, could you please pick her up and bring her to me?" I muttered plaintively?

He didn't answer.

"*Please* pick her up, I'll feed her here," I pleaded, nudging him awake.

I heard him mumble something about having to work early, then ignore me. The baby was hysterical by then. I extended my hand and pushed him in the back again, imploring him to get up and bring the baby to me.

"It's *your* turn to get her, Robbie! I still have to do the feeding," I persisted. "I'm exhausted, can't you see? I can't stand on my feet anymore. Can't you do this for me, for once?"

"I've been working my ass off and you know it, you bitch." He turned around abruptly. "Just you *get* her," he yelled, and he shoved me so hard with his feet, I fell off the bed.

My mind went blank. No, it couldn't be. Not that again. I'd honestly thought somehow that kind of brutality was behind us.

I pulled myself up despite the ton of bricks that had just crashed on me and stumbled to the crib.

As I directed Sophia's little head toward my throbbing breast, I swallowed back tears of hurt and helplessness.

19

Madness

During the months that preceded and followed Sophia's birth, events had seemed to take on a life of their own, spinning in a disconcerting spiral, in quick succession.

Very shortly after I moved to New Jersey, my sister and Hisham, her new, striking, Iranian-Kuwaiti companion, had rented an apartment across the street from me on Boulevard East. The day after my pregnancy was confirmed, around mid-August 1988, my mother had followed, moving from Queens to North Bergen, in New Jersey, only minutes away.

Her catering business, launched some three years earlier, had slowly begun to wane. I had been too busy to help her grow it, and she didn't have enough English, or business knowledge, to do it on her own. At one point, we had entertained the thought of opening a Moroccan restaurant in Manhattan. I'd put together a thorough business plan, had it reviewed by a group providing assistance to community entrepreneurs at NYU's Stern School of Business, and sent it to my rich uncles in Morocco, inviting them to invest with us in an exciting American venture. They had showed no interest and simply ignored our offer.

Greatly disappointed, my mother had continued to get by on a meager income, based on inconsistent catered functions and the same stipend—not adjusted for inflation or place of residence—that her brother Abderrahim was still giving her. My sister and I, and occasionally one of her younger brothers, Hak or Latif, helped her out with a little additional money. Her financial situation was precarious, though not desperate; she lacked for nothing essential. But she felt vulnerable most of the time even as she lived comfortably enough in a pleasant apartment across North Hudson Park.

Then tragedy struck. In July 1989, less than four months after Sophia's birth, Uncle Hak died in a Paris hospital of multiple complications following prostate cancer surgery. His death had been precipitated by the arrest, in Brussels, of his brother Latif, for drug trafficking. Aggrieved by his brother's shocking criminal activity, Uncle Hak had been unable to fight the post-op infections.

Throughout their lives, the two had been there for their sister and her four children. Not only had they been more than uncles for my siblings and me, they'd been father figures for her as well. In the best of times and the worst of times, they had come through for her when she had no one else to turn to. Suddenly, she was orphaned: Neither would ever be there for her again.

This realization was made the more painful by Uncle Latif's latest reassurances. He'd told her that his business was doing so well that she would shortly be free of financial concerns altogether.

"Soon, very soon, you'll never have to worry about money again," he had promised. My mother had been elated by what she saw as an overdue success for her beloved brother.

I was about four months pregnant, in the fall of 1988, when he'd invited her and Nezha to visit him in Paris. The trip, which she prepared for with sheer euphoria, had turned out to be fraught with odd incidents and was a letdown. Uncle Latif, who, after at least two detoxification treatments, had been alcohol-free for a couple of years, had displayed frenzied behavior and volatile moods.

"He was weird, hardly slept at all, chain-smoked, drank excessively, tipped outrageously, and generally acted in an erratic way," my sister had afterward confessed. "He was not the man we knew and loved."

To our dismay, the business, it'd turned out, was not only risky, it was illicit. Uncle Latif, with the collusion of high-profile Moroccan officials, had partaken in a profitable, albeit short-lived, drug trade to Europe. Uncle Hak's untimely death combined with Uncle Latif's offense, had marked an indelible shift in my mother's disposition. She traveled to Morocco for the funeral and, once there, collapsed under unmitigated sorrow. Many in the family viewed her display of grief with concern, even alarm. After that, she was a different woman.

I, however, failed to see any change in Mom's personality until she announced, out of the blue, her decision to marry a total stranger.

What she saw in Chester was a handsome and well-mannered fifty-two-year-old with an affectionate personality. What she did not see was a perennially underemployed, bruised Vietnam veteran, a blue-collar worker from Bayonne who'd never set foot in Manhattan or knew where Morocco was on a map. He had little education, no money, and was prone to heavy drinking and jealous fits.

They had met at Archer's, a Fort Lee restaurant, where she'd gone out for a drink with a friend, shortly after her return from Uncle Hak's funeral. He had been drawn to her exotic beauty, sweet temperament, and refinement. The two had very little in common other than mutual physical attraction and a need for companionship.

She had never been one to date strangers met in bars, and certainly not one to take marriage lightly. Yet they were both convinced they'd found true love and determined to tie the knot without delay and against all advice of prudence and patience. They could hardly wait the mandatory thirty days.

On a beautiful fall morning, October 6, 1989, my mother, then fifty years old and newly grandmother, dressed in an off-white, below-the-knee wedding dress, white flowers in her hair and small bouquet in her hand, married-for love alone-the elegant Chester in town hall. She looked positively radiant.

Over the summer, Robbie and I had decided to buy a larger, sponsor-owned, two-bedroom apartment in the same building to accommodate our growing family. We'd acquired our second mortgage from the coop-sponsor, and original owner, and offered my mother, whose one-year-lease was expiring, the option of renting our one-bedroom. She was living alone and still grieving over her brothers' tragedy, and I had felt it would be good for her to be as close to me and her grandchild as possible. As it turned out, when she moved in to my building, she and Chester had been married for a week.

For Christmas that year, Robbie's parents, who had retired a year earlier, invited us to their new *pensionados'* retreat in Costa Rica. They had bought a little coffee *finca* with a cozy house, and they were eager to meet their grand-daughter for the first time. In our absence, my mother gave a Christmas dinner for the rest of the family. That night, she had her first public argument with Chester because of his drinking and jealousy. On the surface, she displayed a happy face; behind it, the demoralizing reality had begun to peek through.

Shortly thereafter, in early 1990, some seven months after his brother Hak's death, Uncle Latif, in turn, was diagnosed with a terminal illness. So desperate was his condition, the Belgian penal authorities sent him home to spend his final weeks. The news dealt the knock-out blow that caused my mother to lose her mind and sink into the depths of madness. The perfect storm had gathered and finally broke loose, tearing right through the tight fabric of my family.

It is safe to say that my mother always was the central figure in my life. Her happiness was more important to me than mine, and, in my heart, there could be no joy without the certainty that hers was assured. Of course, during my juvenile struggle with insecurity I had taken it all out on her. Still, I forever took care of her and put her needs first.

Since she moved to America, we'd had our share of dis-agreements, even heated quarrels, and we'd pushed each other's buttons on many occasions. Yet we always made up and went on sharing a lot of happy moments. By the time she moved to New Jersey, we'd become even closer and regularly went to the gym and shopping together. Not owning a car, she relied on me for most of her errands. She often cooked delicious meals and called all of us to share them with her, teasing that if it weren't for her food she would never see us.

When she married Chester, I had been particularly busy with my baby and I had also been taking real estate courses in New York with the intention of getting a license and make a living on a more flexible schedule. I'd actually felt relieved that she now had someone in her life to help her take care of things. For years, there had been mounting pressure for both my sister and I to be constantly there to keep her company and help with her bills, doctors' appointments, and other undertakings requiring a modicum of literacy.

By the first week of March 1990, I acquired my real estate agent certification and had not seen Mom for a while, even though she lived only a few floors up.

Until she called me one morning:

"Wafa," barked Mom as soon as I picked up. "I need you to take me for a few errands. I have so many things to do; I need to start right now."

She sounded impatient, irritated, mixing French with Arabic.

"Sorry, Mom, but I can't today. I have to take Sophie to the pediatrician and then—"

"*C'est très important*, I need you now," she interrupted in a commanding tone.

"Come on, Mom, what's so urgent? You can't call me like this, without warning, and expect me to jump. Why don't you ask Chester? I'm already running late. I've gotta go, okay? I'll call you back later."

I hung up, grabbed my baby, and run out the door.

When I returned, I found the tirade she had left on my answering machine:

How dare you hang up on me like that? I'm sick and tired of you treating me like a kid, telling me what to do all the time, controlling my life. I've had it with you, do you hear me? From now on, I'm not your mother. I want you to leave me alone, you little ingrate. Mind your own business. I don't need you... All your bullshit.

She'd gone on with a long outburst of insults and accusations delivered with so much venom that I turned off the message and deleted it right then. The emotional attack I had just been dealt was inexplicable.

Then, nothing for days. It was surprising not to hear from her at all, though not too worrisome. After all, I was hurt and she had her husband, not to mention I was in over my head already—until March 20, when I got a spine-chilling phone call from the cops informing me they had taken my mother to the emergency room.

Apparently, they'd been able to gather some vital information from her in spite of her "condition," which they refused to elaborate on over the phone.

The call left me in a state of panic. My first instinct was to rush to my mother's apartment on the fifteenth floor, hoping against hope to find her there.

The cops must be mistaken, I kept repeating in my head, *they've got the wrong person.*

I found the apartment unlocked and the place in total pandemonium. Scattered on top of the kitchen counter were half-eaten lamb chops, bread crumbs, and other food scraps. Dirty dishes were piled up in the sink. The terrace door was open and swaying in the wind. I ran to check the promenade below, praying she had not thrown herself over.

A glance at her bedroom, and I was struck by the chaos. Clothes were off the racks and out of the drawers, scattered over the bed and floor. Had she tried to rearrange her closet, armoire? Was she meaning to pack? And where was Chester? Had anything happened between them? I called Robbie and my sister at work, asked them to meet me at the hospital. I left Sophia with Nadia, my Moroccan au-pair, and rushed to the emergency room. During the short drive to the hospital, my mind kept rewinding and replaying her message. I wished I hadn't erased it. I needed to understand what was going on and, perhaps, most devastating of all, make sense of the vitriol she'd directed at me.

I found her stretched on her back, strapped down at the ankles and wrists to a gurney, in a cold and dreary hallway of the emergency room. Two police officers were still standing by her side. I could hardly recognize her. The lump in my throat was suffocating me, my belly aching in a warped grip, my mind refusing to acknowledge the reality of what my eyes were witnessing.

Her hair, grayer than I remembered, was sticking out, dirty and unkempt; her face pasty and drained, her eyes full of frenzy and ire, stared back at me briefly. She was saying something in Arabic, mumbled, fast, and barely comprehensible.

"*Here* you are! Where have you *been* all this time? Why am I here? You must get me out of here. These people don't know who they're dealing with." She made a scratchy noise with her throat. It sounded like a repressed cough.

"Mommy! Oh, my god, what's going *on*? What *happened*?"

I looked up at the policemen, tears clouding my eyes,

"What's this, officer?" I asked. "Why is my mother tied *down*? What's going on?"

"Sorry, ma'am. Are you her daughter?" began the younger one visibly contrite.

"Yes. Yes, I am."

"We picked up your mother on the street," he said. "Near your building, in the middle of traffic. She was clearly disoriented. She could've been killed."

"But why is she *tied*? Why is she treated like *this*?"

I tried to fight back sobs of indignation.

"She resisted every effort to take her off the road, started fighting and screaming. We had no choice. The two of us got her here."

He nodded toward the other officer, a bold skinny man holding his cap in his hand.

"We called you."

"Don't listen to them. Morons! They hurt the shit out of me, pushed me around real hard. But they don't know who I am. I know things. Everything is gonna change soon, you'll see."

My mother was seething with righteous anger, ranting in Arabic mostly.

"They don't know who I am. Where *were* you? Now, get me *out of here*," she yelled at me, pulling furiously at her restraints.

I touched her shoulder lightly, hesitantly. I was loath to admit she frightened the hell out of me. Didn't occur to me to hug or kiss her—she looked menacing, her body shaking. Was she scared, too? This made no sense at all.

"Is there someone I could talk to?" I protested.

I turned to the nurse, a somber-looking, sturdy black woman.

"The doctor gave her a shot of antipsychotic medication. It takes a little while to take effect. We also have to clean and treat her leg," explained the nurse in a monotone.

Antipsychotic medication? That's what my mother was? Crazy, psychotic? I wasn't clear about what that meant. These things only happened to other people.

My heart hammered in my chest threatening to burst out. The knots in my stomach were tighter than ever. Fear had gotten hold of me, refused to let go, a growing, gnawing, mind-numbing sort of terror. My mom was psychotic. She was mad, schizophrenic. How could that be? She had never showed any sign; there had been no visible descent into insanity that I could think of, detect, prevent.

"What's wrong with her leg?" I asked a tremor in my voice.

"She's been burnt badly, it seems; probably scalding liquid. It needs to be taken care of before an infection sets in."

The nurse lifted the sheet off Mom's right leg. It looked bright red, almost charred in spots, and blistery all over the front.

"Ah, it's nothing. Hot coffee is all," Mom grumbled, in French this time. "I'm telling you, it's nothing, just let me out of here. I've got things to do."

She looked around her, annoyed.

"Mom, your burn needs treatment. You're not well. You will be taken care of here." I was speaking to her in the same language, trying hard to reach the woman I knew, the rational being.

Incensed, she shouted back at me in Arabic, "*Nooo*, I tell you. Damn, you never listen. I know what's going on. God spoke to me. You don't know who I am, you don't understand, I'm a *prophet!*"

Gnashing her teeth, she tried to sit up on the gurney but was kept down by the straps. "Tell them to *untie* me... You *want* this, don't you? But wait, wait you see what happens, I know everything."

Strangely, at that moment, I was relieved she could not be understood. She, who usually paid so much attention to her appearance, would be so embarrassed by herself, I thought.

Finally the psychiatric resident arrived, a young Indian man with polite manners, who shook my hand sympathetically.

"I'm sorry about your mother," he said. "I gave her a shot of Haldol. She is delusional and quite paranoid at this point."

"What's wrong with her? I don't understand how this could happen. She's always been normal," I blurted.

"She's suffering from psychosis," he explained. "It's a psychiatric disorder like schizophrenia or mania. She's experiencing distorted perceptions of reality, maybe even hallucinations." He paused. "She's never been sick like this before, shown any manic behavior, obsession, or deep depression?" he asked.

"No, never. Well, she's been down of course, maybe even mildly depressed at times, but no, she was never *crazy*."

I frowned, searched my memory for instances that could have signaled something, anything. I shook my head: nothing that I could think of.

"Has there been any particularly stressful event, any great shock lately, like the death of a loved one or a divorce?" the resident insisted.

Then it hit me.

"Uh, as a matter a fact, she lost a close brother last summer. Another one was arrested earlier and is now terminally ill, and also, she married a complete stranger on the spur of the moment, and the marriage shows strains already."

Suddenly it all made sense. Those were the triggering events, the shocks that had pushed her mind to the brink and broken her down.

The young resident nodded quietly.

"Unfortunately, it is very possible that all these things are responsible for her snapping. Do you have any close family member with mental disorders?" he inquired.

"Now that you're asking, yes, one of my mother's sisters, Aunt Aisha, was known to break down after she lost two of her young daughters. In the family, she's considered a kind of harmless mystic. She hears and sees things, often religious manifestations. I don't know really, I'm not entirely sure. Why? Is this inherited?"

My mind was racing. I thought of the way Nezha had spoken of Uncle Latif's odd conduct in Paris.

"It's possible," he said. "These things are never entirely understood. There are indications that this type of mental illness often runs in families."

I glanced at my mother. The nurse had pushed the stretcher behind a curtain, transferred her to a bed, and was attending to her burned leg. The drug was taking hold.

"What should we do? Can she be treated? Can you take care of her?" I asked.

"I think you should have your mother admitted," he said. "But I can't keep her *here—we d*on't have the facility. Check with St. Mary's Hospital in Hoboken."

20

Tricks of her Mind

"That's horrible, no way," cried my sister when she heard the resident's recommendation. "We can care for her at home, we can get a doctor to follow her on an outpatient basis," she insisted.

"I cannot take care of her, Nezha, you know that, not with a baby," I replied. "I know what you're saying. Believe me, I too feel terrible at the thought of having her institutionalized, but I see no other way."

We'd agonized all through the night, waiting around in the cold hospital sitting room, endlessly debating, ignorant of what to do or expect next. Nezha was adamantly opposed to the idea of a psychiatric hospital. Eventually, the resident's firmness broke her resistance, and she relented.

Around mid-morning, Mom appeared calmer and seemed to have regained a semblance of her senses. I checked her out of Palisades and, since she was still clearly resentful of me, Nezha and Hisham agreed to take her to Hoboken.

In the gloomy St. Mary's psychiatric ward, the three of them sat waiting for a doctor to see them. The longer they waited, the more hesitant Nezha became. The sight of the dazed patients was disheartening to her. She was getting cold feet when she looked at Mom, holding her hand.

"Do you think I should tell the doctor that I am a prophet?" Mom whispered.

"*Non, maman, non.* Don't say a word about that," Nezha exclaimed, hit by the dilemma before her, yet shaken by the frightening reality she glimpsed at.

"You're not going to leave me here with these crazy people, are you, honey?" Mom beseeched her. She seemed so lost, so afraid, Nezha panicked. The thought of abandoning her in that place was more than she could bear.

"No," she said. "We're not leaving you here. Come on, Hisham, let's go home."

"Sorry, Wafa, I couldn't do it," she'd told me before I asked. "That place looked awful; there are some scary people in there. Mom doesn't belong there. I couldn't leave her. You'd have done the same."

She helped Mom lay down on her bed. "There must be a more appropriate place for her."

That was easier said than done. For one thing, none of us had health insurance. To legalize her status, I had sponsored Mom as soon as I had been sworn in as a naturalized citizen and she'd been a legal resident since, but that didn't make any difference. A few months after Sophia was born, I had lost my own health coverage from Café des Artistes—and the ensuing Cobra plan had expired. Mom had always worked as a free lance service provider and could never afford any type of coverage. Hence medical cost was a big factor in our delay in hospitalizing her.

When Nezha and Hisham offered to stay with her to see her through her first night at home, I rushed to the nearest bookstore, bought half a dozen books on manic-depression and bipolar disorder, and spent the night reading. The need to learn, to understand her illness, was overwhelming. As usual, only books—and their valuable knowledge—could provide me with dependable answers, calm my fears, put me back in charge of a situation that had gone amok. Her case seemed to mirror the typical text-book mania degenerating into full psychosis. I was made painfully aware of the urgency of providing her with sound psychiatric care.

For days after that I called friends, and friends of friends, for referrals. I also called psychiatrists right out of the phone book, begging them to see her without delay. Their answer was invariably the same: She had to be admitted first; once the psychosis was over, then they could follow her. Our problem was compounded with the fact that she had never been diagnosed with even a depression and had no doctor following her who could help with hospital admission.

For the next few days, we took turn keeping watch over her at home, acquiescing to all her utterances, making sure not to let her out. That alone was no easy feat. Walls, it seemed, could not contain her; every room felt confined, claustrophobic. She had an irresistible need to be outdoors, physically run out the streets, be free, closer to nature, even as, or perhaps because, her mind remained caged in madness.

None of us slept much, if at all, mostly because she didn't seem to doze off more than a few minutes at a time. She constantly got up and rambled around in the dark, muttering to herself, looking around for food in the fridge, fumbling for unspecified items in her drawers. I was terrified, always guarded, could not let myself snooze. What if she decided to go out anyway—how could I stop her? What if she hurt me? Was she not furious at me for all my tribulations over the years?

All along, and at every opportunity, we kept interrogating her. Slowly, a narrative began to take shape. The stories she told with a strange assurance, and much reluctance, were frayed in the extreme, hanging by threads in her shifting mind, unreliable, confusing. It was difficult to distinguish the real from the delusional. Trying to fit all the loose pieces of the puzzle together, careful not to irritate or tire her, we could not help feeling disturbed and discouraged. It was, however, imperative to stay calm in order to hear it all, to try to contain and repair the damage even as her temper seemed to flare up at the most trivial remarks.

One afternoon, she agreed to take us to the new house she had rented, showed us the Chevrolet dealer from whom she had "purchased" a new car. From what we could gather, it appeared she had wandered around aimlessly for miles, often in the park, moved a few things from her apartment to the new place—the second floor flat of a two-family house, off Kennedy Boulevard in North Bergen. The place was still empty save for a few kitchen appliances, a blanket, and a couple of towels.

She never slept and yet never felt better, more powerful or more alive. She was fearless, finally free of others, gotten rid of all the losers in her life; all her burdens had evaporated. She was convinced that she spoke English fluently and had passed her New Jersey driver's license test without problems, though she fiercely refused to prove it. She kept insisting we had nothing to worry about yet was annoyingly short on specifics.

In her heightened state of mind, her limited language ability had vanished, her financial insecurity gone, all replaced with a heavenly certainty. Most glorious of all, she'd seen the Light of the All-Mighty. The Angel Gabriel had come to her and spoken the truth. Lord, had she been frightened, and just as quickly awed, by the miracle.

"I tell you, I saw him just as clearly as I see you now," she said in an eerie tone. "First, there was this roaring fire... burst in the middle of the living room in that blessed house. Out of the flames, *He* manifested himself and spoke to me. And another time, it was in the bathroom. Water was overflowing from the toilet; it was like this amazing river, a waterfall, cleansing everything in its wake. He appeared out of the stream and again talked to me. This time I wasn't afraid. He chose *me!*" She smiled; her eyes sparkled; she was sitting in my living room, wearing an emerald-green caftan—her favorite shade, the color of paradise, she'd often said.

We had just finished dinner, and I had put Sophia to sleep. Robbie and Hisham were smoking cigarettes on the terrace. Nezha patted her hand as we continued to try and understand the extent of the material and financial mayhem she had caused. When I heard her go on about her apparitions, my skepticism got the better of me.

"Okay Mom, listen, please. That's not possible, those were hallucinations, you must understand this," I spoke as gently as I could.

Nezha immediately frowned in disapproval. Mom's expression changed abruptly. Pure exasperation distorted her features and she exploded.

"You never believe anything, do you? Because you think you know everything, don't you?" she snapped, disgusted. "Well, let me tell you, I know what I saw, what I heard. *You don't*. And I know what's coming."

She got up and headed for the bathroom, where she locked herself in.

"Couldn't you just listen?" sighed Nezha in frustration.

She was right, of course. Miss No-Nonsense had once again voiced her doubts, prompting Mom's predictable outburst.

After that, and in spite of all our supplications, she refused to come out. First she seemed to listen silently inside the small bathroom; next it sounded like she was praying, or rather intoning. Then the chant turned into a lament. She was there for over fifty minutes when at last, she unlocked the door, passed by Robbie and Hisham without seeing them, and stepped out on the terrace.

For a moment, she stared, at the familiar cityscape greeting her, the glimmering metropolis, the bejeweled bride that had stolen the stars from the night sky, as she'd once referred to Manhattan-by-night. What could she be thinking? We stayed behind, not daring to interfere. She looked up at the dim heavens above and began chanting again, softly, and then louder. Suddenly, without warning, she screamed, a long terrifying, blood-curdling cry, followed by high-pitched howls, calling out to God.

Stunned by the horrifying sound, Robbie tried to get her back inside, quiet her down, but she resisted, struggled with him, and then kicked him with surprising strength. Throughout, she bawled in the throes of insanity, her reason twisted, eclipsed in the labyrinth of her mind. She called on God, her savior and the only way out of her hair-raising terror. Someone, a neighbor, called the police, and it wasn't long before they knocked at my door. It was now abundantly clear we could not handle her on our own.

I should have listened to the young resident at Palisades, I thought in despair.

Finally, on March 29, 1990, the day after that freakish episode in my apartment, I had my mother admitted to Mount Sinai Hospital. The psychiatric ward looked friendlier, less ominous this time. Still, she was petrified, and so was I. I couldn't help but recall that miserable day, years earlier, when she had left me overnight in the Rabat mental institution and I had felt both unloved and forsaken. I knew she was feeling something similar, and my guilt had no end.

"Why are you doing this? I don't need to be here. *Please* don't leave me," she begged. She looked drained, and confused. She was quite delusional still; convinced everything that had happened was real.

"It won't be for long, Mom. You'll be better soon. We'll visit you every day, I promise."

She doesn't really believe me, I thought. *She's much too scared.*

Throughout her ordeal, never once did Mom ask about her husband, or talk about him in public. In her mind and heart, he was gone; departed—as if he'd never existed. He'd simply vanished and she never wanted to know why. In fact, he had materialized, briefly that first night in the emergency room, and just as quickly, after he was told he couldn't see her, left, probably relieved. I never saw him again.

Nezha told me later that he'd showed up at Mom's apartment, just before she was released from Mount Sinai, and asked for his personal belongings. It happened after Mom had finally related to her bits of the incident that had precipitated her descent into insanity.

**

He had thrust her out on the terrace and locked her out, screaming and kicking.

"You're crazy! What are you talking? I not take your money," she yelled at him in her broken English. "Chester... Chester," she called him back again and again, pounding on the glass door, "Open the door, open *now.*"

How dare he accuse her of stealing his money, how dare he? She didn't even know what he was referring to.

He went back in the bedroom, searching around for the box where he'd stashed his cash, rummaging through her closets and drawers, throwing everything out. He had to have a drink. He was broke, hadn't made a penny at the Sunday flea market where he sold all kinds of knick-knacks. He started drinking upon waking in the morning, still inebriated from the previous night. She'd badgered him in her bad English as soon as he got back home, late, reeking of booze. Where was he again? Where did he find the money to drink? How could he treat her like this?

She got up at dawn, after waiting for him all night, not sleeping a wink. In fact, she hadn't had a full night sleep in days. Her brain was always swarming, her thoughts always jostling. How could she have been so wrong about this man? She was sure she'd found her protector at last—the man of her dreams—charming, good-looking, and such a good lover. He was going to take care of her, give her the security she yearned for.

How quickly things changed. He came short of all her expectations, badly failed her in every way, like every other man in her life, really. He lost his umpteenth job right after they married, went back hitting the bottle shortly after, made terrible scenes every time someone smiled at her. Her parents would be ashamed of her, marrying a loser, again. This time, she *picked* him—a drunken redneck, worse than her first husband in many ways. This one didn't hesitate to shove her around, humiliate her, and even punish her for trying to prevent him from drinking. Not in the morning, she implored him. She only wanted to help him, rescue him from himself. Now she knew not to trust him, ever.

She didn't know how long he kept her on the terrace, prisoner in her own home—worse yet, captive in her head. She tried to force the windows open: all shut tight. Then she watched him leave the apartment, knocked louder, begged, and cried hysterically. Hours went by. She was still in her nightgown, barefoot, cold, and enraged.

It was gray and drizzly that March morning, didn't feel like spring yet. The city, across the Hudson, emerged like tattered slabs of steel in the fog, the crests of the Empire State Building and World Trade Center indiscernible, decapitated. She was going to catch her death but what did he care, the bastard. Oh, that's *it*! She'd had it. She loathed her limitations, weakness, gender. But it was no good simply resenting her fate, she was going to turn things around on her own, never again look up to a man for security. She wasn't stupid. Others had done it. An engulfing rage boiled inside her, a spattering cauldron drowning every last sparkle of awareness.

How long was she glued, like a fly, stuck against the glass pane of the terrace door, after her ranting and raving had died? She couldn't tell. Her body had turned numb, before her mind froze in a paralyzing wrath, hostage of its relentless and obsessive chatter. When she finally saw him enter the apartment, she didn't budge, followed his every step—eyes unblinking—through the small foyer, galley kitchen, dining-area, toward the terrace door. He'd had his drink; his blank gaze said it all. A taste of bile filled her mouth.

He put a hand on the handle, waited for her to back off to let her in. Instead, she threw herself at him with unexpected fury, shouting a torrent of words he didn't understand, tried to beat him, scratch him, bite him. He held her back with both hands, arms outstretched, leaning forward to steady her, his heavy putrid breath filling her nostrils.

Suddenly she spat at him, ejecting a mouthful of saliva and spleen with all the strength and contempt she could muster. The thick, foul spittle hit him smack in the face and that's when he slapped her, hard, sent her flying across the room. She stood back up in a flash, rushed to open the entrance door wide, went after him again, and pushed him out, her eyes popping out of her head, hissing wildly for him to get out, forever, *out of her life.*

She slammed the door after him, ran into her bedroom, got dressed feverishly, and called her daughter, twice. The second time, she let it all out, vomiting all the nauseating rage, frustration, and despair heaped high inside her.

My sister's quiet sobs were clearly perceptible over the line. I listened silently, allowing room for her sadness before resuming her account of the final acts of Mom's doomed marriage.

"When I first cleaned Mom's bedroom and found the infamous tin box, I was shocked, outraged, and very angry at him. Everything was there, perhaps eighty dollars in cash, plus the so-called 'valuables' he'd accused her of stealing. More like cheap trinkets," said Nezha with contempt. "I watched while he packed his clothes, and when I saw him reach under the bed, I knew what he was looking for. Before he left, I handed him the box and told him how vile he was and how I wished he'd disappear from her life for good."

Her tone betrayed her sullenness. "When he saw everything was in there, he turned green, the son-of-a-bitch, and he left like a dog, tail between his legs."

She took a deep breath. "I still have that image of him in my head, the way he walked to the elevator... like a thief."

21

Dead-End

"She means nothing to me," he said ruefully. "We were friends, that's all. I needed someone to talk to."

Robbie leaned over to extinguish his cigarette and glanced at me from the corner of his eye. Night had fallen, and Sophia was already sleeping. It felt hot and humid—a typical New York summer—in spite of the air conditioning. I hadn't seen him in weeks. He looked thinner, and his features were strained with fatigue. The long flight from Tunisia had taken its toll.

"You were *living* at her place, Robbie. I may be naïve, but I'm not stupid. You've made a fool of me for too long already. I've had it, enough!"

I tried hard not to cry. Tears only complicate things, inspire pity and remorse but not always for the right reasons. I felt betrayed to the core. Yet in the midst of my hurt, and perhaps for the first time, there was a flicker of resolve. There was gnawing fear too, though a voice somewhere was whispering to trust my instinct, overcome my dread.

Robbie had just spent a few weeks working with Sami, Nezha's new life partner, in Tunis. Sami had quickly become very close and was considered a member of the family. He and Nezha had met on December 21, 1991. Robbie and I had invited her to Carnegie Hall for Handel's *Messiah*. But halfway through the performance, she'd become restless and, during the intermission, left to meet some friends who were dining at the *China Grill*, a popular restaurant in Midtown. Sami had invited everyone.

A plump and flamboyant man, in his mid-thirties, Sami was a supremely self-confident Tunisian entrepreneur, and he'd instantly fallen in love with her. A couple of months earlier, she'd had a traumatic breakup with Hisham and was determined to learn to live independently, without a man by her side for once. At first, she was rather put off by Sami's flashy style and extravagant generosity. He, however, was not a man to take no for an answer; thence began a relationship that changed, not only her life but mine, too.

It had been a year already since Robbie had accepted a full-time household administrator and butler position with a wealthy New Yorker on Manhattan's Upper East Side. He was well paid but unhappy with his function and mostly resented the many humiliating and unpleasant tasks his employer's cocaine habit subjected him to. So, when Sami talked about his upcoming month-long consulting job in Muscat, in the Gulf of Oman, Robbie expressed the desire to work with him. When they returned, it was decided he would also travel to Tunisia to assist Sami with his textile business.

The whole idea was unplanned and foolhardy—and not just because Sami didn't understand English while Robbie spoke a limited French and knew absolutely nothing about textiles or manufacturing—but also because their temperaments could not have been any more different. Sami was an impassioned doer, a workaholic intolerant of incompetence and laziness, set in his ways, and deaf to criticism. In contrast, Robbie was a laid-back romantic, a cerebral thinker prone to endless discussion rather than action, who viewed Sami as a pathological bully insensitive to the nuances of every situation, particularly when people were involved.

To make matters worse, Sami's business, like the entire Tunisian textile industry, was facing serious challenges and teetering on the verge of bankruptcy. Misunderstandings, clashes, and disillusionment were inevitable. Soon, both men felt growing levels of mistrust and serious dislike toward each other. To cope with such thorny circumstances, Robbie looked for solace in the arms of a Tunisian woman.

"A woman of little virtue, you know the kind. And he stayed in her house!" Nezha had told me on the phone from Tunis. "Sami and I hesitated to tell you, but he really left us no choice. He's not working anymore, not that we can't trust him with anything anyway. Already in Oman, last May on Sami's consulting job, he went wild with the female employees, especially the Asians, you know. It was as if he'd never seen a woman in his life. Incredible! We didn't want to upset you then." She paused. "I'm so sorry," she'd sighed before ending the call.

My mind had gone numb. "Oh my God, oh my God," was all I could manage throughout our conversation. Anger suffocated me. I'd had my doubts about his indiscretions over the years, and we'd had many fights over his infidelity, rumored or suspected. But for the sake of peace, denial, or both, I had always grudgingly accepted his explanations and taken his word at face value, although not without swelling resentment.

Watching him squirming in his seat and chain smoking as he explained himself, I could still recall how, some eight years earlier, I'd lived through one of the most miserable nights of my life. Robbie was a bartender in Midtown Manhattan then, and he worked mostly nights. I'd gone to bed when the phone rang.

"Hello?" I'd answered half-asleep.

"Wafa? Hey it's me, Robbie. Did I wake you?" I'd glanced at the florescent hands of the alarm clock on the bedside table.

"It's two in the morning, Robbie. Where are you?" I'd asked hesitating between annoyance and worry.

"Sorry, the restaurant closed late. I needed to unwind. I'm having a drink with some people," he'd explained. This was not terribly atypical, I thought.

"So when are you coming home?" I'd asked mildly irritated.

"Well, that's why I'm calling," he'd begun, carefully weighing his words. "Listen, uh, you know how we sometime, uh, you know...fantasize...about another woman...a threesome?"

My heart had sunk. "*What?* What the hell are you *talking* about?" I'd exclaimed in a mounting frenzy. I'd pushed the sheets off and jumped on my feet. "Where are you *really*, Robbie? What are you up to?" I'd snarled on the phone.

"Alright, calm down, okay! I told you, I'm at the Sheraton bar on Seventh Avenue and I met this woman. I thought you'd like her. Why don't you come and join us?" he'd persisted in earnest.

Fleeting images of my husband in the arms of a lewd home-wrecker had flashed in my head, the entire scene uncanny to me, outrageous, and profoundly humiliating. What kind of women haunts hotel bars in the middle of the night, waiting to be picked up by libidinous tourists and drunks, anyway? Was he high, or out of his mind? I'd wondered.

"I can't believe what I'm *hearing*. This can't be *true!* You have the nerve to call in the middle of the night and ask me to help you fulfill your fantasy? You know what a *fantasy* is, don't you? It's a dream, it's not meant to be taken *literally*..." Panic-stricken, I'd started crying noisily. "I can't believe you're asking me this. How can you be so cruel? How can you say you love me and do *this*?" I'd choked.

Slivers of light from the street filtered through the drawn shades, casting long phallic shadows on the floor.

"Stop crying, will you? Of course I love you. I just made a suggestion. We both fantasized about it and I thought you might want to try it, that's all. Many couples do."

"Wow, you're really too kind," I'd interjected between my tears. "I only play along because I love you-don't you get it, you *freak*? If you really do love me, care for me, you'd get out of there and come home, that's what you'd do...Unless you wanna be done with me!"

"Don't dramatize now, please. I'll be home soon."

He'd hung up.

In an instant, the small bedroom he'd spent so many days painstakingly painting seemed to slowly cave in around me, compressing the air out of my lungs, muffling my sobs.

My chest had felt like a festering, open sore. I'd sat haggardly in the semi-darkness, the phone still in my hand, with a devastating urge to call him back, beg him to come home and heave me out of my nightmare. But I had nowhere to reach him: He'd abandoned me to my misery, left me in a twilight zone, counting the passing seconds like drips of molten fire on my icy heart.

For hours, tears had ravaged my swollen face until they could flow no more. How to make it stop? A fleeting notion, a survival gasp: I'd put on a coat and shoes and dragged myself down to the nearby Korean store to buy a bottle of wine, a pack of cigarettes, and sleeping pills, anything to drown my thoughts and ease the pain.

When he finally returned home in mid-morning, he'd found me curled up at the foot of the bed, my coat still on, a full ashtray and a half-empty bottle of wine by my side. Neither the pills nor the wine had put me back to sleep; instead they'd left me in a drowsy, migrainous haze with a thick and fetid mouth. Eight hours had passed since his call, an eternity. It'd felt like a miracle that I was still breathing. He'd sat next to me, held me in his arms, and apologized feebly.

My sobs had been my only answer.

Speaking softly, he'd offered his narrative, explained he'd foolishly agreed to follow her home to New Jersey and, when he realized it was a mistake, could no longer find his way back to Manhattan until the morning. He'd sworn nothing had happened.

**

There he was, yet again, lying through his teeth, weaving another mendacious tale on that second week of August 1992. He'd been overseas less than two months and everything had gone wrong. It had been a long time since his last paycheck, and my job as a real estate agent was unpredictable. Unwittingly, I had chosen a profession during one of the most significant downturns in housing in the New York region in a decade. And although I had pulled in decent money in 1991, 1992 was looking very grim, which incited me to accept my sister's invitation—and plane tickets—to visit her in Tunisia with Mom and Sophia. The very day after Robbie's return home, we took the overnight flight to Casablanca, then Tunis. I needed to reflect on the state of my marriage and consider my options.

By the time we came back, on November 11, 1992, I had made up my mind to leave Robbie. His ever-more reckless behavior during the three months he was home alone had made it clear that there was no hope left for redemption. He had not returned to full-time work and never called me for reconciliation; instead he'd invited the woman from Tunis to stay in our home. He had gone through our meager savings and used our jointly held credit cards for his expenses.

After my return, he often wouldn't even come home at night, and when he did, he slept in the living room and we didn't speak. For the following few days, I anguished about how to announce my decision. When the silence took hold, it seemed unbreakable. I had never before in my life held a grudge so big. We had never before felt so estranged from each other. The tension between us had reached its climax; our mutual revulsion was so thick as to be palpable.

"Robbie, we have to talk," I said one cheerless morning as I watched him finish his coffee, throwing his head back, in one motion.

"I don't want to talk right now," he replied without looking at me, putting his cup down in the sink.

"But we must," I protested. "This situation cannot go on indefinitely. It's obvious we can no longer live together. It's bad for us and for the baby," I declared somberly, adding, "You've betrayed everything I could still believe in. I've had enough, I want out." I felt so much resentment toward him; I could hardly control my voice.

"Always playing the victim card," he replied bitterly. "I feel just as betrayed, and I don't want to live with you anymore either, but this is my home. Where am I supposed to go with no money?"

He faced me squarely in the narrow kitchen.

"You *feel just as betrayed*? That's good," I scoffed, itching to add: *I am not the one that cheated, not the one that lied, not the wife-beater, not the one that's squandering our little money. No, that battle had already been fought far too many times, his I-too-am-a-victim argument far too familiar.*

For eleven years, because of my deep-rooted and distorted sense of fairness, I had swallowed it with relish almost, like a penitent nun confessing her sins against God, admitting to my issues and my part in the demise of our relationship. Was I not too demanding, manipulative, nagging, controlling, critical, and nasty even? A slow instillation into the depth of my psyche-that I somehow deserved whatever was inflicted on me-had justified my entire existence with him.

"I convinced Nezha to let you use her apartment upstairs for a little while, until you find a job," I said, trying to put an end to another futile clash.

He looked at me with irritation.

"I suppose you think you can just make those kinds of decisions for me?" he growled.

"Someone has to," I snapped. "The fact of the matter is, we cannot continue like this. Our marriage has been a farce for too long. You and I know that."

"Why don't *you* move out then? I don't want to lose my kid, and I'm just as entitled to keep my home as you are," he shouted back. I realized he was not going to make it easy. I had no idea of how I could manage on my own, I only knew one thing for sure, he'd have to go, and alone.

My intent to avoid a fight crumbled.

"*You* cheated on me, had that whore in my bed for weeks and you're talking of being *entitled?* I want you to get out of my life, *now*. I'm so sick and tired of your bullshit, your irresponsibility, your brutality. I've had enough of you, your lies and pretenses. You're nothing but a fraud."

I seethed, trembling from head to toe. I watched him bite his lower lip, ready to lash out. Instead he walked past me and reached for his jacket on the sofa, then grabbed the car keys on the dining table. That's when he saw Sophia timidly creeping out of her room.

"If that's how you want to play, then I'm taking my kid with me," he barked, took a few steps toward her and scooped her up in his arms.

Frightened, she looked at me with teary eyes. She was not yet four, but she'd already witnessed the violence between us, and told her grandma how Daddy and Mommy yelled very loud sometimes.

"Oh no, you're not," I screamed, disregarding her fear. "Leave her out of this, do you hear me?"

He carried her to her room, rummaged through her clothes.

"Robbie, you're not taking her out of this house, I won't let you. So you just stop this, right now."

He wasn't answering, which only intensified my dread. I picked up the phone, called my brother Larbi, and begged him to come down at once. "Robbie is stealing my baby! Call the police," I implored him.

I ran to the door and threw my body against it. He'd have to kill me before I let him out. Sophia was bawling, calling to me. I rushed back to her room.

"Don't use her to get at me, Robbie," I pleaded.

He was struggling to put on her shoes, his back turned to me, deaf to my implorations. In my frantic mind surfaced all the stories of fathers kidnapping their children to take them away from their mothers, never to be found again, all the untold emotional dysfunctions prompting a man to get back at his estranged wife through her offspring, and I panicked. I wouldn't put it past him. I knew his selfishness all too well. I went back to the phone and called 911. At least I think I did. Or maybe it was Larbi who'd called the police.

All I remember from that God-awful day is that the cops appeared in my hallway, stopped him from taking Sophia, and advised me to get a restraining order, which I did, that very day. For the first time since I'd known him and been subjected to his abuse, I acted decisively to keep him away. I changed the locks, closed our joint bank accounts, and cancelled our credit cards.

He responded violently to each of my actions, threatened me, and went wilder still in his reactions. My brother had persuaded him to move to my sister's apartment where he invited girls over and got high on pot and pornography almost nightly. On the other hand, even though he lived only a few floors above, he rarely saw his daughter and invariably broke his promises to spend time with her under some lousy pretext.

Until he broke down.

He was still unemployed when he called me, well past midnight, one chilly December night, begging me to reconsider my decision. I shivered at the sound of his voice.

"Wafa, this is stupid, we can still work this out," he lamented softly.

I hadn't been asleep when the phone rang. Sleep mostly eluded me in those days. My life was spent showing dozens of apartments to ambivalent buyers and running back home to pick up Sophia from daycare, juggling payments to creditors, and coping with an ailing mother and alienated spouse.

"Work *what* out, Robbie? I haven't seen anything from you that would lead me to believe that anything changed. If anything, your recklessness is adding to my resolve. I went over the last credit card statements. What were you thinking?"

"I just lost everything, Wafa. How am I supposed to cope with that, huh? This is killing me, you know that."

His voice broke. There was a long pause. He seemed to be looking for words.

"I saw a psychic and she told me there was a woman who's out to hurt me. And I know that woman is you."

"What in hell are you talking about?"

I couldn't believe my ears.

"You never used to be like this," he went on. "I guess it's Sami. He's been lying about me, hasn't he? That man is bad, I know his kind, and you don't. You better watch out," he sputtered.

"I don't need Sami to tell me what you're capable of, Robbie. This is just the straw that broke the camel's back. I've taken more shit from you than I could ever admit to. But now there's Sophia, and, for her sake, it's best we separate."

I willed myself to sound self-assured. Inside, I was devoured with doubt and still craving his embrace, like an addict her fix.

"I just don't want to lose you and my kid. I'm *desperate*, I'm telling you. Sometimes, I just want to throw myself out the window." He stopped talking, and I heard him weep on the phone. "I just want to finish with it," he murmured. "Then you'll have my death on your conscience, I swear to you, it's that bad."

I took a deep breath. "Oh my God, Robbie, stop it, that's crazy. Please, please don't do this. I beg you, don't blackmail me with suicide. It's hard enough as it is," I pleaded.

I heard the phone click and he was gone.

What was I supposed to do? How serious a threat was that? I couldn't handle that, too. I had to call his parents, let *them* take care of their son this time.

22

Saying Goodbye

My mother stayed almost four weeks at Mt Sinai. When she came out, she was lucid but her spirit had withered. The drugs she had been administered had restored her sanity but at a great cost. The once bold and smiley charmer had turned into a dull and tired-looking woman barely able to manage a smirk here and there. They had aged her beyond her years, and it took months before she regained some of her spark.

After the brain-numbing antipsychotic pills, lithium became her dreaded nemesis. Regardless of the dosage, it left a pronounced taste of salt in her mouth, a strong tremor, and slurred speech. Depakote soon replaced Lithium, but it, too, caused her to bloat and gain weight, while all side effects did not disappear. Like lithium, it required periodic blood tests to regulate toxicity and mood-stabilizing levels.

After the highs of acute mania, Mom then faced depression, sometimes despair. The anti-depressants battled the mood-stabilizers and, combined with her hormonal replacement therapy, sleeping pills, and pain killers, became part of a daily drug regimen central to her routine. Thereafter, my sister and I were reluctantly inducted into the role of medicine police.

I had been reminded enough, and had read enough, to know that vigilance was necessary to avoid manic relapses. In addition to drugs, the psychiatrist who followed her had also prescribed psychotherapy. Unfortunately, with his imperfect command of French and her minimal knowledge of English, their sessions were less than optimal, and I was often called upon to translate before being sent back to the waiting room.

In the months that followed, and beyond the drugs, the single most important factor that helped my mother reclaim her life somewhat was her children's love and support. Within months of her hospital discharge, all three of my siblings had moved to the Versailles, the apartment building on Boulevard East that had been my home and hers since I moved to New Jersey. Nezha and Hisham were next to make it their residence after their prior lease had expired.

Both my brothers were married by then. In 1987, Larbi had wed Margie, a cute and vivacious Jewish woman from Brooklyn. After a couple of years living in a tiny Manhattan studio, he had finally persuaded his wife to move to larger quarters in New Jersey—a decision which, at the time, she found exceedingly unappealing. Then, in 1989, a month after Mom married Chester, Abdu had tied the knot with Samira, a smart and determined twenty-five-year-old from Rabat. They had initially settled in Queens but soon returned to New Jersey and signed a lease in our building.

Thus, in an unplanned fashion my family and I had come to occupy five units on different floors of the same coop, the possibility of doing so never discussed or agreed on in common. Perhaps my siblings felt an instinctive need to be close to Mom after her illness. Our friends joked then that the building's name should have been changed to ours.

Over the next couple of years, Mom seemed to slowly accept her medicated existence. At least that was the impression she gave—until her second relapse. The debilitating side effects and the fact that she secretly stopped taking Depakote, and then lied about it, were certainly a contributing factor. Even under her daughters' watchful eyes, she still found a way.

Unbeknownst to me then, an ongoing battle was raging between her and her medication, a struggle I could never understand. It was rather simple in my mind; wasn't being "normal" a state that everyone aspired to? I'd never *really* stopped to consider how Mom felt about it. Now that I do, I realize how dreadful it must be to have one's mind hammered, numbed, and then wrung through the narrow bottleneck of normalcy—the insipid need to conform. Aren't our differences what make us stand out in the crowd? Is it any wonder that some of the greatest creative minds, scientists, and artists of all time have been considered eccentrics, wackoes, and rebels during their lifetime?

For the rest of her life, Mom was expected to ingest one type of poison to keep her from too much elation, and another one to avert the depths of despair—along the way wreaking havoc in her body, destroying its exquisite ability to heal itself, and enduring more physical discomfort than one can imagine. How can anyone willingly subject oneself to such treatment? She was hardly alone; most, if not all, mental patients stop taking their medication and go through relapses.

"You seem like you're doing fine, Mom. Did you have a good night sleep?" I would ask her every time she looked well and a bit too happy.

"Yes, I did, and I feel good," she'd answer cautiously, suspecting my motives. Lack of sleep signaled mania, and so did euphoria, but in her case, insomnia could also mean depression. She had to appear neither too down nor too high, just right. How awfully cynical and even contemptuous of our very humanity! Mood changes are part and parcel of the human condition; not even yogis and wise men can achieve an even temper all the time. Moreover, is it not impossible for anyone to *not* want to feel really wonderful? Finally, was I only concerned about her health, or mostly worried about my peace of mind?

"So, Mom, when you start feeling too good, you must tell your doctor, or me, so that we can knock that well-being out of you and drug you down again," is in effect what her doctor and I were asking her to do. Is it any wonder, then, that she rebelled and refused to comply by lying about her growing exhilaration? It's only when her increased brain activity, sensorial sensitivity, and lack of sleep turned into irritability and belligerence, followed by delusion and paranoia, that she would admit to a problem.

But were the lapses in drug intake truly the only culprits in the breakdown of her fragile mind? Today I am convinced that perhaps, more than any other cause, heightened levels of stress can affect the chemistry of the brain and unleash mayhem. And for that, there is no doubt in my mind, that my separation from my husband played a huge part in her first big relapse.

**

When Robbie threatened to end his life, I called his parents and they immediately sent him a plane ticket for Costa Rica. On December 11, 1992, on the eve of his departure, we agreed to put up a Christmas tree together for the pleasure of our little toddler.

"We should probably go now," said Robbie. "I finished packing, and it's getting dark quickly."

"Okay," I answered. "We'll meet you in the garage in five minutes." I ended the call and rushed to get Sophia's coat.

"We're going to buy a Christmas tree, and Daddy is coming with us," I said by way of getting her full attention.

"Daddy coming too?" she asked eagerly.

"Yes, honey, he is." Her eyes sparkled and she did a little dance before letting me put her coat on her. She hadn't seen him in days, and she missed him dearly. And now she looked so happy. I ached at the thought that this was a goodbye to her dad and not a welcome back into our lives. I had thought of it as a way for us to separate in friendlier terms for her sake. Above all else, I wished that he remain present in her life. I knew all too well what the absence of a father meant.

I could barely hold her hand in the elevator ride to our parking floor. She jumped up and down, balancing on one foot, then the other, in her ongoing and awkward monkey dance. Clutched in her other hand, her security blanket—a soft white cotton diaper she called her 'Papette'—flapped up and down her side.

"Sophia! Hi, baby!" he greeted her with a big smile. She tumbled in his arms, squealing with joy.

"Hi, Robbie." I opened the back door and helped him put her in her car seat.

"I'll sit in the back with Sophie, if you don't mind," he said.

"No, not at all," I replied.

The memory of that evening will forever remain with me. In spite of the gloom in our hearts, we strove to maintain pleasant faces and played the part of the happy parents. We drove to Michael's Tree-and-Trim store in Cliffside Park and bought a small artificial tree, and let Sophia choose a few ornaments to add to the ones I'd kept from previous years. After a quick pizza dinner, we set out to decorate and mostly watch our tot run around excitedly, picking shiny and colorful ornaments and handing them to us to hang.

Robbie looked different, thin and so handsome, in his tight jeans and black turtleneck. His sad blue eyes betrayed his state of mind and mirrored mine. I knew well that aching lust, open wound of our profound loneliness. It had been months without any intimacy between us.

"I have some white wine," I said. "Would you like some?"

"Sure," he said as he helped Sophia hang a gingerbread man on a lower branch.

I finished putting a golden ribbon on my side of the tree and went to fetch the wine from the kitchen. He appeared calm and collected, certainly a far cry from the suicidal man I had described to his mother only a week earlier. He didn't even look high, as I had imagined he would. I wondered if he sensed the tension building inside me. It was hard to believe that this was perhaps the last I was going to see him in some time. I poured the wine in two glasses and handed him one.

"Cheers, then." I raised my glass in his direction. "And happy early Christmas," I said, forcing a smile.

"Cheers, Wafa."

He touched his glass against mine and looked into my eyes, piercing through my shattered heart for a brief instant. His beautiful face was etched in sadness. Then he turned toward Sophia.

"You did a good job, baby," he complimented her with a stroke on her head.

I fought back tears; the poignancy of the scene was too much to bear.

She rubbed her eyes with her closed fist, holding Papette tightly. I glanced at my watch.

"It's well past her bedtime," I said quietly. "I think tonight we'll dispense with her bath."

"I'd like to put her to bed," Robbie said. I acquiesced, happy that he had offered, and began putting away the empty boxes.

After all those years, it had come to this. Tomorrow, he would be gone, and none of our individual grievances were close to being resolved or even acknowledged. But at that moment, all that I could think of was how much I had missed his warmth and how good he looked. I felt as if I were falling in love with him all over again.

"She's fast asleep," he whispered, pulling me out of my reverie. His eyes were red. "Is there some more wine left?" he asked, avoiding my gaze.

"Yes, I put it back in the fridge," I said, overcome with melancholy.

He came back with the half-empty bottle and poured some wine into my glass before filling his, still standing on the dining table.

"I'm going to miss her so much," he said. "I can't tell you how it feels."

I knew how he felt, and I ached for him, battled the urge to hold him.

"You will come back when you're better, won't you?" I asked. "You're her dad, and she will need you to be there for her."

I yearned to hear him say that things would be fine, that he would soon return, strong and changed, to take care of us, make everything alright forever thereafter.

"I don't know what to say, except I'm sorry if I hurt you," he said, reaching for my hand. "It was never my intention."

"Robbie, we need to put all of this behind us and focus on what's best for our kid. But first, you need to take care of yourself and be strong. You will be able to do that in Costa Rica. Sophie needs you." And I need you too, I wanted to add.

But words often cut like double-edged blades and must be used with caution lest one's heart get torn to shreds. He pulled me closer and, for what seemed like an eternity, held me in his arms ever so tenderly. On the radio, Whitney Houston's latest hit came on faintly in the background. *I will always love you*, she crooned—words we ourselves could not speak. To this day, that song remains the anthem for our parting. I closed my eyes, inhaling deeply through the soft wool of his sweater, listening to the moving melody and the thumping of his heart. His scent awoke ripples of longing from the depths of my being. Nothing could hold my tears back anymore.

Gently, he pulled my face up and wiped my tears with his hand. Then he lowered his head and kissed my lips. That was all that was needed for lightning to hit and spark raging wildfires through my loins, scorching all thought, all doubt. Wistful winds fanned the flames of my desire, blowing over the dry, drought-plagued grounds of my solitude. His kiss conjured images of paradise lost, memories of blissful times, and all I could think of was how much I loved him still. Gone was any recollection of pain and searing disillusion.

We let ourselves be swept by the waves of our bursting emotions and spent our very last night the same way we had our first—making passionate love to each other. Only this time, our teary fervor was engulfed in a kind of despair known only to those faced with untold tragedy, war, or plague. There is something to behold about human sexual appetites that they find their clearest expression in times of greater loss and uncertainty, as if we, poor souls, need to leave a trace of us behind, should we come to pass and be forgotten.

The next day, Sophia and I took Robbie to LaGuardia Airport. He was not to return to the States until some fourteen years later.

23

New Identity

My mother, who had been following my traumatic break-up and was affected by it, also paid a price. My sister was still in Tunisia with Sami and could be of no help. I became alarmed by Mom's growing petulance and restlessness. Those were early indicators and signaled mania and psychosis were not far behind. In spite of her denials, I was certain she had discontinued her medication, and my arguments could not get through to her to resume taking them. She felt way too good, but when her irritability and anger against one of my sisters-in-law became unmanageable. I literally had to trick her with the help of a friend in order to take her, without delay, to the emergency room.

And so, on March 9, 1993, three months after Robbie left for Costa Rica—and almost three years after her first hospitalization—she had to be readmitted. This time, I took her to Englewood Hospital, where she stayed two weeks. Once again, the whole battery of nightmarish drugs—Lithium, Haldol, Cogentin, Paxil—were force-fed to her. Once again, she turned into a zombie, suffered from slurred speech, impaired memory, a short attention span, slowed reflexes, lack of coordination, tremor, even bladder incontinence, until she stabilized again and recovered a semblance of normalcy.

Her relapse added layers of anxiety and fear to my already overtaxed existence. At a time when I struggled just to survive, I had to drive daily to the hospital to visit her and consult with her attending psychiatrist. My income was dwindling, and I was inundated by hostile calls from creditors. Robbie had left me with two mortgages, two co-op maintenances, and a mountain of credit card debts. He had exiled himself and relinquished all responsibility leaving me to care for a young daughter and an ailing mother, with no steady income, no child support or alimony, and no health care.

Professionally, the real-estate crisis had hit bottom, and there seemed to be no light at the end of the tunnel. Buyers were scarce and housing inventories way up. The values of both my apartments were well below their purchase prices and the amounts of their mortgages—which meant I owed more to the banks than they were worth. Compounding the problem were sky-high co-op maintenance fees and real-estate taxes. Nothing was selling in the Versailles anymore.

Nursery school tuition and basic living expenses were already devouring every penny I earned from vanishing commissions, made worse by the full weight of self-employment taxes. I was forced to liquidate my retirement accounts and faced, not only steep early withdrawal penalties, but also late payments fees, which I then struggled to pay in installments. Not only did I deplete every saving and retirement accounts I owned, I also went through every dollar I could borrow.

The months seemed to fly by at a greater pace than normal, and I felt under siege and ready for the kill. Despite it all, and for over a year and a half, I fought to pay every single bill while frantically trying to supplement my income moonlighting. My efforts failed to keep me afloat and collection agencies stepped up their harassment, pestering me night and day.

All efforts to work out individual arrangements with my creditors failed. They expressed regret and turned me down, my financial profile being simply too grim. My emotional stress was so consuming that the well-being of my child and the care of my mother were seriously threatened. After Robbie left, it took me over a year to find a steady job and, slowly, ways to get back on my feet.

On a frosty January afternoon in 1994, I walked into the tightly packed conference room of a Fifty-sixth and Fifth Avenue office building, inside a Merrill Lynch recruiting seminar. I was one of only a dozen other women in the midst of some two hundred professional-looking men in dark business suits. The floor-to-ceiling drapes were drawn, the room hot and stuffy, and the coat I was wearing felt like a heavy blanket. To say that I was intimidated would be an understatement. My first encounter with Wall Street was literally making me sweat. My knowledge of finance was limited at best. I knew politics, international relations, and diplomacy, and I was familiar with residential real estate, but I could hardly tell the difference between a stock and a bond. Had it not been for the ad in the *New York Times*, I would never have been there.

The quarter-page Sunday ad had explicitly stipulated that all the firm was looking for were people who were personable, charismatic, and had some sales skills, adding *"we will teach you everything else."* I had no doubt I could learn anything I put my mind to. A phone number was listed, inviting prospective consultants to call for an appointment.

"So sorry," the woman on the other end had told me when I called the following Thursday for a reservation. "We're already fully booked. But let me have your name and phone number, and I'll call you if we get cancellations."

"Really? You're completely booked?" I had asked surprised. "You don't have a spot for one more person?"

I had no clear idea of what it was she was referring to, but I had been very intrigued by the advertisement after my sister had brought it down to me insisting it looked perfect for me.

"Not right now, sorry. A lot of people have been replying since Sunday. But you never know," she'd apologized.

I'd given her the information she asked for and promptly forgot about the matter—until I got a call a couple of days before the seminar informing me that there was room for me if I still wanted to attend.

On the day of the event, snow and ice were piled high on Boulevard East and the forecast warned of frigid temperatures. Throughout the morning, I had debated whether I should go to the city at all, hoping to receive a call informing me that the meeting had been postponed.

The session began with a lengthy video presentation of the firm's over-a-century old illustrious lineage and achievements. It was followed by a description of what it meant to be a financial consultant at a prestigious firm such as Merrill Lynch. As I sat fretting on my chair, deep inside the room, and listened to the tall, impossibly blond preppy lecturing the crowd about the necessity of long and hard work hours to succeed in the industry, I kept thinking this was such a waste of my time. I had responsibilities that put limits on how many hours I could spend at work.

Mentally, I was preparing to leave the premises and go back home to my child. Only, the room was overflowing with attentive, middle-aged men jam-packed at the door and along the walls. I was trapped in my seat and forced to wait till the end of the presentation. But instead of releasing us into the icy streets of Manhattan, the organizers directed the attendees line by line to the awaiting interview screeners.

When my turn arrived, I got up and hesitantly followed as instructed. As soon as I entered the small, sparsely furnished office, the young man behind the desk stood up and extended his hand to greet me. Another blond and blue-eyed preppy in a suit! I thought to myself.

"Hi, I'm Prescott. How are you?" he said with a wide smile.

"Faith O'Brien," I answered, shaking his hand.

I had been informally using my married name ever since I began selling residential real estate in the city in the spring of 1990. The first broker who hired me had suggested that I also use a Western first name to advertise the properties we sold. Without hesitation I chose "Faith" the literal translation of my Arabic name "Ouafae", not realizing then that, in so doing, I had completely obliterated my ethnic background.

In October 1993, I legally sealed my cultural individuality by applying to the superior court of New Jersey for a name change. I adopted "Faith" as middle-name and simplified the French spelling of my first name from the clumsy "Ouafae" to "Wafa". By December, I was officially authorized to assume my new identity.

"Nice to meet you, Faith. Take a seat, please. Can I have your application?" he asked.

"Well, to be honest with you, I didn't bother to complete one." I sat on the edge of my chair.

He looked surprised, and I hurried to explain. "Actually, I don't think this position is for me. I'm a single mom. I have a four-year-old daughter and a sick mother. I cannot be working twelve-hour days *and* Saturdays, as they were emphasizing out there." I gave him an awkward grin with my thumb pointing toward the door.

"Oh yeah, I know the spiel," he chuckled, shaking his head. "I can tell you this—I hardly ever work past 4:00PM, and never on weekends. Do you have a résumé, by any chance?"

I nodded. "Well that's a relief," I exclaimed and handed him my CV.

"Where's your accent from? I can't make it out," he asked, intrigued.

"I was born in Morocco. French is my first language," I replied, adding, "And I learned English in England, which explains the British hint."

"Yeah, I can hear that!" beamed Prescott.

I leaned back in my chair, finally relaxed and thankful for the young man's affability. He took a minute to go over my educational and work history. He was in his late twenties, early thirties, I speculated. He was rather nice-looking and oozed self-confidence. I was not aware then that this was all part of a masterful hiring show, not unlike the one Michel had put up for countless reps some twenty years earlier.

"I'm impressed," he said at last, looking straight at me. "You're more educated and have more sales experience than most people starting in this business."

"Do you think so? You know, I never studied or worked in finance," I pointed out incredulous.

"Yes, I do. Don't worry about that. We're in fact interested in your personal qualities, not your knowledge of the industry. If we like your persona, we'll teach you everything you need to know about the business. Trust me, if I could learn this stuff, you certainly can," he chimed.

He went on discussing my background and extensive travel, and closed by telling me to expect a phone call from his branch manager for further interviews. Then he bid me goodbye and handed me his business card.

"Don't hesitate to call me if you have any questions," he said.

The interview had taken almost forty minutes. When I stepped out of the building, it was dark and snowing but my outlook was bright and sunny. Prescott had uplifted my spirit and made me feel good about my prospects. I waited two weeks to call him back, wondering why nobody had contacted me yet.

A couple of weeks later, I went on a string of meetings with various middle managers and senior consultants, and successfully took a few tests, before ending in a final face-to-face with a branch manager.

"What makes you think you can excel in this job and work with wealthy individuals?" he asked me point blank the minute I introduced myself.

His tone was measured but provocative. He was an imposing man, heavy and tall with grayish hair. He commanded respect in his large office with panoramic bay windows framing shiny skyscrapers behind him. It had finally all come down to this; this man's opinion was the one that counted. Though, by then, I felt more confident about my abilities and self-worth. I was not going to let him intimidate or bully me, I reminded myself.

"I have a great deal of sales experience; I'm well informed, highly educated, and worldly. I'm comfortable with wealthy people coming from a well-to-do family. They know they can trust me," I explained.

"What's the highest annual income you've made so far?" he continued, unimpressed.

The question took me aback. No one had asked me that so far. I tried to think fast; numbers flashed in my head.

"I made upward of seventy-thousand dollars selling real estate in a lousy market," I said nervously, exaggerating the figure.

His eyes twinkled with amusement. "You understand that's peanuts around here, don't you?" He wasn't asking, rather stating a fact in a derisive fashion, as if he were mocking me.

Is he poking fun at me? I wondered. Nobody had spoken about money or salary yet, though I really wished they had. I was in such financial distress; my trepidation went up a notch.

"I suppose it is!" I retorted. "I'm actually glad to hear that. I'm certainly ready to make much more money than I have so far."

I looked him right in the eyes, willing myself into sounding determined and supremely confident. He finally smiled and, leaning forward, extended his hand.

"I like you," he said. "Welcome to Merrill Lynch."

On March 7, 1994, I started my training as a rookie Merrill Lynch financial consultant.

Despite the manager's assertion, my compensation that first year was barely enough to cover the most essential bills. I had nowhere to turn and was terrified at the thought of losing my new employment. At long last, after seven more agonizing months examining every conceivable option, doubt and guilt-ridden, I decided to seek protection under the law and allow myself and my family a so-called "fresh start." Out of desperation and the necessity to face the dismal facts, I filed for bankruptcy on October 7, 1994. On February 23, 1995, I was released from all dischargeable debts under Chapter 7. My debts were wiped clean, but I had also lost my apartments.

Had it not been for the kindness of a stranger, the co-op sponsor, who, when told of my predicament, offered to let me continue to live in my home and pay only the monthly maintenance charges until I could get back on my feet, Sophia and I would have been homeless. It had taken me fifteen years to build a spotless credit history with not a single late payment or returned check. It took less than a year to shatter that perfect record.

On a few occasions, throughout my financial ordeal, I tried to appeal to my in-laws for help, but they turned me down flat every time. I'd had the brilliant idea to write a letter to them in which I laid down all my grievances and their son's responsibility in the breakup of our marriage. My mother-in-law's first response was to disbelieve every word of it.

Evidently Robbie had denied all wrong-doing or transgression, and it was obvious that his word had more weight than mine. After this fruitless attempt at requesting financial assistance from them, I tried to appeal to their grand-parental sentiments by asking that they and Robbie keep in touch with Sophia.

In a long letter, Charm had replied that, as a child, she herself had been abandoned by her biological father. She'd gone on explaining that, far from being hurt by her father's absence, she'd found great happiness with her step-father. She had then advised me that I ought to look for the same solution for my kid's well-being, and concluded that I should stop trying to contact them or her son altogether.

I was dismayed by her callousness. I had always held her in the highest esteem and viewed her as a compassionate woman. Her heartless reply was utterly unexpected. I understood that her empathy with her son had blind-sided her and that she was angry at me for the pain he suffered, but to reject her innocent grand-child out of their lives and offer such an insensitive answer inflicted a blow to my psyche that I could never forget.

24

Endings & Understandings

"I want my Daddy. I want my Daddy," whined Sophia over and over.

It was not the first time she had cried for her dad. Sometimes it was unpredictable, although often it followed his phone calls. I cuddled her as best I could, bewildered by her heartbreak but powerless to relieve it and full of hate toward its source.

"I'm sorry, honey, Daddy is far away. He's not well. He can't be here now. You know he loves you very much."

What was I supposed to tell her? How much could a four-year-old understand? How could I explain that I had no idea why her father had decided to stay in Costa Rica instead of returning to her side?

In the weeks that followed his exile, every time he called and asked for her she ended up distraught or tearful. Despite my reluctance, one day, I picked up the second phone and listened in on their conversation.

"I miss you so much, baby, and I want to be with you very much, but I can't right now," he wept.

"But why, Daddy?" she insisted. "Why? Why?"

"I just can't right now, baby. But I love you and I miss you."

His voice broke, and I could hear him sob.

I listened in disbelief. There was a grown man talking to a tiny girl and not for a moment did he show restraint or understand the implications of his indecent show of self-pity. What did he think she could make out of that? I'd heard enough. I hung up and went to her.

She was sitting on the sofa in front of the television set, ready to watch her favorite program on that cloudy Saturday morning when the phone had rung.

"Say goodbye to Daddy, honey," I said with a kiss on her head.

"Bye, Daddy," she said in a little voice, handing me the cordless phone.

"Hi, Robbie?" I said. "Hold on a minute, will you? I need to talk with you."

I covered the receiver and looked at Sophia. "You want to watch Barney?" I asked.

She nodded and put her left thumb in her mouth. I turned the TV on, gave her "Papette" to hold on for comfort, and went into the bedroom. She watched me walk away before turning to the screen with a deep sigh while kneading her blanket.

"Robbie? What do you think you're doing exactly?" I asked in dismay.

"What do you mean?" he retorted on the defensive.

"I mean, here you are, once again, crying on the phone with your child who is already traumatized by your absence. How do you imagine your infantile display affects her?" I struggled to keep my voice down.

"you're a bitch," he replied in disgust. "I'm just being honest. I can't pretend everything is okay when it's not. I can't talk with her without thinking of you, and I'm hurting. You don't understand..."

"No, as a matter of fact, I don't," I snapped. "I do get that you're in pain. We all are. But Sophie is a baby, and hearing you weep breaks her little heart and makes her cry, too. You do that every time you call. It's incomprehensible. She doesn't know why you're not here. She thinks she's somehow responsible for that. She often calls her uncles 'Daddy' and asks for you all the time. You're inflicting immeasurable damage on her. How can you not *see* that?" I choked on my last words.

"I'm not there because *you* kicked me out, Wafa. You think it's easy, don't you? You have no idea what I'm going through, how much I miss her—"

"Then get back over here and *be* there for her," I interrupted. "I wanted you out of *my* life, not hers. You've been away for almost *six months* now. Why are you still acting like a helpless victim? How long does it have to take you to separate our situation from the fact that you are a father and have responsibilities towards your child? She has *nothing* to do with *us*. She is not *me*. You must think about *her*, and her well-being, alone. Is she not your highest priority?"

"I can't do that yet. I have no money, and I've been sick. I need to take care of myself. I can get treated here," he said.

"Then you better get well fast," I snarled. "You can find a job and live nearby. You can be with her as much as you want. We can work out flexible custody terms. Listen, she *needs* you, period."

I paused, besieged by memories of my absent father and the pain that had caused me. My child had to be spared similar torment. But there was another pressing matter.

"By the way, I need you to sign the divorce petition. We both have to put this mess behind," I ventured, aware of the thorniness of the subject.

"You wrote all that shit about me in the complaint. I can't agree to that," he said sullenly.

"I had to give a cause for wanting to divorce immediately. 'Extreme cruelty' is a common ground for expeditious action. Besides, it's all true, and why should it matter to you, anyway? It's not costing you a penny! Just sign it, and let's put an end to this." God, he really tested my patience.

My anger simmered at the surface. I was certain his reluctance to sign the petition had more to do with innate procrastination than with a valid sentiment of offended honor.

I had him served when he was still in New Jersey, but he had ignored it altogether. I had sent him at least two more petitions to Costa Rica, which he'd dodged yet again. I had no clue what else I could be doing to get him to sign the documents *and* return them. My lawyer was pretty inept, and I couldn't afford someone more competent.

There was no financial dispute because there were no assets to speak of, only piles of debt, which I wasn't even asking him to help with. There was no request for alimony or child support, and I had agreed to joint custody. I knew he was still unemployed, broke, and living with his parents. I just wished him completely out of my life. Divorce was the only way out, and a quick signature should have been easy. Apparently not!

My only expectation was that he stayed in touch with Sophia, though even that was a challenge. His egotistical and cavalier attitude toward his daughter was a source of greater distress than I had imagined. As much as I had been missing him and yearned for his presence for months, I'd come to see him as a fiend.

Love is a treacherous mirage, appearing like an oasis in the wasteland of our desire and neediness, only to metamorphose into loathing once our expectations are trampled.

That turned out to be our final conversation. He stopped calling, writing, or otherwise communicating with his daughter—not even on her birthday or Christmas did he feel he needed to express his attachment. He just let it go, let *her* go, as he did me, as if we were one and the same. What did fatherhood mean to him? Did he imagine that relinquishing his responsibility to her freed him from me? For the life of me, I could not comprehend why, as intelligent as I knew him to be, he was still incapable of separating his feelings for me from his love for her. For that very reason, I never trashed him in front of Sophia.

Throughout my childhood and teenage years, I had deeply resented my mother's horrid portrayal and savage criticism of my father—no matter how true or well-founded. It was, hence, paramount in my mind never to speak ill of Robbie to my daughter. Quite the contrary—I described him in the best light possible. Ironically, it was *his* behavior over the years that revealed his true character to her, making her despise him for a long time.

In the end, he never signed any of the divorce petitions I sent him and never filed his own. We were at a standstill. As a last resort, on September 29, 1995, I entered a request to be granted a divorce by default. To do that, I had to publicly publish the complaint in newspapers in both New Jersey and Costa Rica, wait thirty days, and then be granted a hearing. On November 28, 1995, three years after our initial separation, a final judgment of divorce was issued.

"My parents were insulted to have their name in the Costa Rican paper associated with your appalling petition," he afterwards had the nerve to complain—as if he had left me any other option.

What exactly had he expected me to do? If my petition was so offensive, how was his child abandonment to be qualified? Where were his and his parents' sense of honor then? Furthermore, had he really wished for the whole matter to remain private, why hadn't he signed and returned any of the complaints that were sent to him on multiple occasions for three long years? My questions had remained unanswered.

Most outrageous yet was his request for a copy of my final judgment of divorce, a couple of years later, when he was ready to marry a Costa Rican woman he had impregnated. Even more egregious was his phone request for a loan to divorce the same woman years later, and obtain legal custody of his then two young children. All those years, I agonized watching Sophia aching from his absence, and as much as I felt bad for him, my reason would just not let me show him any sympathy. I ignored all his appeals for help, and he had the common sense not to insist.

There was, however, a bright spot in the midst of those sad circumstances—it came from his mother, who, despite her prior insensitive statement, had in fact maintained a rapport with Sophia, writing her every birthday and Christmas and sending her a check on each occasion. Had she not been there, I am convinced Robbie would have vanished without a trace from his daughter's life.

**

As I finished writing those words, I was struck by a flash of awareness. I stopped and mulled over the tone of my narrative. The voice was all one-sided, stubbornly smug, and sanctimonious. If I felt that way then and, for years afterward, wallowed in self-righteousness, I was no longer that person, I realized.

"It's like I still want to have the last word!" I said out loud, the sound of my voice breaking the silence.

The sun had sunk behind the horizon, leaving a red-orange smudge in the dimming sky. I stared back at my computer screen. Is it possible for me to ponder over those times and reassess my life with Robbie objectively, without prevarication or bitterness? I never had the opportunity to hear *his* side. I never cared to find out. My pain had sealed me off from him, and I'd had no desire to be compassionate.

I closed my eyes and revisited our relationship in my mind, trying in earnest to stay detached.

When Robbie first admitted his pot problem and expressed his desire to free himself of his dependency, he'd also described the goodness toward which he'd aspired, and I'd believed I had found my prince. I was going to help him heal, be his savior, change him for the better-just as he had thought he found his "beau-ideal," as he put it, his Greek goddess, in me. We'd each childishly clung to those imaginary deities out of selfish need and in total obliviousness to the real other.

Behind my lover's beautiful physique, intellect, and sensitive soul, had lurked an anxious and depressed young man, who self-medicated with marijuana, masturbation, and pornography. My disappointment had been so immense, I'd kept obsessing over *his* problems-in denial of my own. I had thought myself in control and dealt with my own anxiety by taking charge, with regular physical exertion, running, and gym workouts, never once indulging in drugs or alcohol excess, all of which enabled me to claim the moral high ground. I do recall him pointing to just that, prompting a swift refutation from me.

"You and I are the same," he'd once said, stretching full length on the couch in front of TV on one of his days off. "Behind your self-righteousness and poise, you too are doubt-ridden and afraid. We simply deal with it in different ways, which does not mean you're better than me."

I'd been getting ready to go to the gym and had asked him to watch Sophie; he'd said no, arguing that he needed to relax and advising that I take her upstairs to Mom while I was gone. I was infuriated by both his statement and his refusal to take care of the baby in my absence.

"How is getting high and habitually dallying in front of the TV the same as going to the gym and working out?"

Thinking back, the idea had hit a nerve and lingered in my head. Indeed, I'd often mentioned it to friends and relatives in expectation of reinforcing my view of him, which they invariably did.

The thought had, however, finally seeped through my psyche and was staring squarely at me. I could see now what he meant and how true it had been.

There was no question he had been guilty of some creepy and brutish things over the years. But *I* couldn't be absolved of all blame in our demise. For one thing, I was so insanely insecure about money that it had become second nature to confront him with images of imminent Armageddon. Time and again I had disparaged his natural generosity and desire to please, going so far once as to yell at him for bringing me flowers for no reason other than to celebrate me. In his hand, the bouquet had looked like a posy of overdue bills. Forever since, I have felt like an ogre for that unremitting tyranny.

I should have known the first time I had caught Robbie smoking pot in hiding, that there was something fundamentally wrong, deeply dysfunctional, between us. He, on the other hand, who had lived for my approval, was just as oblivious. I had become his father figure under his very eyes. Pleasing me was his *raison d'être*, and he submitted to it, albeit

rebelling and striking back every so often. Like a disobedient teen, he had wanted to avoid criticism, while I'd behaved
like a nagging parent, reprimanding and judging his every
act. I'd put him down, made him feel worthless, incapable of
achievement. The longer he put off his college graduation and
career goals, for instance, the more my reaction contributed
to further stunt his dreams. Was I solely responsible for his
failure to succeed? No, but my displeasure had contributed
to it.

Change, for most of us, is inherently difficult. But it is next
to impossible when we live with people who don't believe in us
and wear their discontent on their sleeves. Instinctively, I had
also emulated my mother in her criticism of my father, who
had not been strong, or ambitious, or a good provider. In my
eyes, Robbie too had fallen short on every count.

To make matters worse, we had both been opinionated
and aggressive in our beliefs and conversation, always locked
in a bitter power struggle and resorting to vicious arguments
about everything, from political issues to household chores, to
Robbie's on-again off-again drug use. Physical violence and
verbal cruelty had infected our encounters and worn us out.
We'd each had to have the last word. Neither would give in,
as if our lives depended on it. Disagreements turned to accusations and slights. Quickly we'd learned which buttons to
push and, when words failed, I had hurled insults and he had
thrown physical blows.

In the end, our early infatuation had quickly been deflated
by reality. We were no angels, just earthlings struggling with
our inadequacies. Because we only saw what we wanted to see
in each other, we had no recognition of our failings, no clear-
eyed acceptance of our shortcomings, the inevitable other side
of our all-too-human selves. When we grasped the illusory

nature of our expectations, the ground shifted under us and we came face to face with our frailty.

In the midst of our passion, we had paid only lip service to our flaws, resorting to understatements and indulging in subtle, secretive games for fear of falling short in the eyes of our beloved. At other times, we so believed the strength of our love would somehow triumph over everything; we were so fascinated with the ideal of love in all its perfection, that we stripped ourselves naked by revealing vulnerabilities that put us at the mercy of each other. When, in the course of daily life, the honeymoon ended and our faults made their way to the surface, they no longer seemed trivial or surmountable; they caused us instead to feel betrayed. Before we knew it, the seeds of resentment had grown into thickets of discord.

I leaned back against the back cushion, deep in reminis-cence. The room was almost completely dark, save the glow from my computer screen shedding a single point of light. I reached for the glass on the side table and took a sip of luke-warm water. The monotonous ticking of the clock in the kitchen, and the faint roar of planes in the night sky, were the only discernable noises besides the clicking of the keyboard and the vent of the computer notebook on my lap. I could feel its slow burn through the fabric of my jeans. Later my thigh would display the telling red, marbled marks. I had no desire to move back to my desk, feeling comfortable in the living room chair, legs propped on the coffee table. For the first time, as I dug into long gone memories, I felt completely at peace with my past. I took a deep breath and went back in time.

But what else was there to say than that our love had undergone a hideous transmutation? Trust had been violated repeatedly in a relationship that lasted more than a decade, small waves of bliss quickly drowned by tides of acrimony. All along, what was missing was compassion and, ultimately, true love. Robbie's abandonment of his child was only an indication of the depth of his despair and anguish over the failure of a long-cherished and idealized romance with a fairytale beginning and a nightmarish end. That, in a nutshell, was all of it.

25

Wall Street Waltz

At the very moment my financial and marital life unraveled, my professional career progressed, albeit on a wobbly course. When I first joined Merrill Lynch's financial advisors, I imagined I had found my calling. The first three months were entirely devoted to the study of industry rules, regulations, and practices, and taking the licensing exams. They were followed by twenty-one months of grueling training while I built a client base. That particular side of the job I abhorred, for to create a customer book from scratch, new hires had to learn to network ceaselessly, make countless cold-calls-often right out of phone directories—and otherwise metamorphose into annoying, thick-skinned telemarketers day in and day out.

Every six months, recruits were supposed to reach a higher level in the firm's Professional Development Program (PDP), and a new amount of commissions and assets, to move on to the next stage. I missed my first two echelons yet still managed to survive. Underneath a brave smile and winning composure, every day, from nine to five, I dwelt in a tunnel of anguish beset by tides of rejection. I felt lonely and despondent and found no support from management whatsoever. I was far from being the only one suffering from the pressures of the job. Jana, a dear friend to this day and a bright and beautiful Scandinavian-looking woman I had met during the Series 7 training, developed such a prospecting phobia and fear of rebuff that she became physically ill and lost an absurd amount of weight. She felt she had no choice but to quit and look for another line of business.

I could not do the same. My Master's Degree was in politics and international relations, and I had an incomplete doctoral thesis, which did not open too many lucrative fields for me. I needed to make money-which is not to say that I did not try to find another job when the going got tough; I even went on a couple of secret interviews.

I didn't know then that the dreadful burrow of rejection was not inhabited equally by all recruits. Not unlike many others in the industry, my branch manager had his pets, predominantly waspy young men, on whom he lavished rich accounts and numerous opportunities. They were unashamedly aided and thus succeeded rapidly, building substantial client books out of thin air and turning into prosperous advisors. I recall attending office meetings and naively listening to male brokers vaunting their meteoric rise at the top even as they admitted, in moments of unguarded candor, how it "helped to have friends in high places to *feed* them" when they needed it. All were alpha males, members of an exclusive club created by the branch manager, who treated them to three-martini lunches and golf outings.

As well-publicized class-action gender discrimination lawsuits later revealed, it turned out I had joined one of the firm's most chauvinistic branches, managed by a man who felt no remorse over ignoring his flailing female consultants and hired them only because he was under great pressure to do so. I had been warned about the notoriously male-dominated Wall Street but I had no idea what that meant until then.

Fortunately, I soon became acquainted with a handful of successful women consultants who told me how they had surmounted the inequity and prejudice, and I persuaded myself that if, in spite of the odds, they'd been able to make it big in the industry, so could I. I was far from imagining the price I would have to pay eventually to be in that league, even so briefly. Still, I knew from earlier experiences that I could be a terrific salesperson, and so my natural ambition and competitiveness kicked in, I hung on, toughed it up, and within five years I had gathered over a hundred million dollars of clients' assets, and almost double that amount in the following three years.

I do, however, need to acknowledge one person for mentoring and guiding me at a critical moment of my career. At the time of my hiring, Linda Bartelli, who up until then had managed Merrill Lynch's flagship office at the firm's World Financial Center headquarters, was named New York City district director. Her office was located in the same Fifth Avenue building as mine, a few floors up. As I became more proficient in my job and started to hit my marks, I showed up on her radar screen, and my career as a rookie consultant finally took off—not because of free accounts and special dealings, but because of her steadfast encouragement and personal recognition of my efforts.

Linda was one of an unconventional breed of female managers who took Wall Street by storms. A tall woman with a big voice and thunderous laughter, an uncommon sense of humor, boundless energy, and an imposing yet down-to-earth presence, she at once charmed and conquered. Physically, she was a sight to behold. A cloud of short blond hair with wavy bangs covering her forehead and framing her blue eyes, gold hoops adorning her ears, a sunny white smile that could lighten up any gloomy day—she stood out in her bright suits as a flash of dazzling yellow, orange, red, or green in a sea of dark suits.

The first time I laid eyes on her, my notion of appropriate dress and style was tested. I thought the woman was too much—too flashy, too ostentatious, too crazy, and then she gave me a taste of her warmth and people-management skills, and I fell in love with her. I only wanted her praise, wished to please her, craved her appreciation. The more she acknowledged my accomplishments, the better I performed.

Her advice was rather straightforward: "Work hard and be focused on your goals. Continually help yourself grow and get better. Maintain a high level of personal integrity, always do what's right, and care about your clients and the people you work with." This was more than an aphorism; she backed up her words with concurring deeds, personal phone calls, congratulatory notes, verbal encouragements, invitations to special events, and otherwise made sure you knew that you counted—no matter how small a producer you were—and that she was there for you, should you need a sound piece of advice or simply a kind ear.

To grow my production, I had begun targeting my prospecting efforts on the business community in Manhattan and Northern New Jersey and met with some success when Linda invited me, along with a group of other promising consultants, for a two-night-and-two-day meeting with Merrill Lynch Business Financial Services (BFS) officers in Chicago. During our second night in the windy city, we were treated to a great dinner at a well-known steakhouse and then offered a drink in a nearby blues venue. The rest of the team chose to party on a little longer; Linda and I had decided to call it a night.

"This was a wonderful evening, Linda," I said emerging in the cold blustery air. "Thank you. I feel lucky to be part of this trip."

"It has nothing to do with luck, Faith," she replied with her trademark smile as we reached Magnificent Mile and walked in the direction of our hotel. "You have exactly the personality you need to become a successful broker."

"Thank you all the same. You always know how to boost my morale."

"I mean it, Faith. You're smart and articulate, and it's obvious you care, but you're also charismatic and optimistic. And a positive attitude is key in our business. I've worked with many people over the years. I've come to recognize greatness," she added without missing a beat. "It's gonna require hard work and perseverance, no doubt, but you're going to succeed beyond your greatest expectations, I'm sure of it!" She pulled her cashmere scarf over her nose and gave me an expressive glance.

Her words triggered a whirl of excitement inside me.

"Wow. That's really good to hear from someone like you. You have no idea how much your support means to me. I have tremendous respect for you, as you can imagine. You're the best manager I could ever hope for."

I stopped talking and pressed my coat collar against my ears to fend off the penetrating wind that was gushing down the deserted avenue. "It got so cold!" I frowned, shivering to my bones.

"Yeah, let's hurry up before we freeze here," Linda mumbled in her scarf. "I'm not sure it was such a good idea to walk back to the hotel instead of waiting for a cab...You can tell it's not Manhattan-taxis are awfully scarce at this time of night."

A couple of years later, for family reasons and to my great chagrin, Linda decided to move to Florida and relinquish her New York City district directorship.

It was around then that Ralph Giordano assumed the management of my branch. An elegant and mild-mannered man, he immediately set out to overhaul the culture of the office and worked to make it the best in the district, in direct competition with the World Financial Center branch. An ambitious and hands-on kind of man, he picked up where Linda had left off, encouraging and backing all financial consultants, small and big producers alike. Under his watchful eye, my revenues to the firm rapidly mounted, far exceeding the hurdles that had once eluded me. Soon after his promotion, he moved the whole branch to bigger, more imposing, quarters occupying almost two floors of the Citigroup building.

I enjoyed working with him even as he kept daring me to reach higher. If, within a year, I grew my numbers further than I'd projected in my annual plan, he would reward me by moving me to a better office—a larger, more beautiful space with East River views and a conference table. I have always been a sucker for challenges, often following my egotistical impulses to the detriment of my better judgment, so I aimed to please. I worked relentlessly on my revenues and climbed the corporate title ladder smoothly and seemingly effortlessly. I became a senior financial consultant and vice president and made an income of close to a quarter million dollars a year at the height of my career. I was one of Ralph's darlings and the envy of my colleagues. In those swinging Nineties, I was at the top of my game.

It was around that time, my mother came to pay me a visit.

My assistant poked her head in the doorway, her long jet-black locks cascading down her shoulders, and announced merrily: "Faith, your appointment is here."

I gave her a puzzled look. "Which appointment are you talking about, Leslie? I don't have anything scheduled."

She broke in a big smile, moved aside, and showed my mother in.

"Oh Mom, what a nice surprise!"

I jumped on my feet and planted a kiss on both her cheeks. Despite several invitations, this was her first visit to my new Citicorp Tower location.

"Can I get you something to drink?" Leslie asked her sweetly.

My mother looked striking and cheerful. She had makeup on, and her hair was done in the style that she favored and suited her most-pulled back in the front by a black headband and let loose in the back.

"Just a glass of water, please," she replied.

"You're sure you don't want a coffee? We have an espresso machine here, and Leslie can make you a coffee just the way you like it, black and strong," I said.

"Okay, then, a black coffee and a glass of water," Mom told Leslie, still standing there looking at the two of us.

"You look so much like your mom, Faith," she grinned.

"Yes, I know." I giggled, put my arm around Mom's shoulders and gave her a little squeeze. "So, what do you think?" I asked. "Do you like my office?" I tilted my head, peering at her from the side.

"First, let me show you the view from here."

I walked her to the vast bay window and swept the air with my hand, pointing to the glistening river under the crisp, sunny sky and the boroughs beyond.

"At home, I enjoy the mighty Hudson, and at work, the East River—the best of both worlds," I said.

She looked on and then turned around to admire my office.

I had spent a great deal of effort and expense decorating it. Carefully chosen impressionist reproductions and prints hung on the walls; an Indian rug lay under the conference table and a smaller one in front of my desk. Directly under an ornate mirror, a console table contained a bouquet of flowers and a lamp. It looked quaint and elegant at the same time, a page out of a catalog. Not a day went by without a perfect stranger popping their head in to tell me what a beautiful office I had.

"I love how you decorated it and made it so stylish," beamed Mom. I smiled with contentment.

"Okay, now I'm taking you around the rest of the branch. You know we occupy the entire forty-seventh floor as well as the forty-sixth," I said, taking her by the arm.

I knew Mom was proud of me, and I felt like indulging her sense of pride even more. Her dream for me, for her, had come true, and she reveled in the moment. She looked around enthralled, shaking the hands of colleagues I introduced her to with delight, charming them with her alluring smile and friendliness, often asking with her disarming accent, "Do you speak French?" by way of excusing her poor English and as if she were about to engage in a lengthy conversation if they did.

When we came back in my office, she sat back in one of the large chairs facing my desk, sipped her coffee, and watched me answer a client's call in silence, taking it all in quietly.

It was not hard to guess what was going through her head. The sacrificed teenager, married against her will at a tender age in a medieval time and place, was witnessing something she could not, in her wildest dreams, have ever imagined. The frightened little girl whose hand she once held to school, some three-and-a-half decades earlier had turned into a successful Wall Street advisor managing million-dollar portfolios and reaching the pinnacle of American society in a transformation that baffled her mind.

I ended my call and gazed at her, filled with emotion. Tears were welling up in her eyes, but she was smiling at me. She had finally won her battle with destiny. I got up, sat next to her, and reached for her hand in silence.

On the eve of the new Millennium, Merrill Lynch, like all of Wall Street, was shooting for the stars by taking full advantage of the new Financial Services Modernization Act, also known as the Gramm-Leach-Bliley Act (GLBA), that permitted commercial and investment banks to consolidate, in effect repealing the landmark *Glass-Steagall Act of 1933*, one of the central pillars of Roosevelt's New Deal. Throughout the preceding years, the banking, investment, and insurance industries had joined forces and furiously lobbied the Clinton administration and Republican majority in Congress with the single-minded determination to relax the remaining Glass-Steagall restraints, already loosened by Reagan in the early 1980s. Ironically, legislation that had been put in place to protect American capitalism after the 1929 Wall Street Crash was abolished at exactly the time an unprecedented speculative bubble in the technology industry was sweeping through the global markets.

Merrill Lynch was getting ready for big mergers and record-breaking revenues, both through underwritings and acquisitions. Branch managers were directed to set the pace at every level, in every department, and encourage the craziest material dreams from their consultants—the more unimaginable the goals, the better. We were told to map out yearly written plans with the most ambitious material aspirations, from million-dollar homes to lavish secondary residences, luxury cars, private yachts, exclusive country club memberships—no vision was too big—and back them up with ever higher annual commission and revenue numbers.

More than ever before, consultants, thrust down the path of greed, found themselves trapped in the race for flagrant wealth, brazen spending, and audacious borrowing. A rat race of unparalleled proportions ensued. Meeting after meeting showed us the road to success and the way to get there. And to give us a taste of things to come, and fantasies to aim for, every year Merrill Lynch rewarded its best and brightest with fabulous club trips to five-star resorts in the United States and abroad.

In December 1996, Alan Greenspan, the Federal Reserve Chairman, spoke of "irrational exuberance" when referring to the "undue escalation of assets," and sent the market into a spin. Three years later, that memory had all but vanished and the markets were again gorging on fast profits and obscene greediness. Some internet and computer stocks were selling at prices over a hundred times earnings; sometimes they had no earnings at all. It was all pure unadulterated speculation.

I found myself in the midst of the madness and not knowing quite what to make of it. It all felt weird and, at times, uncomfortable, but I had neither the desire nor the guts to stand up and express reserve or dissent. Indeed, I partook as best I knew how. Barely a year after the co-op sponsor had officially repossessed my apartment I re-purchased it and closed in the summer of 1998. Six months later, in December, I bought Mom her very first home, a corner two-bedroom apartment she had been renting for two years in my building. And exactly a year after that, I helped my sister buy her own, identical to mine, two-bedroom two-bath apartment, on the sixteenth floor of the Versailles, by co-signing her mortgage loan.

But instead of feeling satisfied with my achievements, under a year later, in the summer of 2000, just as the market had begun what would become a prolonged decline, I bought the apartment adjacent to mine, expanding my home from thirteen hundred to twenty-two hundred square feet, and embarked on a complete, hugely onerous renovation that went on for over fifteen months.

I had never before experienced a serious bear market, only short-lived downturns, quickly followed by heightened speculation and volatility, and renewed market highs. Furthermore, no one, neither clients nor experts-save a few doomsayers, seemed to be noticing the looming crisis.

Over the years, my clients had been pushing for greater returns. A carefully balanced portfolio with moderate returns was deemed a shortsighted strategy, and I was increasingly under pressure to meet or beat those unbelievable S&P returns.

"Come on, Faith, the S&P yielded thirty percent annually between 1995 and 1999-don't tell me that fifteen percent is a good return!" the voice on the end of the line argued in frustration.

"But, Alan, you're not invested only in stocks. Thirty percent of your portfolio is in bonds. You're almost fifty years old. That's a prudent allocation," I replied with vehemence. "We already discussed this."

"I'm speaking of the freaking stock *index* returns, Faith. I'm not even talking of the small tech stocks. Those are doubling within months," he went on, deaf to my argument.

"Well, would you be ready to take on that kind of risk and lose as much as you're willing to gain? That's how it works, you know. There's no free lunch out there," I protested.

"Look, I've been doing some online trading on my own, and I can tell you this, I made more money with less investment in five months than you have in a year," he said, exceedingly agitated. "I really don't know why I pay you so much money!"

There it was the familiar threat; if it was so easy anyone could do it. Why pay a broker? The menace never failed to send shivers down my spine and tie my stomach in a knot.

"You pay me to responsibly help you invest your savings, manage your liabilities, and grow your assets, not gamble them away," I retorted. "I know you're upset because some people have made a lot of money in a very short period of time, but they're betting on a few speculative stocks, not investing. There's a big difference."

"I understand that, but couldn't we, at least, spike those returns with a few IPOs here and there? Merrill Lynch underwrites many of them, and you never offer me any. Some of those skyrocket in a single day of trading."

That too I'd heard before. The truth was I didn't get any of the highly sought-after initial public offerings to propose to my clients. Those were allocated to the big wigs, the mega-producers and their clients, and to institutional investors. My clients, many of them with million-dollar portfolios, were still considered small fry. When I was presented with IPOs, they often were lesser or undersubscribed issues or leftovers.

"Tell you what, I'll go over your accounts again, and I will identify places where we could afford a little more risk. I think we may be able to add some of the best tech stocks, like Cisco Systems, Yahoo, and Amazon, although they may be a bit pricey. But before I suggest anything, I want to make sure and scan not only Merrill research but also other firms' ratings on those companies. I'll put together a list for you with only the best recommendations. How's that?"

"Sounds good, Faith. And let's see what you can do about some good IPOs, too," he said grudgingly.

I put down the phone feeling drained. Few of my clients were willing to hear the voice of moderation anymore; playing it safe was outdated. They all wanted a piece of the action, a position in all the sexy Internet stocks that everybody talked about.

At first, I resisted the temptation to give them what they begged for, sticking with what I had learned, buying blue chip companies with a long history of profits and experienced management. Then, slowly, as I began to learn more about the so-called "new economy," I too became complacent and fell prey to the widespread hi-tech lure, buying more technology stocks and funds for my clients and my own personal accounts. Soon, my clients loved the superior returns, and I loved pleasing them. My sole concerns were how to minimize the fiscal impact of short-term capital gains and avoid wash sales.

26

Up Close and Personal

My first affair as a single woman took place almost a year after Robbie left for Costa Rica. Financially, I was bankrupt then; emotionally, I felt lonely and empty. My mind tortured me with elaborate schemes of my ex seeing the light and returning to be the man I had always dreamt he would be. For in spite of the wretchedness of our marriage, our sex life had always been rich and satisfying. Finally, after much mental wrestling, I answered a personal ad in *New York Magazine* with a short note and no photo.

The header had advertised: *"Extra-Special Man,"* and gone on:
I am a very handsome, 6'4", slim, fit, salt-pepper hair, brown-eyed businessman. Adventurous, uncommon sense of warmth and caring. I am a complex, very special man with very deep values and a good heart. I am looking for a very special woman—probably someone who rarely, if ever, answers ads. You are a very attractive brunette, who is totally fit (physically, emotionally, and spiritually) Warm heart and soul. Passionate about life. Nonsmoker, 32-42.

After all, I was a fit and attractive thirty-seven-year-old brunette with a "warm heart and soul," I thought.

I didn't hear back from the "extra-special man" until some eight weeks later, after I had all but forgotten about him, and when we met for the first time, I was stunned by his good looks and dazzling smile. A well-off, Hungarian-born fifty-year-old, Elek was indeed warm, loving, and caring, and a divorced father of two grown children. We dated for a little while, and he seemed to be doing everything right, working hard to please me in every way—that is, until we became intimate and all our efforts failed to accomplish their purpose.

"I'm so sorry," he said, contrite. "I don't know what's wrong with me. It never happened before."

Shit! I thought, just my luck. It was too good to be true. No wonder it took him so long to get me in the sack! I took a deep breath and silently prayed that my disappointment did not show.

"Oh, no," I reassured him. "Don't worry about it. It's not all that important."

Like hell, I kept thinking. I should've known from the moment he kissed me, on our second date—such a lousy kisser! Still, with my help, the kissing had gotten a lot better. Perhaps, if I were patient enough, he might recover from erectile dysfunction too!

"We can have fun in other ways," I teased to relax the tension.

We did indeed find other ways to enjoy each other but what was missing did not get much better with time. These were the days before Viagra! His ED never went away, but it was not the only reason for me to want him out of my life after only three months.

In fact, I'd liked him so much at first that I really convinced myself I could live without a fully satisfying sex life, and we began to spend more time together. A highly accomplished skier, he took me to Vail for a long weekend and helped me perk up my skills. He met my mother and the rest of my family. Then Sophie and I spent the holidays with his friends and relatives. But, at four and a half, she disliked him. He was strict and not much fun with her.

"You have to finish your spinach if you want your dessert," he had once insisted, leaning over to push the plate toward her. "My kids always ate their vegetables." And to make it easier to swallow, he'd sprinkled sugar on the green leafy vegetable.

"Come on, baby, it's good for you," I'd encouraged her, not wishing to overrule him.

She'd beseeched me with teary eyes, aggrieved that I had taken his side, tried a tiny bite, and almost immediately spit it out. Elek had been incensed, and I'd had to intervene to calm him down and rescue her.

Furthermore, it turned out he suffered from pronounced obsessive compulsive disorder, which, during the first weeks, he'd masked as best he could, until I started going to his upstate house and discovered the full extent of his battle with germs.

The place was covered with thick, white carpeting, a small child's nightmare. Shoes were banned indoors, of course, and no child drinking cups, outdoor toys, or pets were allowed. Bath towels could not be used more than once after which they were thrown in the wash. He ran a washing machine daily and cleaned his hands at every turn. He showered before bed and upon waking, and meticulously cleaned the bathroom every single time he used it.

I could not sit or lie down on the bed still wearing street clothes, since one never knew what those public seats had been through. If we sat on the carpet to watch TV and ate popcorn, God forbid I picked up a fallen kernel and put it back in my mouth! The very thought of ordering a delivery-pizza made by some filthy pizza-men was an anathema.

He began criticizing the way I cooked and how well I cleaned my hands or washed the veggies before preparing them. I failed to recognize then that his OCD may well have been the primary cause of his ED.

Perhaps, most damaging of all was his steadfast "conservatism" as he viewed it, more like unswerving hypocrisy in my eyes. As an entrepreneur, he railed against high taxes, but he cheated on his returns and admitted reporting only a small portion of his actual revenues. He helped his elderly mother conceal all her assets so that she could be eligible for Supplemental Security Income and then fumed against wasteful entitlement programs. Slowly but surely his true nature was revealed. The last straw came one night when he referred to homosexuals as "faggots and dykes," and Italians as "dagos." I hadn't even heard the latter term before. Suddenly his "very deep values" appeared shallow and prejudiced in the extreme.

I wanted nothing more to do with him. Oddly, the news came as a shock to him. Even so, four weeks later he showed up at my door with flowers and an engagement ring and asked me to marry him! I turned him down flat and never again answered a personal ad in print.

A few days later, I came across the Merrill Lynch ad in the Sunday *Times*, and my life quickly got very busy. I had no time for a relationship anyway, and before I knew it, it had been more than three years since I had one. By the summer of 1997, my professional life had begun to show some promise, and I was badly in need of a vacation. That summer, Sophie and I were invited to my cousin's beach house in Morocco.

I first saw Najib, a distant relative I had never met before, at a family wedding we attended and was instantly drawn to his wide grin, warm sexy voice, and confident laughter. I immediately ached for his toned, tanned body and I pursued him until I had him, which took all of twenty-four hours. Our first night together was at once ardent and blissful. At thirty-six, he was tender, loving, and infinitely giving. Every inch of my body hankered after his touch like a starved animal presented with a raw steak. It had been far too long.

By the next morning, I had barely slept a wink. Everyone was deep asleep still. The big house was full of children—his young son, my daughter, my cousin's three boys, all occupying different rooms. I had sneaked into his after the house settled into nighttime slumber and found him waiting for me. All through the hours of darkness, long after love-making, I had felt his soft hand caressing my body, my back, my hair. At dawn, I slipped out barefoot onto the sandy beach, my feet sinking in the wet sand taunted by the flirty waves, watching the sun rise behind the dunes, tears of elation streaming down my cheeks. I breathed the salty marine air, blown away by the sensorial overload of the night, already longing for another embrace.

Forty-eight hours later, he drove me to the Casablanca airport. Sophie was staying behind for another two weeks with her little cousins, and he was going to take care of them. I gave him a long good-bye kiss, invited him to the States, and left with a heavy heart. A month later, I picked him up at Kennedy Airport. I had fallen in love with him and had been counting the minutes that separated us.

"I'm falling for you, hard," I confessed one night as we lay side by side in my bed. "It's crazy how fast that happened." He gave me a kiss, gently, but did not say anything.

His reluctance to respond to my declaration became a source of consternation for me. On our very first night he had admitted that I was the first woman he had been intimate with since he left his French wife three years earlier. He'd also told me that he was still not completely over her. I quickly assumed he hadn't met the right woman yet, and I was certain, even cocky, that I would be able to make him forget her in no time. After all, the woman had betrayed him in the most despicable way, humiliated him time and again, and was still living with another man.

"I do care for you a whole lot," he'd said to me. "More than I have any other woman in a long time. Only I'm not sure I can love again the way I loved her."

"You think you loved her so because your ego won't let you accept the fact that she preferred someone else," I snarled once as we drove back from a late party in Manhattan. "She cheated on you, fucked a man in your own bed, twice, and you're still hoping she'll recognize her mistake and take you back." The thought of competing with a long-gone spouse infuriated me. "You know what they say, nice guys really do prefer bitches," I snickered.

After his first month-long sojourn, he left for Morocco to take care of some business before returning to live with me in America. At least, that was the plan. But only two weeks later, I had made up my mind. I packed up all his things in a large carton and sent them back to him, signifying in no uncertain terms that I no longer wanted him.

"I'm sorry," I told him when he called, astounded. "I love you, but I'm not willing to play second banana in your heart indefinitely. You first figure it out for yourself, and then we'll see."

"But you're not giving us a chance," he replied calmly.

"Oh, yes, I did, for five months. The more love I showed you, the more you held back. I need a man to be madly in love with me, without the slightest reservation. If there's one thing I have learned in my life so far, it's that I will listen to my instincts and not settle for less than I deserve. I can't let you make such a huge move and then find out we're stuck in a dead-end."

I hung up the phone and put my face in my hands, holding back tears.

"Are you okay, Faith?" Leslie inquired at my door.

"I'm fine, thanks," I answered without looking at her. "I just broke up with Najib."

"Oh. I'm sorry to hear that. You want me to get you a glass of water?" she asked. I shook my head.

"No, thanks. But I'd appreciate if you could hold my calls for a moment."

Within days, I got a call from his sister, an older high-school friend of mine, urging me to reconsider.

"I realize it's none of my business, but I thought I'd give you a call anyway. My brother loves you, and he's very hurt by your break-up. He doesn't care about his ex anymore, I assure you. And I hadn't seen him as happy as when he was with you in a long time. I don't think you've thought this through," she said with her customary bluntness.

"Well, actually, I *have* thought it through, Laila. For once, I haven't let my emotions override my deep instincts. He's your brother. Of course you'll take his side. But he missed the boat with me. That's all there is to say!"

I threw myself back into work, delved into more material indulgence, and put my emotional life into prolonged hibernation yet again. The mood of the time, cleverly depicted in *The*

Long Boom, the bestseller by Peter Schwartz and Peter Leyden, conspired to make me believe in a new gilded age of prosperity, a dawning twenty-five-year period of "radically optimistic meme." So what if I was still single and alone? I was neither lonely nor friendless, but independent and more self-assured than ever, and I had no time for affairs of the heart.

It was in that spirit, and to celebrate the turn of the century in style, that I decided to throw a huge New Year's Eve party—perfectly scheduled for Friday, December 31—complete with great Moroccan and international food, French champagne, multicolor hanging balloons, and an artful music medley. Some forty friends and relatives were invited, including Carlos, a young, striking Argentinean diplomat I had met only a couple of days before in a Manhattan nightclub. That, in and of itself, was bizarre because I had not set foot in a club in ages, and I had only agreed to go after having been literally harassed by two of my old Moroccan friends, one of whom was visiting from Geneva. I had asked him in jest, not expecting he would actually show up at my party—in New Jersey.

He did, arriving late and in great form. He danced a lot, laughed with abandon, engaged in animated conversations with a fat and hilariously funny Spanish accent, and shamelessly flirted with me.

Within an hour of his arrival, he asked me if he could use the master bathroom, since the second one was occupied. He followed me to my room and, without further ado, kissed me with fiery passion, giving me a taste of what I'd been missing for two and a half years.

As the party drew to a close, with Sophia in bed and all gone, he was still pretending to help me pile glasses and dessert plates in the dishwasher. In my head, I was struggling between bidding him farewell and using him to quell my repressed sexual craving. I needn't have worried. Before I had time to close the appliance door, he bent his six-foot-four frame over me, picked me up, and carried me effortlessly to the bedroom with the resolve of a man who knew what he wanted. The rest of the day, I still remember as one of the greatest, sleepless stretches of love-making ever. I barely took a few minutes to take Sophie upstairs to my mother's. The following Monday, to Leslie's astonishment and my mildly embarrassed, glowing look, four dozen long-stemmed red roses were delivered to my office.

"My God, what did you do to this guy?" a colleague joked.

I blushed. "You don't want to know," I said slyly, quivering inside.

Thus began a crazy, entirely lustful relationship, which I instinctively knew from day one could not be anything more—he was much too needy, twelve years younger, and wanted children—but which I was unable, or unwilling, to abort even after I realized that my impetuous Latin lover's initially innocuous acts had become unacceptable.

In the beginning, I was so utterly conquered by his charm and extravagance that I felt flattered with all the attention, flowers, and small gifts. I did not really question his constant calling and turning up at the most inappropriate times in my life, twenty-four hours a day, until I found myself a prisoner of his obsession.

At first, I found it endearing that he met me at work and walked with me to pick up Sophie from school; appealing that he looked for me at the gym and waited for me to finish my workout; loving that he accompanied me to the grocery store and made shopping suggestions; and, titillating that he arrived in the middle of the night at my apartment because he couldn't sleep without me.

Slowly, however, it did not feel so right, and I questioned why he showed up at the salon where I had my hair cut. I resented his appearing, uninvited, at the restaurant where I had dinner with my sister and girlfriends. Eventually, he began to check my personal mail, checkbook ledger, and daily agenda. His love for me soon turned into a fatal attraction of sorts. I revolted and began to fight back, to no avail. He, by then, accused me of being heartless, unfaithful, and a liar.

"Listen, Carlos, I've been thinking about Saturday night, when you said that I didn't miss you the way you missed me when you were away, and that I didn't love you the way you loved me, and I've come to recognize that you were quite right on both counts."

I tried to keep my voice down and not get agitated. I did not want to hurt him unnecessarily, but I needed to make myself absolutely clear.

"I feel like my love for you has died a slow death, killed by your obsessive behavior toward me. I'm no longer comfortable with our relationship, not that I ever was, really. From the beginning, I didn't approve of your irresponsible work ethic, your competition with Sophie for my time and attention, and your *insane* jealousy. But I was blinded by lust and passion."

I paused, waiting for him to say something, but he just sat there, staring into his cup of coffee in silence, his long fingers tapping the table.

I went on, "Over the last few weeks, your love has felt like a prison. I feel abused by your mistrust, and I've finally reached a point of no return. I'm sorry."

"You met somebody else," he sourly blurted out in heavily accented English. "Why don't you just say you're with another man?"

He looked me straight in the eyes. I sensed his anger mounting. I stared back at his strong handsome features, stubbly chin, black shoulder-length hair, white skin, and full lips, and forced myself to remain calm and collected.

"No, I'm *not* with another man," I said patiently. "I know it's hard for you to believe, but not seeing you as often lately, I've realized that I don't want to spend any time with you anymore. Not because I found someone else, but because I don't love you anymore, Carlos. I'm free of you, and I'd like you to respect my decision. Please don't keep calling me; I have nothing more to say to you."

"You lied to me all the time, from beginning," he said bitterly. "You never loved me, it's the truth. I'm crazy for you, want a baby with you, and you play with me like a puppy!" He clenched his fist and jaw.

I felt relieved to be in a public place and not at home—not that he ever was violent, but I was not inclined to find out.

"I never mislead you or lied to you. Every time you expressed the wish, I told you that I had no intention of having children again at my age. Remember I'm forty-four and I already have a child. Don't get me wrong—I did have wonderful moments with you, which I will always cherish. Please, let's not destroy those memories with sour grapes. I like you very much, and I really wish you the best. I simply know we're not right for each other. And, Carlos—" I reached for his hand gently—"I want my apartment keys back, please."

He pulled his hand away, pushed his chair back, stood up, and with a last anguished glance, briskly walked out of the coffee shop without looking back.

He never did return my keys. In fact, he went back to my apartment, without my permission, to retrieve a few things he had left behind and all the photos we had taken together over the last nine and a half months. This last incident terrified me, prompting me to change the locks and alert the doormen.

For months afterward, he called me and remained speechless.

Only once did I hear him say, "Hi, baby, how are you?" with his unmistakable, guttural pronunciation of the 'h' sound.

I hung up on him and kept doing so until I changed my phone number, years later.

At the time of my break-up with Carlos in mid-October 2000, the market had persevered in its decline following its all-time heights of the spring. But the general feeling was still bent on optimism. It was widely believed that the crisis would soon pass, just as it had before. Productivity was still up, unemployment and inflation still down, the economic expansion still alive and well, and the consumer was still giddy from the long stock market orgy that had been going on for what seemed like an eternity.

Only, this time, the Federal Reserve, which, after a string of interest rate cuts related to the Asian financial crisis in 1997-1998, had been bent on a tacit laissez-faire policy, changed course in mid-1999 and initiated a series of interest rate hikes totaling a hundred and fifty basis points in less than a year. The abrupt reversal promptly derailed the mood, and the economy came to a screeching halt quickly followed by plummeting markets.

27

Gathering Storm

It is difficult now to remember the kind of hysteria that spread through the Western World as the dawn of the new Millennium approached. The Y2K bug, as it was dubbed, was going to wreak havoc in the global economy: Computer networks everywhere were expected to not recognize the new date, then crash and burn. In fact, there were more people concerned about the millennium bug than the tech bubble, suggestive of the tree hiding the forest analogy. But then, I too was living a fantasy of my own making, working hard and heedlessly spending money, living a sexual fantasy with no grounding in reality, and overlooking signs of my mother's impending relapse.

Both my sister and I had been vigilant over the years, watching her medication intake closely even as neither one of us actually lived with her. Because my sister spent half the year overseas and I was living in the same building, I was at least close enough to monitor my mother's mood and general health almost on a daily basis. By then, it was clear to us that she could not be subjected to any stress without paying a price. Overall, however, and for seven and a half years, she had led a healthier life-until the early fall of 2000.

That summer Nezha had been away with Sami in Djerba, an island off the southern coast of Tunisia, and Carlos and I had gone to France to collect Sophie at the end of her summer camp in Brittany. After we reunited with my kid, we decided to skip the rainy Parisian weather that August, chase the sun, and join my sister and her husband on their Mediterranean island for a beach vacation instead.

In Djerba, the news from Mom was not good. On the phone, she seemed to be more dejected than usual, and her mood did not improve much after I returned. She'd had a terrible summer, with long stretches of depression and insomnia. She'd also been sensitive to stress generated by money and family problems. Her brother Abderrahim had cut off the monthly stipend he'd been allocating her for decades under the pretext that the money was sent to my father, in Morocco.

In fact, I was using Mom's checking account in Morocco to send Dad his monthly stipend and I gave Mom her money here. The idea was to minimize money transfers back and forth with the ensuing bank fees and currency rate fluctuations. Mom had been hurt by her brother's decision and wanted to call him and explain the situation in an effort to change his mind.

"No, Mom, you don't have to do that. Your brother has been very generous all these years. You don't need him anymore. I can take care of you now," I'd reassured her.

"But you're already helping me, and you have your daughter and dad, too. My brother is so rich; it's like a drop in the bucket for him. I've got nothing. Why does he have to do that?" she'd wept.

The issue of two of her brothers' extraordinary wealth had always been a source of both great pride and veiled envy. She was convinced she'd gotten the short end of the stick, and that life had been unfair to her and her children. All her life, she felt that as the youngest and most wronged sister, they could have done more to help her financially.

But perhaps it wasn't just the stress. The seasons seemed to play a part, too. Over time, a pattern became evident. Toward the end of the summer, in September-October, and again at the end of winter and the onset of spring, in March, her disposition grew noticeably somber. This time, she was the one who asked to be admitted. She said she could feel her mood shifting, although without reaching an acute manic stage.

It was decided to take her to St. Mary's Hospital, in Hoboken, the very same place she had dreaded in the days of her first delusional blowup. Sadly, this last confinement, although lasting less than a week—from September 21 to 26, 2000—left her with lasting physical impairments.

As soon as she reached the psychiatric ward, she was administered the customary basket of drugs, including Zyprexa. In the spring of 2000, the FDA had approved it for the short-term treatment of acute manic episodes associated with bipolar disorder. It was believed that it acted more quickly to stabilize the patient's mood. In my mother's case, the drug triggered strong side-effects, and she fought hard against taking it.

Her main complaints were that she felt weakness throughout her body and impaired range of motion. So difficult were her movements, she could not make it to the bathroom on time, she admitted in humiliation. She described it as a sort of paralysis. Then there were the usual dizziness, garbled speech, and drowsiness. Finally, she suffered from severe edema in her legs.

Despite her protestations, she was administered the drug and required to stay on it until Depakote stabilized her mood. All attempts at discussing the issue with the attending psychiatrist at St. Mary's were fruitless, and my calls were never satisfactorily answered. I cannot begin to express the depth of my regret for having her admitted. The hospital staff, for the most part, was unresponsive, or rather anesthetized, to the plight of their patients and their loved ones. My poor mother had unwittingly entered the gates of hell.

After her discharge from the hospital, she never returned to normal. The first signs that something very wrong had occurred were her persistent leg edema and skin disorders. She had dry, flaky, and itchy rashes on the skin all over her body and in particular on her hands, ears, and scalp, even inside her nose. Her nails had thinned out and become prone to some kind of fungus. Other symptoms included a sore mouth and raw genitalia, making eating any spicy or acidic food impossible and urination a burning agony. She visited a couple of dermatologists, who performed various skin tests and reached different conclusions: she was told she suffered from psoriasis, then eczema, and finally allergies. The different creams and ointments prescribed had no effect whatsoever.

In the meantime, her hands were so sensitive she had to wear cotton gloves at all time. Weeks later, the discomfort turned into acute pain, spreading from her hands and wrists to her arms and shoulders. The stiffness and difficulty of movement were evocative of the Zyprexa days. The pain was so intense; she was confined to bed, where her suffering seemed to intensify at night and upon awakening. Around that time, the news of her older sister Aisha's death reached her and her emotional distress translated into increased physical dysfunction.

She reached a point where she could neither get dressed on her own nor turn over in bed. She could not sleep without sleeping pills—and sometimes even they didn't help. Her life became an endless misery marred by great frailty and unrelenting pain. She could not open a jar and dropped objects because she could not maintain her grip. She was incapable of going up or down a flight of stairs. She entered a car with difficulty and was subject to cramping in the legs and sometimes the arms. Occasionally, she had blurred vision, and she remained depressed, crying for hours and wishing to die rather than live under such conditions.

I began researching her condition in medical books and journals, thinking she might have some sort of neurological problem or neuroma. I took her to see Dr. Michael Davis, a neurologist at Cornell-New York Presbyterian, who speculated that she could be suffering from a chronic episodic condition known as 'polymyalgia rheumatica'—an inflammation of the large arteries with the exact same symptoms she had been describing, often affecting people over sixty years of age. He ordered a blood test to check her erythrocyte sedimentation rate, or ESR. It confirmed his diagnosis of increased inflammation, albeit non-specifically.

Dr. Davis prescribed Prednisone, a popular immunosuppressant corticosteroid prescribed for a broad range of autoimmune and inflammatory ailments. He also suggested a follow-up with a rheumatologist and a psychiatrist, since Prednisone could trigger mania in manic-depressive patients.

A renown specialist in rheumatology at the Hospital of Special Surgery, Dr. Susan Freedman was, however, quite certain that polymyalgia rheumatica was not the right diagnosis, and she ordered another slew of exams to determine what was responsible for the high level of edema and pain. Her tests resulted in no additional positive diagnoses, and Dr. Freedman, besides recommending decreasing Prednisone's dosage, sent us back to Mom's internist, Dr. Ronald Klein.

The pain came under control thanks to Prednisone, the severe edema was unabated. Soon though, irritability and insomnia, as well as kidney and lower back pain, reappeared and prompted Mom to discontinue the steroids. She would get on, or off, depending on whether the searing pain subsided or recurred. Meanwhile, Dr. Klein referred her to Dr. Philips, who proceeded to order the complete cessation of Prednisone to allow for yet another test, a muscle tissue biopsy, which was performed in Holy Name Hospital. After three weeks off Prednisone, Mom's physical pain reasserted itself and had become unremitting by the time the results of the muscle tissue biopsy were received in another three weeks.

From the result of the muscle tissue biopsy and an electromyography test (EMG), Dr. Philips diagnosed a condition called diffuse peripheral neuropathy, or degenerative disorder, which, in lay terms, indicates pretty much any type of nerve damage with all kinds of causes. In the end, nobody really knew what ailed her. She, however, knew, without the shred of a doubt that Zyprexa, had been at the root of the damage to her nerves, only there was no way to prove it-not that we ever thought of taking any legal action. Finding lasting relief was her only wish. All along, and after months of searching and wishing for a miracle, her symptoms had seemed to subside, only to give way to new complaints.

Her depression worsened. Depakote and her anti-depressant were ineffective in preventing, or even alleviating it. She was constantly crying and could almost never sleep. Worst of all, the inability of so-called specialists to come up with an accurate diagnosis aggravated her emotional state. She was appalled at the physicians' inability to determine the cause, or causes, of her symptoms—even as she continued to put her faith in them and hope for a diagnosis. The fact that they just passed her along and appeared to drop her case, or more deplorably, hinted at some form of hysteria or psychosomatic disorder, while distancing themselves, caused her great grief.

By then I was just as discouraged as she was. If there was any redeeming grace, it was that I was fortunate to have Mom fully covered by my health insurance. Since I was unmarried and she was my dependent, my Merrill Lynch health plan was extended to her. I had taken her to so many doctors and specialists that I had an entire address book set aside just for that. And every single time, I held my breath and prayed that we would soon see the end of her purgatory.

Each time I faced a new physician, I went through her entire history, symptoms, aches and pains. Invariably, he or she would comment on my familiarity with the drugs and conditions, frequently inquiring whether I was a doctor myself. And indeed I was very knowledgeable, from all those hours spent on the internet, reading medical publications. I talked fast, aware of the time constraint of my interlocutors. Too often, I had too many questions to be answered, and their replies were invariably fuzzier than I hoped.

My mother's health was not the only issue I was forced to contend with at that time. Besides my work obligations and my daughter's care, I became involved with the renovation and expansion of my apartment. It was timely that I had ended my relationship with Carlos: At least I didn't have that headache to deal with.

The first phase of the construction went on pretty smoothly, until I was ordered to stop all work and wait for all permits to be duly filed and approved, and all fees-and fines-paid.

"What happened?" my sister asked me on the phone from Tunisia.

"Well, do you remember that older lady who lives one floor below me?" I asked.

"I'm not sure. The one with the dog?"

"No. I'm talking about that tall, dignified-looking Cuban woman with silver-gray hair? You've seen her; I'm sure—the one who called to complain about the loud music on New Year's Eve in 2000. In any case, she's been living one floor below for the past twelve years. We know each other, and we've always been on pretty good terms. She started to complain about the noise, and all of a sudden, she decided to send her big son—the giant who also lives in the Versailles?—she made him get the town's building inspector to visit my apartment. She did that without ever calling me personally to tell me about her grievances," I said in disgust.

"Didn't you inquire about this before you started?" asked Nezha.

"I did, but I was told I would be required to hire only state-licensed contractors with proper seals, file all the necessary permits, and pay all the fees, all at once. And everything had to be approved before I'd even be allowed to begin. I had a general contractor, an electrician, a plumber, a window contractor, a Home Depot kitchen designer, even an architect, at one point. All of them told me that, because of the bureaucratic delays and cost involved, most people tend to overlook the permit requirements. And I foolishly listened. Now I'm paying the price for my negligence."

"I don't understand how that could be. You've always been so organized and on top of things!"

"Yes, right? Here I'm planning a huge renovation-three bathrooms and a kitchen with upgraded electric wiring to accommodate top-of-the-line appliances. I'd ordered the installation of brand new windows, AC units, and wood floors. I knew I'd be breaking through walls and re-configuring the design flow of two apartments, and I really thought I could get away doing it all without applying for a single permit! Crazy and irresponsible, I know!"

"I'd say that sounds quite unlikely! So what's going to happen now? You've done half of the work already, right?" Nezha inquired.

"Yeah. Everything's been stopped. It's been four weeks now. I had to straighten out everything. I had to go to the building inspection office I don't know how many times. Each time, I had to wait and wait and plead with them to attend to my requests and send the inspectors quickly so that I could resume my renovation."

"That's terrible!"

"The grumpy old lady got a few weeks of respite, but barely. For the remainder of the work, I'm going to encourage as much noise as we can possibly make, especially on Saturdays... That's the thing—she works weekdays and wasn't even home during the time of the construction work."

Nezha laughed. "Revenge is sweet, huh?"

I sighed. "To tell you the truth, not really," I admitted. "I'm the one to blame here. I'm pissed off at her for not contacting me before taking action, but it's my fault for listening to bad advice. Hopefully, the work will be done by the time you come back." I paused and added: "I wish you were here, honey. I miss you very much, and so does Mom."

**

When Nezha finally came home on August 20, the renovation was almost completed. I was putting in the last touches and overseeing the installation of the remaining fixtures in the apartment.

On one such day, on a beautiful Tuesday in September, as I was waiting for the plumber to fix a bathroom fitting, I got a call from my brother, a little after 9:00AM.

"Are you home?" he asked point blank.

"Yes," I said. "I'm leaving now for the office. I had to wait for the plumber—"

"Go on your terrace," he interrupted. "Something terrible just happened."

"*What*? What's going on?"

My heart skipped a beat as I run to the terrace, stood outside, and looked around, my cell phone glued to my ear. The river was shimmering like a ribbon of liquid silver under the shining sun. There was not a cloud in the clear blue sky—a crisp and balmy, perfect autumn day.

I turned my gaze downtown—huge billows of smoke were swelling out of the Twin Towers.

"What's that?" I asked Larbi still on the phone. "It looks like there's a fire—"

"No, they're saying a plane hit. They don't know what's going on. You stay home, don't go anywhere. Put on CNN. We'll talk later."

I run to the den and turned on the television set. The large window was facing south and I could clearly see the fire now raging out of the Towers.

My chest barely contained the mad pounding; fear seeped through my flesh, flowed in my veins, and built clasps of steel in my guts. A feeling of doom overcame me.

Stay home... How could I stay home? Sophie's in school in Manhattan, I thought.

I flipped channels, hoping to comprehend the incomprehensible, grasp the meaning of the madness. Reporters were talking non-stop, mostly speculating. A growing sense of dread was sweeping through the city.

Videos of the Towers being hit by the planes were showing on a loop. Images of horror flashed on the screen as bodies begun flying out the windows to escape the blaze, choosing the void over the inferno. My sister and mother, who'd come down from their apartments, were weeping uncontrollably.

At 10:05, the South Tower collapsed, plummeting like a castle of cards into the streets below in a giant cloud of dust and debris, under the eyes of the world.

Oh no, Oh my God, Oh my God, I kept repeating in my head, trying to reach the Lycée Français by phone. The school, where Sophie was in sixth grade, was way uptown, on Ninety-Fifth and Fifth, thank God!

Then the news that the Pentagon too had been attacked was announced.

Full-fledged terror was now gripping the collective psyche.

At 10:30, the North Tower, in turn, crumpled from the top down, forming a tsunami wave of thick white and black powder mixed with fragments of the wreckage. It mushroomed and drifted through the narrow streets of lower Manhattan, swallowing everything in its wake. People were running, crying, turning around to watch the monstrous cloud threatening to bury them.

A horror movie, no doubt—it couldn't really be happening in my city.

For two long days, Sophia stayed at the home of a school-friend in Manhattan. All tunnels and bridges were closed; nobody could go in or out by land. On the third day, she really wanted to come home and I encouraged her to take the ferry. There were literally hundreds of thousands of people using the New York Waterway ferries to leave the city. She had to wait for hours on line before she finally boarded the boat that took her home.

I received her in my arms, relieved that she was well and unharmed.

28

The Eye of the Storm

The world as I'd known it changed forever after that day. Nothing could have prepared me for such a terrible event both emotionally and professionally. The markets had been on a free fall for a year already; I had become a therapist to my clients, comforting and supporting them in their moments of doubt and fear even as I had to overcome my own uncertainty. Every down day was followed by yet another down day in an endless downward spiral.

One of the greatest tests of will I passed in my own mind came the day I fired a fifteen-million-dollar client because I refused to be abused by him anymore.

"I need to talk to you about something that's been causing me a lot of grief lately," I said as I took a seat in my manager's office.

"Sure, Faith. What is it, and how can I help?" Ralph answered in his usual affable manner.

"It's about Juan Costas, one of my largest clients," I began uneasily. "You know how much work it was for me to get his account in the first place. I think I told you that I was introduced to him by his accountant, also a good client of mine, who thought that Mr. Costas was in need of a serious financial plan and good money management. I travelled to Florida twice to meet him, and we got together again a couple of times here. I also introduced him to you when we were still in the Fifth Avenue office."

"Yes, I remember well," Ralph said. "You did a good job getting that account."

"Yeah, I think so. I presented him with a whole plan and a strategy for a sound asset management. Finally, he transferred his accounts to Merrill Lynch. That was two years ago. Ever since, I've done everything possible to keep him satisfied. He's not only a demanding client, he lacks discipline, he's very controlling, and he has a hard time listening to professional advice. That would be okay if in fact he had an adequate knowledge of the financial markets, but he doesn't. *He thinks* he does, but he's moved entirely by rumors and unrealistic expectations."

"Have you tried to talk to his accountant about this?" Ralph asked.

"Yes, I did. He said he was aware that Costas was an impulsive and very difficult man to deal with, and to be diplomatic with him. Well, I've been more patient and diplomatic with him than with any other client. He has a quick temper, and he readily resorts to verbal abuse. He's very high maintenance. He calls almost every day under one pretext or another. It's gotten so bad that even my assistant now refuses to deal with him. Imagine—he'll even have his assistant call me, asking to get him a corporate discount on his five-star hotel stay in the city. I didn't even know we could *do* that, but he apparently did." I paused.

Ralph's phone was ringing. He gestured for me to hold on briefly with his finger pointing up.

"Excuse me for a second," he said, and, speaking in the phone, "...Tell him I'll call back in a few minutes. Thanks...

Sorry, Faith. So what do you want to do?" he asked. "You want me to talk with him?"

"No, unfortunately, it won't help. The first time I ever met this man, I knew he acted like a spoiled brat with his assistants, accountant, even clients. It's been no different with me. The truth is he's the type who has no respect whatsoever for others. He thinks his money entitles him to abuse people, especially those who work for him. Well, I'm not his employee, and I want to *fire him*," I said with determination.

Ralph looked at me surprised, half-smiling, and nodded in silence.

"Ralph, this guy is a real jerk. He's always been a jerk, but now that the markets have been going down, he's turned into a tyrant. I know it's a huge account, but that cannot justify the amount of stress and anxiety that I have to live with to keep it."

I felt tears welling in my eyes and quickly tried to change the tone of my argument. I'd been feeling increasingly emotional.

"I agree, you shouldn't," said Ralph.

"Don't think that I haven't tried to deal with this. But you saw the state I was in last month when I was lying flat on the floor with that horrible back pain. Well, I've been going to a chiropractor three times a week. I've already been struggling with the brunt of the turmoil in the markets before and after 9/11. I cannot also argue daily with an angry, vindictive customer, no matter how big." I paused, relieved I'd let it all out at last.

"You're right, Faith. Nobody should disrespect you. If you want to fire Costas, you have my support."

He stood up and put his hand on my shoulder. "I know you. I trust your judgment, and I want you to take care of yourself during these trying times."

He walked me to the door. I was grateful to him. It had been much easier than I'd thought.

I went back to my office, picked up the phone and called Juan Costas.

As soon as his assistant put him on the line, I blurted out: "I'm sorry to tell you that I no longer wish to manage your accounts. Please have your assistant get in touch with mine to transfer them out of Merrill Lynch. We'll do our best to make it as seamless as possible... Best of luck to you, Juan."

I put the phone down with a sigh of relief. Thankfully, he'd remained mostly calm.

Less than six months later, I had to terminate another relationship that I'd been cultivating since the summer of 1996, almost six years earlier. I had first met Richard Cohen when I opened a new 401k plan for his employer, then in South Florida. For the following weeks, I had a great deal of telephone interaction with him as I proposed to organize his finances, do some planning and consolidate his scattered assets. Two years after the accounts were open and funded, he and his wife Judy closed a mortgage for a new home in New Jersey with Merrill Lynch Credit Corporation.

For four years, the Cohens' assets grew significantly. The couple was thrilled with our relationship and ecstatic at the prospect of achieving a seven-figure portfolio so quickly. Throughout, their investment style drifted from a long-term growth strategy to a more aggressive one, and we added more technology stocks to the mix. Richard was always expressing the need to make "as much money as possible, in the shortest period of time." His wife and he were then contemplating early retirement. Two financial plans were completed, only two years apart, followed by extensive meetings and portfolio adjustments.

During the second half of 2000, with the market entering its downturn, Richard was calling me constantly for reassurance and hand-holding. I had always been in close touch with him; he was often unemployed and had a lot of time on his hands. But then he became increasingly fearful of losses and in search of sure answers that no one could provide.

For my part, I continued to build my knowledge and information of events in the financial markets better than most, and I kept on top of Wall Street research, economic analysis, and the global environment. Even so, no certainty about short-term market direction existed anywhere. Richard would keep me on the phone literally for hours at a time, draining me of every bit of energy. He inquired again and again about the market's prospects, always questioning whether he should "sell everything and wait for the turn around."

At one point, I introduced him to Ralph, who stayed on the phone with him close to fifty minutes and then gave the phone back to me for another thirty-five minutes of the most twisted and contradictory reasoning a human being could bear. I kept preaching investment discipline and patience and advised against market timing while slowly increasing the couple's exposure to municipal bonds and fixed income. Then, in March 2001, he and Judy ordered the liquidation of all their equity positions, maintaining only the annuities and fixed income portion.

In July, four months after pulling out of the equity market, the Cohens decided to return and invest their cash in a diversified mix of mutual funds I had researched and discussed with them. Unfortunately, the events of September 11 brought a fresh round of mayhem to the global economy and stock market. The pressure to provide Richard with "crystal ball" insight was unrelenting. At the end of October, my new partner, Cliff, and I met the Cohens in New Jersey and spent two hours explaining the importance of market allocation and discipline as well as the concept of professionally managed money.

Judy seemed to approve of the strategy immediately and was ready to sign on the process right away; Richard could not let go of the idea of "recouping" their losses and only then adopting a new discipline. He was reluctant to lose control and worried about not making his own decisions. He kept going on ad nauseum about whether the time was right to adopt a new strategy.

Cliff and I left the meeting exhausted and decided then that, if they did not agree to the new discipline and did not acknowledge they were fully responsible for their current positions, we were going to terminate the relationship altogether. The retention of assets was not worth the level of stress and ongoing emotional mistreatment Richard had been inflicting on my assistant and me. I felt I had gone beyond the call of duty. In January 2002, I sent the Cohens a letter officially ending our relationship and inviting them to transfer their accounts to another firm.

Three months later, in reprisal, he wrote to management, using my words out of context and alleging negligence and mismanagement while demanding remedy from Merrill Lynch. In response, I sent a long letter defending my position:

In almost five and a half years of a close relationship with me, the Cohens have had ample opportunity to appreciate my extensive experience as a financial advisor. Indeed, the level of trust they placed in me during all those years speaks for itself. It is because of my integrity and belief that their interests would be better served that Cliff and I elected to direct them toward professional money management.

Mr. Cohen's lack of discipline and market knowledge, and his irrational fear and greedy reactions to daily events, which led him to rush decision-making, were standing in the way of a successful long-term investment strategy. That fact, more than any other, guided us to terminate our relationship with the couple. If anything, the brutal bear market of the past two years has taught us that strict discipline and asset allocation based on sound financial planning must become the very foundation of our team's business.

Therefore, it is our strong belief that we cannot in good faith accept to work with clients who refuse to heed our advice. I only regret that Mr. Cohen interpreted our insistence as negatively as he did.

Unfortunately, the overall gloom was not about to lift up any time soon. For months, the stock market persisted in its retreat. The NASDAQ 100 technology-laden stock index dropped a whopping eighty-three percent from its high of 4800 in March 2000, to about 825 in September 2002. Furthermore, for three excruciatingly long years from March 2000 till March 2003, the broader S&P 500 Index itself lost fifty percent of its value.

Nothing I did seemed to work. Any restructuring of portfolios into more moderate allocations appeared only to highlight the weakness of the equities I had advised to keep. No company seemed immune to the debacle, and investor trashing of all industries alike kept me and my clients on edge at all times. 9/11 had thrown all of us, clients and consultants, into a doldrums that no amount of optimism could shake. Governments embarked on an all-out war on terror on the terrain. I had already been living in a world of apprehension and disbelief that no one but I seemed to be aware of.

Huge corporations were going out of business because of the greed and corruption of their upper managements. Reputable accounting firms were increasingly coming under attack for aiding and abetting their corporate clients. Brokerage firms and their analysts were found guilty of the same while issuing misleading stock ratings and analyses to the public. For the first time, my fairy tale world of success and material achievement was looking like a snake pit. I could not trust anything or anyone with impartial advice, least of all my managers.

In meeting after meeting, management persisted in showing confidence and optimism, continued to call for those annual business plans, insisted on increasing assets under management by aiming at bigger accounts, and urged the annualization of earnings by recommending money managers as the best way out of the crisis. Broken consultants were dropping like flies and their best accounts went to the top male producers in every office of the firm. Those of us who remained saw their numbers fall and their despair grow. I lost many clients, my income plunged, and I was moved physically back into a smaller office. My morale and my self-esteem were badly shaken as days went by, and I felt totally misunderstood by those around me.

Worst of all, I could not tell my clients, often people I cared for immensely, to just move on with their lives and wait for the storm to pass. I was reminded time and again that clients were like patients; they needed a prescription to feel that one was doing something for them, even if the prescription was only a placebo. I was told numerous times that I cared too much and took things too personally, that I had to understand that the bear market was not my fault and that I had to learn this was a survival game, nothing more.

Meanwhile, for the previous two years, my mother's health had continued to deteriorate, culminating in her inability to stand or walk normally. For years, she'd been suffering from

osteoarthritis of the knees—in fact, she'd grown pretty accustomed to the aches of arthritis, as well as the throbbing of
corns and bunions, which had presumably been corrected with
surgery a couple of years earlier. But this was quite a different sort of pain—the sort that would not quit. Arthritis pain
prescription drugs like Celebrex and Vioxx had little effect.
She also relied on huge dosages of over-the-counter pain killers, and Tylenol Codeine 3, for some modicum of relief. She
became dependent on a walker and, sometimes, a wheel chair.
Her pain-stricken knees could no longer carry her; the osteoarthritis that plagued them had rendered her legs completely
useless.

I became depressed, experienced sleepless nights, and sudden anxiety attacks. Most days, just getting out of bed in the
morning was a test of will. When I made it to the office, I
was met by another challenge: continuing to feign a calm and
self-controlled appearance when handling my panicked clients'
calls. The year 2002 went by slowly draining me of every last
bit of energy I could still muster. I tried everything from exercise to meditation to anti-depressants as I tried to cope with
the unyielding stress I was confronted with day in and day out.
I felt strangulated by my circumstances: my suffocating job,
my mother's deteriorating health, her continuous demand for
my attention and care, and my now-teenage daughter's competing needs.

As it were, the coup de grace occurred in February 2003.
In the middle of the month, my mother was hospitalized for
a bilateral knee replacement operation. The procedure was a
success from a mechanical point of view, but Mom never again
walked unaided. When most patients needed a month of rehabilitation to regain the full use of their legs, she spent almost
three months in a reputable New Jersey rehabilitation facility

and still could not walk, or even stand, on her own. Even worse, the pain never lifted.

My own health had become a concern, too. My mental distress had been feeding multiple physical problems for quite some time, including a growing uterine fibroid. Eventually I succumbed to a nervous breakdown, and I went on a prolonged medical leave under both a psychiatrist and a psychologist's care.

29

Dying Inside

I walked to my psychologist's office on Park Avenue, blind to the vibrant palettes of tulips planted on the grand avenue's mid-section and deaf to the birds' chirping on the blossoming branches. The full splendor of spring was everywhere on display that warm May afternoon. Only I was a prisoner of my mind, aware only of the ten-thousand-pound elephant crushing my lungs. My chest felt achy, my breathing shallow and hard. I barely cracked a smile at the doorman of the old pre-war building and rushed inside. The doctor's office was right off the lobby. I pushed the buzzer, and the door opened. As I sat in the dowdy armchair, alone in the small waiting room, images of my mother lying in her bed in the rehabilitation center occupied my thoughts.

**

A curtain was drawn between her bed and the other patient in the semi-private room. The white light shed a cold glow on the greenish walls. The small TV set, hanging from the ceiling at her feet, was muted. A strong and unpleasant hospital odor filled my nostrils, a nauseating mix of illness, detergent, and urine I fought to ignore. She seemed almost not there, pale and feeble, absent in her gaze. She'd lost a lot of weight and appeared smaller.

"I can't sleep; the pain keeps me awake in spite of the pills," she moaned with a small voice, adding: "and I've been constipated for days..."

I reached for her hand and kissed it.

"Haven't they given you any laxatives?" I asked.

"I take them every day, but nothing works anymore. I'm so bloated..."

She closed her eyes in resignation.

I patted her hand. "Let me go find the nurse and see what else can be done!"

I left the room and headed for the nurses' station.

I had been going to the center almost every day after work, driving more than an hour from home on the notoriously busy New Jersey highways, stopping only to pick up a favorite dish or zesty salad for Mom, and staying until past nine most nights.

I found a couple of attendants engrossed in animated conversation when they spotted me waiting uneasily to explain the problem.

"She didn't have a bowel movement in *how* long?" the tall, black woman in charge asked, her eyebrows raised.

"I don't know exactly, but she said it's been several days and the laxatives aren't working. She's been complaining about it the last two times I visited her."

"All right, I'll send someone over. You're her daughter, right? You come every night, huh?"

I nodded, thanked her, and left without further questions. I wondered if she was going to order an enema to relieve my mother of her discomfort. Twenty minutes later a nurse with a friendly demeanor showed up at the door. I had already helped

Mom to the restroom and I could hear her groan in frustration behind the curtain that served as a screen.

"Okay, lady, let's see what we can do," interjected the middle-aged woman cheerfully in the direction of my mother.

Before I could understand what she was up to, I watched her put on a pair of plastic gloves and walk inside the bathroom. I stepped back, puzzled. She had no other equipment but her gloved hands and what appeared to be a tube of lubricant.

"Just relax, darling. I won't hurt you, just take a deep breath and relax," she was instructing behind the curtain.

My mind went blank.

I heard Mom utter a feeble, "Okay, thank you."

"You're going to feel a hell of a lot better in a minute, I promise you," said the attendant with conviction.

Mom was presently grunting in discomfort, but no vocal protestations came out of her mouth.

Baffled by the turn of events, I was ready to intervene. This was definitely not what I had been expecting. I felt sickened and inexplicably filled with sadness at the indignity endured by my poor mother when I heard the sound of the hard droppings in the bowl and the deep sigh of relief that followed.

A few minutes later, the nurse laughed at my discomfited look.

"It's called *manual disimpaction of the bowels*," she informed me in passing while helping my mother slowly regain her bed. "It's quick and very effective. Your mom will sleep better now."

She smiled with a compassionate look at her. "Aren't you relieved now?" she asked gently.

Mom nodded and touched the woman's forearm. "Thank you," she sighed.

**

Sitting in the psychologist's waiting room, the images of that night were carved in my memory. Mom was now living with me and was again complaining of constipation, among many other things. The pain killers were responsible for that. I felt so tired, so overwhelmed...

Dr. Damon interrupted my thoughts and waved me into her office. She was a thin, older woman with the look and manner of an old-fashioned school principal.

"How have you been since last time?" she inquired after I sat down on the sofa facing her.

The room was small but clean and comfortable in spite of its near darkness. A faint old-book smell lingered.

"Not well, unfortunately. My mother was sent home from the rehab clinic after three long months of little or no progress. I have her staying in my apartment. There isn't much more they can do for her. I got the insurance to agree to more physical therapy sessions at home." I tried to take a deep breath. My tight-sealed lungs wouldn't let me.

"It's very frustrating; she simply doesn't seem to want to work too hard. I can't understand it. Her effort in therapy is timid and filled with complaints. It's like she gave up on walking or something. Her willpower is shot..." I paused again.

Dr. Damon patiently waited for me to go on.

"She used to be such a fighter, a real trouper... now she can't stop complaining of inexplicable pain, nothing helps... I feel useless... There are times, I... I..." The words stuck in my throat, my sight clouded with tears...

Dr. Damon reached for the tissue box and put it in front of me in silence. I hated the predictability of her gesture, of what was to come.

"I don't know how to say this... I wish she... I'm a monster for thinking this... I know," I shook my head and reached for a tissue to wipe my face. The tears were flowing slowly down my cheeks. "Sometimes, I wish... I wish her dead..." I finally whispered.

A torrent of tears gushed through and I wept and wept, a high-pitched wail, twisting my hands, leaning over in agony and shame.

"Can you imagine? My own mother... I love her so much, and yet...I hate her, too..."

What was I grieving for so intensely? My admission, my guilt, myself? I had no idea!

"It's completely normal to feel that way, anyone would under the circumstances," offered Dr. Damon. "You're under a lot of stress. You shouldn't feel guilty for your feelings."

Her soothing words did not interrupt my cries. I was a mess, sensed my eyes, nose, and mouth swelling, my face throbbing. This was a typical session marred by hysterical weeping leading nowhere but more heartache. I was sick of my own voice, tired of talking to this complete stranger. Still, I went on, choking with self-pity.

"It's killing me... If only she could try harder, you know? It's like she's regressed; I can see it in her eyes. After all those years of fighting for her independence, she just gave up. At sixty-four, she's a cripple like her mother before her. But unlike Grandma, she's always in agony, always whining."

"Don't you have anyone else who could help take care of her for a while, your sister or brothers, maybe?" asked Dr. Damon.

I shrugged. "My sister is overseas, and my brothers... well, let's just say they're oblivious." I said it without a second thought, and yet, I realize now, I had never really asked them for their help, or even opinion, never contemplated such a possibility. As usual, I had single-handedly taken over the duty of caring for our mother, assuming all along they were unable or incapable of caring for her and doing as good a job as I was. But then they barely even visited her.

I was the head of the family after all; I controlled everything, especially when it came to Mom. I had willingly been managing her life to the last detail since I was a teenager. Our roles had been reversed for as long as I could remember. She was as ensnared by me as I felt trapped by her. My burden was my own doing. Only I didn't know it then. I viewed myself as a helpless victim.

"How do you feel about your job? Have you given any thought to when you think you can return to work?"

My psychologist's voice brought me back to the second matter of utmost importance. I had gone on a medical leave within a few weeks of my mother's operation, almost twelve weeks already, and a decision had to be reached regarding my return. She had authorized my prolonged absence, and the company was again asking about my condition.

"I can't even fathom going back to work at this point. How can I be of help to my clients, anyway? The markets are still so far below their highs and crippled by the uncertainty associated with the war in Iraq."

I shook my head in disgust. This was yet another topic feeding into my overall anxiety.

"The Bush administration is lying to the American public so that they can wage war in Iraq. There's this growing general hysteria about Muslims."

The question flashed through my mind: *What does that have to do with me?*

"I can't really explain this. My mind is shrouded in dread and impending doom." Another futile attempt at a deep breath disrupted my thoughts. I blew my nose hard.

"I guess I know what you mean. Many of us feel that way," volunteered Dr. Damon.

I looked at her in surprise.

"Really? No, I mean I think it has something to do with *me*, my background."

I was born a Muslim, of Arab parents, but since I started working in sales, both as a real estate agent and Wall Street broker, my identity had carefully been concealed, at least at a professional level. After my divorce, I had dropped my Irish married name and started using my new and improved, albeit truncated, western-sounding last name.

"You know my original last name is really 'BenHallam'," I explained looking in her eyes. "I officially shortened it to 'Hallam,' which, I always volunteered, was also a very 'British' name, referring to the Victorian writer and historian Sir Henry Hallam. There's even a Hallam Street in the heart of London." I breathlessly recited my oft-repeated validation as I had countless times with clients over the years. At this point, I literally believed it myself.

"So you see, 'Ouafae BenHallam'," I went on in self-derision, "became 'Faith O'Brien,' then 'Faith Hallam,' western raised, French speaking, with an undefined religious background. People around me know I celebrate a pagan Christmas, don't practice any Islamic rite, and that my brother is married to a Jewish woman from Brooklyn. I wholeheartedly assimilated Americana. In my professional circle, no one can tell you with any certainty what I really am at this point," I sneered.

"How does that make you feel?" asked Dr. Damon.

"I've avoided asking myself that question. I conveniently justified it as the only way for me to succeed in a city and an industry overwhelmingly dominated by Jews and WASPS. It's very difficult as it is to acquire new clients. It would've been virtually impossible with an Arabic name. Imagine me calling a prospect and introducing myself as *'Ouafae BenHallam, Arab-Muslim-American, asking you to trust her with your money.'* No, that was not really an option. But to answer your question, I guess it did make me feel ill at ease. I deliberately hid my background, lied by omission, cunning even. But you know it was more for survival's sake than in dishonesty. I've always believed my integrity to be one of my strongest assets."

I stopped to ponder my words.

"Still, around my family and old friends, I found pride in my roots and lineage. I wasn't ashamed of that," I reminded myself. "In spite of the appalling state of the Arab world throughout my existence, I've never stopped identifying with its magnificent culture and past glory."

"In what way do recent events affect you, then? What has changed for you?" she asked pointedly, forcing me to face issues I had been sweeping under the rug for a long time.

"This war, this new hatred of Muslims, is definitely affecting me deeply, although not overtly. It's more of an inner struggle. For the first time in more than twenty years, I feel I don't belong anymore. There's so much ignorance of the world out there in this country, a lack of knowledge that is being used for a bloody conflict, and the majority approve. Thousands and thousands of innocent Iraqi civilians, women and children, who have nothing to do with 9/11, are going to die because of a handful of so-called Islamic terrorists. How is that supposed to make me feel? I despise terrorism too, Islamic or otherwise. It's a curse that must be defeated, but this war is only going to strengthen it. Of that I am certain. It's so obvious to me. I cannot believe it's not to most Americans!"

My tone had turned contentious; I was incensed. The subject of the war in Iraq never failed to inflame me.

"You know that many people agree with you," said Dr. Damon, shaking her head.

She may agree, but she couldn't possibly understand, I thought to myself.

I was at a point where I had begun to feel rejected, if only in my head. It was a bizarre thing to experience. Yet I knew my family and close friends all were in agreement with me. It was not as if I was living in America's heartland, cut off from similar opinions, or that opposition to the war was not in fact widespread in New York and most of the Northeast.

But this felt much more personal, and it beckoned me to come clean about my identity, to close ranks with all the other Arab-Americans who felt stigmatized and cast off. I felt a pressing need to speak out, condemn the murderous fringe that cloaked itself in Islam only to defile it. Theirs was not the religion of my father, I wanted to shout out. His peaceful, tolerant creed had nothing to do with those barbarians.

Only I did not speak out, did nothing in fact but fret and fuss in hollow frustration and anger. My mental and emotional health was under attack from so many sides, they rendered me inept and hopeless. I retreated, kept reacting to events that seemed out of my control, and never took any action, save popping anti-depressants in a futile attempt to lift my disposition.

"I'm going to sign off on a few more weeks of therapy and medical leave. You have another appointment with your psychiatrist, right? He may need to adjust your medication. I'll contact him. I don't think you're ready to go back to work just yet," concluded Dr. Damon after a furtive glance at the clock on the side table. My time was up.

I stepped out in the dimming light with huge dark glasses hiding my puffy face and rushed back home, praying I would not meet anyone I knew. Those therapy sessions were exhausting and for what? All I did was rehash the same current plights and wallow in the same old remembrance cesspool.

30

Costly Choices

The Manhattan skyline shimmered in the blue velvet sky, its etched reflection mirrored in the Hudson. My thoughts were darker than the river water. The front door of my apartment opened and closed. I barely budged. My sister stuck her head through the terrace door behind me.

"What are you doing out here?" she asked. "Come in, it's getting cold."

I turned around without answering.

"Well, you've been crying a storm again, I can see. I really wonder how much good those therapy sessions are doing you. It's been almost three months, right?"

She wrapped her arm around my shoulders and pulled me inside.

I ignored her question.

"I've decided to put both my apartment and Mom's up for sale," I said after I sat on one of the high chairs of my kitchen island.

Nezha looked at me in astonishment. Before answering, she switched on the hanging lights over the black granite counter and stood facing me.

"Both apartments? Mom's too?"

I nodded in silence.

"Did you tell her? After all, that's her home. I know you bought it and it's in your name, but you gave it to her." She only articulated what was tearing me up inside.

"Listen, I know. I didn't come up with the idea lightly. This is an extreme decision for drastic times. That's why I need your help to announce it to her." I bent my head and added under my breath, "I feel bad about it. But I'm in bad shape in every way... My income's dropped significantly, and it's no longer enough to cover everything. I've been borrowing money every month just to keep up. I need some financial relief."

Carrying both mortgages and maintenance payments was ruining me, and I had nowhere to turn.

I hurried on, "I will not sell hers if mine finds a taker first. Since I'm not sure of that, I'm putting both on the market at the same time." I looked at her for moral support. She was well aware of my situation.

We had been in contact the entire time she was overseas, and we had spent hours together every day since she returned from Tunisia to close on the sale of her own apartment. I would have asked her for help if I knew she could afford it. But she had been struggling to pay off her own mountains of debt.

Before she could answer, I added: "I also wanted to ask you to take Mom to Morocco and have someone—a family member perhaps—take care of her around the clock. I can't do it anymore," I sighed.

I knew she was the only person I could turn to for this sort of thing. She had been going to Morocco far more often than I had, and she'd even been hinting at moving back there. She was convinced that it was far easier and cheaper to hire help and live more comfortably in that country.

But at that moment, my sister's expression betrayed her bewilderment.

"Oh my God, Wafa, these are big bombs you're dropping on me. Mom isn't going to like this. Living in Morocco doesn't appeal to her at all anymore. It hasn't in a very long time!" she moaned.

"I know, sis. But I *cannot* do it anymore. I'm at my wits' end, and broke. The truth is I can barely take care of my own daughter... not to mention you'll be going back to your husband soon," I lamented, my anguish oozing through every word.

"Well, why doesn't Sophie go spend some time with Sami in Tunisia? He'd love to have her there, and you'll get a break. She'll have a good time with him and the dog. And you and I can join them in a couple of weeks after we straighten things up with Mom."

That sounded like a worthy idea to me. I was also aware that Nezha needed to pacify Sami's feelings. Sending Sophie to stay with him for a few days was another way of further postponing her own return. He protested that she was abandoning him every time she went to the States. She would promise to be gone for a month and end up staying two or three instead, leaving him lonely and distressed. But it was a real torture for her to live away from her family. It was not something she would have chosen to do were it not for him.

"Sending Sophie alone to Tunisia will not be a walk in the park either, I assure you," I said.

At fourteen, she wasn't easy to deal with. Her school results were atrocious, and her principal had informed me they were keeping her behind in eighth grade, a catastrophic prospect in my eyes. But since the tuition cost a fortune, taking her out of the Lycée Français was really the only option.

The problem was compounded by the fact that the public schools in our town were overcrowded and populated by children of working-class Hispanics, which in itself did not bother me in the least—diversity rather appealed to me—but the crowded classrooms, limited resources, questionable discipline, and substandard education caused me to reject that possibility.

"What to do with her schooling this fall is going to be another problem... God—" I muttered.

I closed my eyes and massaged my forehead with my fingers.

"Why is everything so difficult? I'm so confused. I've got to find a way out of this shit somehow..."

"Let's deal with one thing at a time," advised Nezha. "You send Sophia to Sami while I convince Mom to go to Morocco," and added, "I'll take her myself on my way to Tunis. And I think you should join us there for a couple of weeks to rest and clear your mind. A brief escape will help you recover from your despondency."

I was grateful to her for presenting me with solutions, no matter how short-term.

**

Everything seemed to go smoothly at first.

Nezha had booked their trip to Casablanca for July 9 and helped Mom pack. The ride to JFK was uneventful; it was only when they reached the gate area crowded with passengers anxious to board the plane that the mood changed.

"You want to get rid of me, don't you?" Mom blurted out all at once.

She was sitting in her wheelchair, waiting to be taken onboard.

Nezha had had Mom agree to go to Morocco with her to be cared for by Fatima, her recently widowed oldest brother's second wife, and her two teenage daughters. She was to live in their large villa in Temara, south of Rabat. Uncle Khalid, Mom's youngest brother, also lived nearby with his wife and three children. We hoped his presence would make it easier for her to feel comfortable and get better.

"I can't go back," she whimpered. "There isn't anything there for me anymore."

Her eyes filled with tears. She pulled Nezha down by the hand to face her.

"My home is here now. I don't want Wafa to sell my apartment; I don't want to go to Morocco. Please don't send me away, let me stay home," she pleaded, sobbing softly, unmindful of being in public, devastated by the sudden realization of her imminent departure.

"My God, Mom, what's this? How can you say these things? I thought we'd talked about this. We love you and only want you to be properly taken care of. You'll be surrounded by close family, not strangers."

We had been nervous all along about Mom's uncharacteristic submissiveness. It was now clear she had only been concealing her torment.

"You know our circumstances, Mommy," Nezha went on, wiping her tears with her bare hands. "We have too many things going on and nobody to care for you at the same time."

Mom shook her head in disbelief, squeezed her daughter's hand. Nezha grabbed her other hand still squatting by her side. Her legs ached. She was aware of the stares around her.

"You've already fallen down twice at night just trying to go from your bed to the toilet in your room," insisted Nezha, "It's a wonder you didn't break a bone, or worse."

Luckily, she had fallen down on the carpeted floor of her bedroom. It took the help of a big man to get her back in bed. My sister, who had been staying with her to relieve me, had had to call one of the building's porters in the middle of the night. None of that seemed to matter to Mom.

"So you want to get rid of me, I can see that... I'm too much of a burden for you!" she wailed, submerged in dread.

"It's not true. You're crazy to think this way," retorted Nezha.

"Is everything alright?" inquired a flight attendant. "We're about to start boarding shortly, and you're going first."

"Yes, thank you. We'll be ready in a minute," said Nezha. She turned to face Mom again.

"Mom, please, this is not helping. And, you're wrong. We're not leaving you forever, only a short time, I promise. Just give us a few weeks to settle things out and for you to get well. But you too must do your part and get better."

Leaning over, she kissed her tenderly, dabbed her face with a tissue she pulled out of her purse and cleaned the makeup smudges.

"It'll be okay, Mommy, you'll see," she said.

Then she walked behind the chair to wheel her onboard. She was trying hard not to burst into tears herself.

**

I was resting on a lounge chair under the large beach umbrella provided by the hotel, shielded from the fierce Mediterranean sun, when my cell phone rang and pulled me out of my torpor. I scrambled to answer.

"Hello?" my sister's voice immediately shook me into full alertness.

"Nezha? Hi, I've been waiting to hear from you," I muttered at last. "How's Mom doing?"

"Badly," she said, "she's doing very badly." Her voice broke, "Last night, at around three in the morning, a few hours after she took antibiotics, she began vomiting and passing blood in an uncontainable diarrhea. She was rushed to the emergency room of the Polytechnic Clinic nearby and given an intravenous."

My heart skipped a beat. A few days earlier, upon their arrival in Morocco, my sister had called to tell me what had happened at boarding time, and all I could do was vehemently defend my decision. She had concurred with much sadness. After that the news had been that Mom was suffering from a burning sensation in her mouth and throat which made it very difficult for her to chew or swallow. The symptoms kept getting worse until she could no longer eat, drink, or talk. All the doctors who examined her had diagnosed the ailment as an oral yeast infection, but the latest physician she'd seen had prescribed antibiotics, insisting that it was an inflammation rather than a candidiasis.

On July 23, Mom had taken the first dose of the medication only to be hospitalized a few hours later. The following day, giant, white, thrush-like ulcers had appeared on her tongue and oral cavity. The sores had erupted very quickly and spread to her throat. After five days, she still hadn't had any food or drink and was still incapable of speech.

"None of the many specialists who examined her had any idea what was wrong with her," explained Nezha. "So yesterday I had her admitted in one of Rabat's most reputable private hospitals, Sheikh Zayyed."

I could hardly believe my ears. This was the worst imaginable scenario, a nightmare.

"But what are they all saying? What the hell is wrong with her?" I pressed her; my guts knotted.

"No one knows, Wafa. The ulcers were so severe, they were eating away at her tongue. She almost lost the tip of it. She's being kept alive intravenously."

I could hear her heave a sigh. I so shared her grief.

"When I saw those lesions, Wafa, I swear I thought she had Aids. Thank God, that was ruled out. Still, the only thing her doctors agree on is that this is caused by some kind of human immunodeficiency. In other words, her immune system has collapsed," she went on. "Multiple tests have been ordered. Most have turned out negative, and the rest are inconclusive. Her doctors are mystified, to say the least. They can't figure it out. And, trust me, there are some really good specialists here."

"Oh my God, honey. I'm so sorry you're dealing with this on your own," I said.

I never offered to go to Morocco to help her, though. I had already done my part. And Nezha never asked. In fact, she seemed grateful that I was in Tunisia with Sophia and Sami.

"Look, I'm already spending hours in the hospital every day. Also Hanan, Mom's new young maid, is amazing, with the sweetest temperament. She has not once left her side and attends to her needs day and night. Truly, there isn't anything more you could be doing," she reassured me.

Still I couldn't help feeling mortified that I had let Mom down, no matter how defensible my choice. Her worsening condition did nothing to alleviate the remorse of having sent her away and not being there. This was my punishment, and not a day went by when I wasn't haunted by an eerie sensation of absolute disconnect between my presence in a beach resort and my mother's near-death state far away from me.

When Sophia and I returned home from our Mediterranean retreat, Mom was still on intravenous support; she remained so for the first twenty-five of the thirty-nine days she was hospitalized. When the oral candidiasis seemed to lift and she began to eat and talk a little, other lesions appeared on her scalp. These were painful purulent pustules, which first showed up on her temples and within two weeks spread to her entire skull together with shooting throbbing pain. She was discharged on September 5, still suffering from these head lesions, and pretty much undiagnosed. The vast number of talented specialists who had examined her had not been able to identify her illness with any degree of certainty.

**

Back home, I had to figure out what I was to do next. My mother's condition was consuming me, and I could reach no solution that did not include her. Materially, I had already drastically downsized my lifestyle and reevaluated my priorities. But there was no escaping the fact that my financial situation had continued to deteriorate. My managers were demanding that I return to work or else face the consequences. And after months of therapy, I reached the inescapable conclusion that I could no longer go back. My psychologist agreed, deeming it challenging for me to fully recover without changing careers altogether. And indeed, the mere thought of returning to pick up my personal belongings was so unbearable, and generated so much terror, that I just abandoned them until the bulk of it was shipped back to me months later, I never having set foot in my office again.

There was nothing rational about any of it. All I knew was that I was living in a state of incomprehensible dread and, even more so, loathed the very idea of returning to my place of work. The stress had already materialized by taking shape within my womb. But the once small embryo of fear that had germinated months earlier in my uterus had grown into a snarled, melon-size mass of blood and tissue, causing random hemorrhages and prompting pre-menopausal symptoms that woke me in the middle of the night, drenched in my own sweat and paralyzed by my own destructive thoughts. Yet not even that monstrosity, and the fact that I was sure to lose my health insurance as well as my mother's invaluable coverage, was enough to make me reconsider my decision.

I was sailing in the fog without radar or lighthouse to guide me through the rocks and shoals of my destiny; and once I crashed, I kept making haphazard decisions without conviction and with shattering consequences for me and the people I loved most. My apathy and confusion had shut off my horizon, and no hint of light was visible to me anywhere. My instinct, and determined old self, had deserted me for good.

As I suspected, and apprehended too, my mother's apartment sold first that summer, relieving the financial pressure though deepening my remorse. In the fall, my daughter did not go back to the Lycée Français. I opted to home-school her with the help of an online program in Florida. Before long, my sister and I came to the conclusion that, if we all lived in Morocco, our immediate problems would be solved. Mom would be forced to recognize that we had not abandoned her, and I would leave the stress of working on Wall Street, and the prevalent xenophobic hysteria, behind. I began dreaming of a more catered and peaceful life in my native country.

In time, with our know-how and experience, we were confident we would also be able to start a business in Morocco. Nezha was already exploring the options. Moreover, we had invested in a good piece of land on the island of Djerba in

Tunisia just before 9/11. And even though the ambitious project we had capitalized on never saw the light of day, the property was still there, appreciating in value. If nothing else, we thought we could sell it at a good profit when the time came.

In December that year, and despite Sophia's ferocious opposition, we left home for Morocco—with express instructions to my broker to double his efforts to find a buyer for my apartment.

31

Back to Morocco

The return to my birthplace was therapeutic. My sister and I spent the first two weeks looking for the perfect house, big enough for all of us: Mom and Hanan, her young live-in maid, Nezha—and Sami later—and Sophia and me. We settled on a brand-new rental, a sun-drenched villa facing the Atlantic Ocean a few miles south of Rabat, in Harhoura. We furnished it with Nezha's and Mom's furniture, which I had shipped from the States along with Mom's small Chevrolet Cavalier. The house was so large I had to order an additional custom-made, Moroccan-style salon, and furniture for two extra bedrooms. There were a total of four bedrooms and three full baths on the second floor.

The master-suite alone, which was immediately designated Mom's special private quarters, was as big as a very large studio apartment, with another 140 square-foot terrace facing the sea. It easily accommodated her king-size bed, TV set, dresser, make-up vanity chest, desk, and a comfortable sitting area. Downstairs, on the ground floor, in addition to a vast foyer and a powder room, there were three living spaces, divided by a working fireplace. The dining area opened into a large tiled terrace facing a small garden with two solitary palm trees and the ocean beyond its iron gate. Next to it, a huge kitchen led to a laundry room and garage.

My goal was to create a perfect environment not only for us, but also, and primarily, for Mom. I threw myself into this task, meticulously decorating each room. I bought dozens of roses and tulips from a nearby flower farm every week and scattered them in beautiful arrangements throughout the house. In addition to Mom's live-in maid, we hired a cook and a young man who could perform various tasks—driver, gardener, server, and handyman.

As we settled in, we also extended warm invitations to our multiple cousins and friends, some of whom we hadn't seen in two decades. Many came to visit and welcomed our return "home." The only person we did not reach out to was our father.

I had not seen my father in seven years, and even then our encounter had lasted half a day. Actually, in the thirty-two years since my parents' divorce, I had visited him perhaps three times in all and always briefly. Throughout those years, I continued to send him a monthly stipend and paid for his pilgrimage to Mecca. But overall, I inquired only rarely about him despite his constant nagging for more attention and financial support. I can't explain precisely why I had so little desire to be close to him, only that I still resented him and felt guilty for not doing more.

The one sure thing was that, in his presence, or on the phone with him, I was never free to be myself. All my life, I had felt compelled to pretend and lie to him simply because it was more expeditious. He had not a clue who I was or what my life was like. On the rare occasions we met, it was impossible to catch up since our communication was constrained by my poor Arabic and his deteriorated French. After years of absence, our conversations were limited to my platitudes and his inevitable religious questioning.

"You do pray, don't you? How do you cope with fasting during Ramadan? It must be difficult in America, isn't it? You're raising your daughter as a good Muslim, right?" and so on, all of which I brazenly assented to or promptly evaded.

So when, most unexpectedly, my father called one night to ask that we take him in to live with us, we were caught by surprise. According to him, he was being mistreated by his wife and adopted daughter and demanded to leave. Needless to say, the mere thought of his visit literally made my mother wince when she heard of it—not that it was ever likely that my sister and I would ever envision such a thing. By every measure save social convention, we were strangers to him, having lived a vast ocean apart for decades.

After a full investigation of his latest grievance and discussions with our relatives, it turned out he was the one who had made life miserable for his family. My mother's old depiction of him had been validated. He was still the Grinch of old, and ever as mean-spirited, his searing and demeaning verbal abuse often directed at his twenty-four-year-old daughter.

He had adopted her, immediately after birth in 1980, some eight years after his divorce, because his wife was barren and wished for a baby. I never really knew the exact circumstances of her adoption, only that her biological mother had died in childbirth and, following Sharia Law, my father gave her a different last name from his, which caused the child a great deal of emotional pain during her growing years. Orphans in Morocco are often viewed in a disparaging way, seen as nothing more than "bastards."

Nonetheless, she had found a home, family love, and caring, especially from her adoptive mother and her side of the family, and she had been schooled. Unfortunately, my father had never failed to remind her of her origins when his unpleasant streak kicked in. I can only presume his cruelty was caused by his unhappiness or customary bitterness. Both daughter and wife had suffered silently then but were far too respectful to shun him or shut him up.

His wife had continued to attend the special recital nights at the Sufi shrine founded by her ancestors, even as he had long severed his affiliation with the Tariqa, contending that he did not need a spiritual leader to connect with God. Unemployed for most of the past thirty years, he was mostly friendless and without known hobbies or interests besides religion, his daily routine mainly consisting of five extended daily prayers, followed by readings of the Koran, and, in the evening, TV watching.

He repeatedly complained about his children's abandonment of him, comparing it to his brother Hassan's very close relationship with his own children, who, despite the fact they also lived overseas in France and Canada, stayed in close touch with their father. Apparently his new family was not enough. His religious ardor did not seem to help him find inner peace and contentment in any lasting way. And his judgmental, negative mind set had not changed much despite his faith and authoritative command of Islamic scripture, from which he quoted at every opportunity. And yet one of the most central concepts of Islam is that of daily praise and gratefulness to God, no matter how difficult our human circumstances.

Hence, after an initial moment of uneasy, guilt-laden discussion, weighing his request, my sister and I did not debate the issue for too long: His presence was neither desired nor welcomed. The subject was dropped and never again brought up.

**

Winters in Morocco are short and spring arrives early; 2004 had begun on a groundswell of hope and optimism. A home facing the sea had been a long-held dream of mine. Ours was so close to the ocean that, during high tide, the surf reached all the way to the back gate, threatening the small grassy backyard.

Nightly, from the comfort of my bed, through the large glass windows, I was treated to a spectacular dance of breakers pecking and crashing against the black cliff in sudden eruptions of sparkling froth. With only the moon and stars lighting the gigantic sprays of bubbly spume, the display of aqueous fireworks looked like an ever-changing white celestial lace. I could have watched all night had I not been lulled to sleep by the endless roar and rumble of the Atlantic. I woke up only briefly at dawn, to close the shades for a late slumber.

"Don't you love it, Mom?" I asked at breakfast. "I can't get over the beauty and awe-inspiring presence of the ocean so near."

"I find it rather scary myself... all that noise!" Mom answered with a sheepish grin.

I laughed out loud at her expression and cuddled her in my arms. I so wished for her to find happiness at last.

Morocco had never felt so good. We were all elated with our picturesque setting; the luminous house with the sun streaming in from sunrise to sunset, the army of seagulls standing at midday like miniature guards, facing the same way, saluting the sun on the rock-strewn, moonlike scape.

Not even the full hysterectomy I had in January, less than a month after my arrival, could dampen my new buoyancy. The fibroid had become so big, and caused so much bleeding, it interfered with my daily life. I could no longer wait; it was already too large to expect it to shrink on its own.

I was cut open and my entire uterus and ovaries taken out, and even though I no longer had health insurance, the entire cost of the operation, with two brilliant young surgeons and three nights in a private room in a brand new clinic, came to fifteen hundred dollars. Finally, finally, with the irksome growth removed, I was confident; the bad times were behind.

To be sure, Mom was still disabled and mostly confined to bed, requesting assistance merely to stand or walk. Her scalp lesions had not yet healed even though she had had her hair shaven to facilitate their treatment. Doctors and physical therapists were now paying her regular visits at home, and, occasionally, I drove her to a hospital or laboratory for further testing. She was still complaining of pain, insomnia, and other ailments, though the overall circumstances of her care had vastly improved and only required her to be more fully engaged in her own recovery. But every so often, she appeared happier and willing to be less passive. At such times, all of us encouraged and cheered her up as if she were a baby taking her first steps.

On March 4 I wrote an email to my friends in America in which I rejoiced:

Mom is finally showing signs of improvement. She was prescribed Prednisone at 60 mg a day, and the results are pretty amazing. We're keeping our fingers crossed that she doesn't have any side effects, like edema, bone loss, or mania. We're watching, cheering, and praying all at once...

Adding,

Life in Morocco is delicious. Every day I delight, not only in the sumptuous sunsets over the Atlantic and the crisp sunny days, but also in being taken care of by no less than three house staff. That's such a luxury still for me, I feel like royalty, and I'm not sure it's for real yet...

32

The River and the Sea

"Noooo!" The inhuman howl ripped through my thoughts like a cyclone across a barren plain, a sound utterly surreal. It felt like a piece of my own liver had been savagely bitten off and was being chewed up. My entire being was screaming in agony, even as merely a whimper came out of my throat.

"When did it happen?" I asked, though I was incapable of hearing the answer. "We're on our way... Thank you..." The phone dropped out of my shaky hand. I struggled to keep my eyes on the road. My daughter, sitting in the passenger seat next to me, began weeping silently.

We had resisted, we had fought, and then we stood defeated. Thence we surrendered in the vilest of nightmares to Death, the ultimate victor.

Glum stares followed us through the grim walls of the hospital. Mom was lying still on her hospice bed, pale and serene, just as we had left her the night before. All the tubes had been removed. Strangely, her head lesions had all but vanished. Hanan, her eyes red, stood up when we appeared. Sophia and I approached Mom on either side of the bed, and each took a hand. They were soft and cold. I leaned over and kissed her cheek. Sophia caressed her face.

"Mommy," I whispered. "You're at peace now."

How does one deal with bereavement? How can it be put into words? When thoughts fail, bodily perceptions endure, and my flesh, heart, entrails, every inch of me was dissolving into wrenching, mind-numbing, engulfing revulsion, even as the loss had not yet registered in my mind. From her face and demeanor, I knew Sophia was coping with a wretchedness her young heart was never prepared for. I turned to Hanan.

"How did it happen?" I murmured.

"She just stopped breathing, no struggle," she assured me. And that simple statement I received with a measure of gratitude.

**

Mom had been back in the hospital for less than a week. Ten days earlier, on Friday, March 5, the day after I wrote my friends describing our new idyllic and hopeful existence, she began complaining of a severe leg pain. I called the doctor and left him a message. This was the start of the weekend and we were not overly surprised that he did not call back. Late on Saturday afternoon, the physical therapist came for his scheduled appointment.

He spent a lot of time trying to alleviate her pain, massaging and exercising her limbs. Hot compresses were applied, and lots of pain killers administered, none with lasting results. For the next couple of days, Mom did not sleep at all. On Monday, my sister and I had a business appointment in Casablanca and on the way there called her doctor again. This time he returned our call.

"She's been in agony since Friday, and it's been getting worse, Doctor. Could you please find the time to visit her today?" beseeched Nezha while I was driving.

"Tell him that her foot is getting blue and very cold," I interjected.

"Also, her foot's turned blue and cold..." she began. "What... what do you mean?" Her tone had changed, and her sudden distress hit me like a punch in my solar plexus.

"To the hospital? Right away? Yes... okay..." She hung up.

"What's going on? What did he say?" I urged.

"He got very alarmed when he heard her foot was cold and changed color. He said it was very serious. He's calling Professor Lakhal, a vascular surgeon, right now. He wants Mom to see him immediately."

"Why? He didn't even examine her..." I cried in full panic mode.

"The cold foot, that's terrible... that's an indication, probably an obstruction in an artery, something called an ischemia, I think," she went on. "We have to take her to Sheikh Zayed hospital. That's where this surgeon is. It's extremely urgent, he insisted."

"Oh God, I can't believe this has been going on since Friday. He didn't even call us back over the weekend."

"There's no point in blaming anyone," said Nezha. "Mom has been in pain for so long it was impossible to tell whether this was any different." Adding, "All we can do is hurry back and drive her to the hospital."

The surgeon was unreachable that Monday, and a lot of damage had already occurred before an endovascular procedure was attempted in Sheikh Zayed Hospital the following day. It did not go well, and the prognosis was disturbing. The next day, Mom was transferred to Avicenna Hospital, the largest and best equipped facility in Rabat.

When she reached the operating room, and while her attending surgical team was still considering their options, her heart stopped before they restarted it and got it going again. She was in no position to undergo a lengthy, complicated procedure. Her surgeons were now talking of a leg amputation above the knee, but, first, all their efforts had to be focused on saving her life.

All hell broke loose in my family. Call it instinct, or presage—we were guided to act and spread the ill-omened news to our loved ones with urgency. Our mother had been hospitalized multiple times in the past, and as recently as the prior summer in Sheikh Zayed, often with dramatic, life-threatening ailments, yet never with the same foreboding. We called our brothers in America, our uncles and cousins in Morocco. We sought support but also guidance and assistance.

My sister was convinced that, given a choice, Mom would rather die than accept the amputation of her leg, although this was hardly a matter of choice. Many patients who undergo a major leg amputation often do not survive the complications that follow their bedridden state. Mom had already been confined to bed for more than a year, and her health was severely compromised; an amputation would surely lead to her demise.

By the middle of the week, there was a sense of events slipping away from us. I called on Mom's older brothers, Brahim and Abderrahim. They were rich and powerful men; they could get the best specialists to take on their sister's case and help save her. And indeed, a few phone calls from them, and soon an army of eminent professors and specialists examined her and offered their expertise. Uncle Abderrahim came to visit her in

Avicenna the next day, visibly upset to hear of his little sister's bleak prospects.

She had been placed in intensive care and remained mostly unconscious. The few times she regained consciousness, she'd asked for her children and brothers. Uncle Abderrahim had reported that when she saw him, she looked into his eyes, attempted a feeble smile, and muttered something. Both my sister and I knew how much his visit meant to her. She had such adoration for him, his presence felt like a gift, even as her life was hanging by a thread.

In the intensive care unit, it had become blatantly clear that the longer she was unconscious, the less likely that even the best medical team in the world could do much for her. Her attending physicians had pretty much given up; it was only a matter of time. As her ischemia progressed, so had arterial thrombosis. A stroke or heart failure was not far behind.

All we had left was hope that she would awaken from her near comatose state and undergo the amputation of her gangrened leg, thus saving her life. In my prayers, I implored God to help ease her pain in ways He alone knew.

Her heart stopped beating on March 15, 2004. She was only sixty-five.

Perhaps God had pity on her and spared her any additional misery.

From that moment on, my sister and I went into a deep stupor, relinquishing all decision making. Aunt Touria, Uncle Brahim's first wife, took charge, with the help of her youngest son, Cousin Nabil, who expertly handled all the legal formalities. Then she called on Uncle Abderrahim to bankroll everything from the hospital costs to a huge, fully catered funeral.

Finally she asked Fatima, Uncle Mohamed's widow, to make her large villa available for the traditional, three-day-and-night gathering marking the beginning of a forty-day morning period.

All we had to do was be there and greet family and friends, plus a few dignitaries who showed up to pay their respect to Uncle Abderrahim. Over three hundred people attended the funeral, some of whom we had not seen for twenty-five to thirty years. The single most conspicuous absences were those of Uncle Brahim and my father. My uncle was traveling in India, and his second wife, who was alerted, had not deemed it reasonable to interrupt his trip since he could not be there for his little sister's interment anyway. As to my father, he was eighty-four and in weak health, and to endure a day-long bus trip from Tetouan was too much for him to bear. In truth, his absence was a relief.

As for Nezha and me, the only request we made was that the burial be postponed until our brothers could arrive from the States. Under Islamic law the dead must be buried within twenty-four hours. Hence Nabil had to arrange for the body to stay in the hospital morgue overnight to gain an extra day. Larbi flew in the following day with Margie and Jaad, his wife and son; they landed a few hours before the burial. Abdu, who lived in Orlando, was delayed overnight because of a snowstorm that interfered with airline traffic and prevented his transfer to JFK airport. He never had a chance to say a last goodbye.

**

Behind me the religious chants grew louder, the men's voices completely drowning the women's. I entered the small, quiet chamber with apprehension. The sun filtered through the window shades lending a hallowed aura to the place. Her body had been laid on a mat in the middle of the room directly on the floor. An unworldly glow floated over her figure. Her head and entire body were fully draped in an immaculate white cloth. Only her face was showing, framed by the tight scarf covering her short hair. The shroud was reminiscent of the white garments Muslim women wear during the pilgrimage to Mecca.

Two experienced women, although not professional undertakers, had been hired by Aunt Touria to wash her body and hair with only soap. She was rinsed a few times until the water run clear. Then, her body was dried carefully and her arms crossed right over left. My mother's un-embalmed corpse was finally shrouded in a white cotton sheet to be buried immediately in a modest wooden coffin without jewelry or items of value. A strong, fragrant scent of rose water and B'khur—an ancient and pricey incense made of agar wood and highly valued in Morocco—emanated from her and infused the air in the enclosed space.

I bent over her face, kneeling on the ground, not noticing the women who had just performed the solemn ritual, and barely recognized my mother. She looked younger, relaxed, and peaceful. Her skin was flawless, nearly translucent, but also distended. Not a single wrinkle was visible, and yet not a trace of makeup or lotion had been used. An intimation of a smile was apparent on her lips. I couldn't help but think the smile looked unnatural, forced almost, as if it had been arranged, her lips turned upward intentionally by mortal hands.

What did it matter? This was but a shell, not my mother, I reminded myself. She had relinquished her earthly vessel, was no longer there. The thought struck me—not so much a spark of awareness as a stark realization that I too was a shell, filled but with an immense void encouraging me not to linger.

Shaken, I hurried outside the room and gestured to Sophia to go in.

"They're going to take her body away in a few minutes. Do you want to see her one last time?" I asked, not without hesitation.

"Yes, I do. Can you come in with me?" she asked.

Like most females present, she was wearing a blue Moroccan *djellaba* borrowed from a cousin. She looked awkward and uneasy in her unfamiliar garb, but she did not complain. In a country where Western dress is widely used, important events are attended in traditional clothing. While Moroccan women favor richly decorated kaftans on festive occasions, they attend funerals wearing *djellabas*, garments which are understated and more modest in color and shape.

We entered the chamber. I waited at the door while Sophia approached the body. This was her first real encounter with death since that last hospital visit, and I worried about her reaction. She loved her grandmother deeply and throughout her young life had built a strong bond with her. I should not have been concerned; she stayed calm and collected through her tears and sorrow and demonstrated more maturity than I had expected.

After Sophia, my brother and his wife went in briefly. We were being urged to speed it up. The body had to be taken away to be buried by noontime prayer. Finally, four men walked in and came out carrying the coffin. The religious psalms and praises to God and his prophet intensified, building into an intensely emotional chorus, a temple of invocations that filled even the least spiritual of listeners with unwitting awe and reverence.

All of a sudden, the shrill, cascading *yooyoos* of women punctured the loud religious incantations. I was shocked to hear them. They were no different from the staccato ululations heard at weddings, and they prompted a weird analogy in the theater of my mind: The scene of my mother's funeral had turned into an eerie departing party for her corpse; she was Death's bride. And I couldn't help but think that, while her terrifying wedding night had signified the death of her childhood's innocence, her funeral meant the re-birth of her soul, which I suspected she had perhaps secretly longed for during her ordeal.

Still, that image of deliverance was little consolation for us pitiable mortals left behind. As everyone rose to their feet to witness the procession moving toward the door, tearful faces mixed in the crowd with chanting mourners. I held on to Sophie and Nezha's hands, all three of us sobbing uncontrollably, bleeding tears of grief.

Someone behind me grabbed my shoulder.

A woman's voice urged me, "Please don't cry. Don't let your daughter and sister weep either. This is a time of celebration, not tears, don't you know? Your mother's soul is returning to God, her Creator, and her body back unto the earth it's made of."

I shook my head as if to say, *Yes*, I knew that she spoke the truth, though my heart simply wouldn't listen.

"It'll sadden her to see your sorrow in her moment of glory," the woman insisted with compassion.

At the small, scruffy cemetery, Mom's body was buried in a little plot not far from that of Mohamed's, her oldest brother, in the shadow of an unpretentious neighborhood mosque. Weeds and wild plants had invaded the graveyard, a vision of neglect and lack of upkeep. A tiny prayer room, a *sayyed* enclosing the tomb of a saint, had been built on the premises, and a few people gathered there after Friday prayers. There was no organization designated for the cemetery's maintenance save for an old guard and destitute woman who watered the planted tombs and closed the gate at night to prevent unwanted access. They survived on public alms and charity, mostly from visitors. Poverty and an absence of civil and social structures were to blame.

I was saddened by the shabby resting place we were offering our mother. It seemed unworthy of her somehow. Not that I would have preferred a rich mausoleum, just a tidier and better groomed graveyard. A few tombs were built with the top shaped as a basin the length of the crypt, filled with soil and planted with daisies and geraniums. My first thought was that I wanted the same for Mom, later, when, after forty days, her tomb was built.

There were more prayers and incantations during the interment and after the coffin was covered with dirt. The space around the grave was so tight, we had to carefully watch where to put our feet not to step on other tombs.

On the return to Fatima's villa, the funeral had taken on the allure of a singular ceremony. People kept coming back for three long days and nights and were fed breakfast, lunch, dinner, and tea and coffee in between. Emotionally, it was a roller coaster of tearful and, oddly enough, joyful moments too as we reunited with people we held in deep affection and whom we had left behind decades ago.

The massive show of support was a great comfort to all of us, but we were glad to regroup in the intimacy of our home. Larbi, Margie, and Jaad only stayed a few days and promised to return in the summer. Abdu extended his visit for three more weeks before going back to Florida. When everyone had left,

Nezha and I felt like inflatables from which the air had gone out. We shriveled and recoiled, each in the emptiness of our hearts, unmindful as we were of the poet's words of wisdom as he celebrated the oneness of all existence.

> "For life and death are one, even as the river and the sea are one...
>
> For what is it to die but to stand naked in the wind and to melt into the sun?
>
> And what is it to cease breathing but to free the breath from its restless tides,
>
> that it may rise and expand and seek God unencumbered?
>
> Only when you drink from the river of silence shall you indeed sing.
>
> And when you have reached the mountain top, then you shall begin to climb.
>
> And when the earth shall claim your limbs, then shall you truly dance."
>
> The Prophet, Khalil Gibran

33

Sleep Walking

My mother's sudden death had come at a time when I was convinced my dejection had finally ended. It was a short reprieve. My aimless walk in the all-too-familiar wasteland of my mind resumed anew. There were days when I was no more than a living corpse; carrying my ache and mourning my flesh, I went through the motions, pretending to be alive. That, in essence, was my life for the next four years.

The only thing that kept me anchored in my sea of angst was my daughter, her well-being a constant concern to me. Even before her grandmother passed away, she had been homesick and, not unlike many teenage girls, subject to mood swings and periodic gloom. Suddenly, she had to cope with the unimaginable, death and its finality. On her fifteenth birthday, just a few days after the funeral, a friend offered her a three-month-old puppy, a tan female Labrador she called "Bonnie." Alas, the instant love she felt for her new pet was not enough to ease her sporadic fits of unhappiness.

We had frequent clashes that erupted without much warning, like rolling thunder in a clear sky, triggered by a little more than a nagging remark about her lack of studiousness, or discipline, or tidiness. And she would just look at me with unbridled anger, spitting with fury:

"I *hate* it here. I hate it with all my heart. I want to go back home in America. I don't want you to sell our apartment in the Versailles. My family is there, my best friend is there, I have no one here, especially now that Grandma is dead." She'd choke and start crying.

"Listen, baby, I know you feel lonely and hurt, I know that, and I'm really sorry," I'd say to appease her. "I quite understand you don't want me to sell our apartment, but I *cannot afford* it anymore! It costs me a fortune. Just so that you understand, it costs as much to keep it as to live a whole month here, all expenses paid. Not to mention the worries and maintenance problems. And I cannot go back to New York. After twenty years of living the rat race, I'm done."

It broke my heart to see her in such pain. Still I felt I had to stand my ground.

"Then *you* can stay here," she'd argue. "*I* want to go back home, live there. I can take care of myself, and it's not like I'd be alone. My family's right there also, only a few flights up. I'm ready to go to Memorial High School. It won't cost you a dime. You're always complaining about money, and now you're looking to spend over fifteen thousand dollars a year on tuition again."

She had thought it all through. She was fed up with Morocco and the isolation of home-schooling.

"I decided on the Rabat American School because it's the best place for your education, regardless of the cost. Plus you'll make friends, and you'll feel a lot better about living here, I promise. In any case, only three more years and you'll be going to college. So it's not like this is a permanent move for you." Far from soothing her, my words fell on deaf ears.

"Mom, this is *your* country, not mine. I'm an American! I don't feel at *home* here. The problem is, you don't understand me, you never do... you're so *selfish*!"

Then I'd start shouting as loudly as her. "That's not true! You know how much I care. It's really quite unfortunate you can't see what a great experience this is for you! You think everyone can have an opportunity like this?"

"But I *don't care*, don't you see?" And, with that, she'd run to her room wailing, making sure to slam the door behind her and not reappear for hours.

Sophia was right about one thing: Money was haunting me yet again, though nothing mattered more to me than her education. If necessary, I was ready to borrow to pay for tuition. The bigger worry was my vacant apartment in the States. It was depleting my resources and more than doubled our otherwise manageable expenses in Morocco. The business venture I had started with Nezha in January was fast turning into another drain. Not only was it slow in taking flight, it was very far from even sustaining itself, let alone generating any income.

In Morocco, to build a successful venture one has to have a lot of influence, endless patience, and very deep pockets, on the one hand, and an essential acquaintance with the country's mores and practices on the other. I thought I had that understanding. I was mistaken. Luckily my sister was far more adept. Still, we encountered multiple difficulties generally related to an overly laid-back temperament and a widespread lack of efficiency, expertise, or professionalism. These problems were made worse in our dealings with public officials and navigation of the bureaucratic maze by protracted corruption.

Moroccans, like most Middle-Easterners, are genuinely warm, charming people, but their natural tendency is to more readily tell their interlocutors what they want to hear than keep to their word. Missed deadlines, poor quality controls, recurrent cost overruns, an unapologetic lack of punctuality, and endemic overpromises are but a few of the ills we encountered regularly.

To be sure, suppliers, vendors, and government officials were often polite, even gracious, but they did not care for straight talk as much as they did for nuance, subtlety, and elusiveness, if not half-truths. God forbid I displayed any hint of frustration or aggravation with them, for they were most easily offended. I had much less patience with such nonsense than my sister, and the task of mending miffed feelings always fell to her.

Thus the subject of money, fueled by our inability to get a business going, loomed like the darkest of clouds, more ominous every day, creating a huge wedge between my sister and me. I felt I was carrying the whole burden alone; she thought otherwise. Within a few months of our mother's death, we turned on each other with ferocious indignation.

On a warm and rainy May morning, I was going over my banking statements online and my anxiety was mounting with the amount of expenditure and my diminishing resources. My sister was moping around still in her pajamas asking me something when I lashed out at her.

"I've been spending all my money to support us, and I think you should at least show some gratitude," I complained bitterly pushing my laptop aside.

"Hey! Where did that come from?" she asked stopping in her track. "I've been spending as well, not just you. Besides, you're the one who insists on all the lavish expenditure on decoration, flowers, and what not," she retorted.

"You forget the house was new and needed a lot of fixtures to make it inhabitable. Plus I wanted to create the best environment for Mom. But I didn't think I'd have no help from you at all."

"That's not true. I got transfers from Sami. And all the money you've spent comes from the sale of Mom's apartment, right? Well, then, I'm just as entitled to it as you are."

There, she'd blurted it out, laid out her assessment of a controversial subject we had been avoiding all along.

"Yeah? And how's *that*?" I shrieked. I had been dreading the time we would be sparring over that very issue.

"Sure, you bought the apartment for her. But you also *gave* it to her, didn't you? Then, as her daughter, I get to share in its sale. In fact, come to think of it, so do our brothers!"

"Really, and who else?" I scoffed. "They never spent a penny to help her out, ever. Quite on the contrary, she was more often giving *them* money. The bottom line is this, and please put it in your head once and for all: I gave her the apartment to enjoy during her *lifetime*, certainly *not* to pass it on as inheritance to her heirs. I paid the mortgage and the maintenance. Not to mention, you have a husband to provide for you. I don't. Why doesn't *he* help out a little more?"

Somewhere in the back of my mind, I felt abashed at my petty, pathetic self but swiftly covered my shame with outright hatred.

"He does as much as he can. I choose to live here while he's still in Tunis. If he lived here, he'd contribute his share. I can see how the shortage of money demoralizes you and undermines your judgment. I've seen you act like this many times before. I know those symptoms in you," she hissed.

"Well, I'm glad you recognize the symptoms of my dysfunction. I wish you could come up with solutions instead," I spat out in disgust.

"I don't worry like you, Wafa. I feel sorry for you, really. Money doesn't define *me*. We've never gone hungry or homeless; I_*know* everything will be fine eventually. Besides, I never asked you to support me in the past and I don't expect you to now."

Her words felt like insults, hitting all those sore buttons at once.

"But you're doing just *that*! In fact, the whole idea of coming to live in Morocco was *your* idea. Starting a business here was your idea. Hearing you, Morocco was the Promised Land. Look at the mess we're in now. I'm so sorry I listened to you and your stupid dream!"

I felt a searing pain inside and my head began hurting. I could now clearly see the disgust in her eyes.

She lowered her voice but couldn't hide the rage in her tone. "Nobody forced you. You were so depressed and confused, you jumped on it... Do not pretend otherwise."

She turned to leave the room but stopped, threw her head back and looked me in the eyes, fuming. "Why don't you go back home with your daughter and stay away from me? I don't need you here. I'm sick of your constant criticism. Your pessimism is sabotaging all our efforts to create something. Better you go back to America."

I very rarely saw that side of her. Her soft, gentle nature had been taken over by an incensed, peremptory woman.

"You have no say in what I do. I have too much invested here financially and emotionally to just turn my back now. I really resent your arrogance."

She was gone already, leaving me livid and trembling from head to toe. I closed the door, threw myself on the bed, and wept.

On the surface, the cause of our mutual bitterness was money, though, of course, it was not only that. We were both filled with grief at the loss of our mother and had no one else but each other to blame it on. For Nezha as for me, Mom had been everything, our sole purpose in life to cater to her every need, fulfill her dreams. But for my sister, not having children of her own, Mom's happiness had become her most pressing priority, almost an obsession. After the death, she had completely lost her drive and zest for life, had withdrawn, mostly kept to herself, and fallen ill often.

Sophia and I returned briefly to the States that hapless year, she in mid-May and I at the beginning of June. My apartment was not moving, and I needed to change brokers or find a way to rent it if I couldn't sell it. The trip, which took place at the time of the rift with my sister, turned out to be a source of infinite sorrow. Everything reminded me of my mother. I stayed indoors and went out only to visit close friends. Despite all their best efforts, I was a walking husk, alienated and forsaken, intensely hurt by my loss and my sister's animosity.

Back in Rabat at the beginning of the summer, I was glad to find Sami had left Tunis and agreed to join us in Morocco for good. Both my sister and I needed him to relieve the pressure of pursuing a venture in a patriarchal society that I, in particular, had lost touch with. He immediately endeavored to reconcile us and soon we had regained some of our lost trust, understanding that the pain of bereavement had contributed to our clash.

In the fall, Sophia entered tenth grade at the Rabat American School. As I had predicted, before long, her overall disposition changed entirely. She made new friends and participated in several sports, joining various teams from swimming to basketball to volleyball and cheerleading.

But, even as she felt better about her life in Morocco, I was going the other way. My thoughts were marred by yet another challenging aspect of life in my native land. I was plagued by resurging doubts, a mixed bag of enduring misgivings I thought I had long left behind. No longer was I happy to just watch the sun set over the ocean and feel complete. As I had often in the past, I was drowning in my old fears and negative thinking, closing myself to life's simple pleasures.

Could I really accept, and adapt to, the reality of life in Morocco? As much as I wished for our business to succeed, could I reconcile my desire to make money with the guilt of doing so to the detriment of so many who lived in abject destitution? Would I be able now, almost a quarter century after I had left this country behind and it became but a distant memory, return to a make-believe existence denigrated and reviled in my youth? Could I hide in a bubble of privilege with once-rejected compromises because the young rebel in me was now a tamed, middle-aged woman?

Undeniably, there were advantages to living in Morocco, but they were largely due to the country's unbroken state of backwardness and social inequalities. In that respect Morocco was not much better than the rest of the non-oil producing, Arab states. Labor remained so very cheap relative to everything else that it was difficult to believe in the trickle-down argument that a new enterprise would help build the nation's economy, create new jobs, and thus feed more families. Since independence, there had been very little trickling down.

Some say that labor was cheap because the work force was mostly either uneducated or undereducated. True, but why was that still the case? In thirty years, the country's elites had only looked after their own self-interest, not renouncing an inch of their excessive privileges or backing any reform to combat illiteracy, and that had had repercussions on all other social and economic indicators. According to United Nations data, the kingdom's literacy rate was still only fifty-six percent, a percentage much higher among women and girls.

Moreover, to my chagrin, the status of women in the cities seemed to have gone backward instead of forward. The use of the *hijab* was now ubiquitous even among well-educated middle-class professional women, who often contended to my face that their *hijab* was their own choice. But was it really? Like the habit and veil of Christian nuns, is the *hijab* a simple uniform worn to show renunciation of ego and earthly desires as well as identification with the Almighty? If such is the case, then I was ready to salute them. But what to make of the many women wearing the *hijab* with elaborate face make-up and other embellishments, oftentimes without any religious principle? Was that mimicry, fear, or subtle intimidation born from a new wave of religious sentiment?

The spread of Islamic fundamentalism had not spared Morocco even as the government led an aggressive campaign against Islamic extremism. And its insinuation into the social fabric had an impact on all kinds of civil liberties, which made me feel a lot less free than I had in my youth. To be fair, the young King Mohammed VI, who succeeded his father in 1999, had shown a great deal of resolve in advancing women's rights, but forces beyond his control had infiltrated the social psyche regardless of his wishes.

Suffice it to say that, in my mind, I was back where I had been three decades earlier, only worse. Not only was I struggling with the same long-standing issues of inequality and social justice, torn between my selfish need to indulge in cozy materialism and the blatant poverty at the periphery, I also found myself met on a religious plane by a social disconnect within my own stratum I had never encountered in the past.

And finally, I became concerned about the type of influence Sophia was being exposed to. In the American School, she associated with the children of American expatriates but also, and mostly, with those of the very rich and influential Moroccan bourgeoisie. I could witness in her the subtle and not-so-subtle signs of a spoiled teenage girl, unaffected by the social disparities around her.

Within a year of Mom's death, I had come full circle. My initial enthusiasm was dampened by mourning and personal reservations regarding Moroccan society.

By the spring of 2005, I was ready to go back home. Ironically, this time, Sophia did not. As I had predicted, she had fallen in love with her school and friends. Beyond all my other qualms, I felt I had no choice, my apartment—hanging like an albatross around my neck—had still not found any taker, and tuition only increased my burden. I could hardly wait for the school year to end.

At the end of April, I wrote Marie, a dear friend of mine,

I have been battling with an overwhelming feeling of loneliness since Mom passed away, and neither my sister nor my daughter have been able to fill the void inside. I feel like a stray, lost in the wilderness, looking for a new meaning to her life.

At the end of May, just as I was ready to reconsider the whole thing, I got a decent buy-offer and a contract on my apartment. It had taken two long years, an eternity. By then I had made up my mind to return home. Since December my sister and I had been struggling to get a second venture off the ground and the prospects that once seemed encouraging had again been quashed. On June 25, as my sister and Sami began exploring yet another promising project, our third, Sophia and I flew back to America permanently.

**

During the summer of 2005, I kept busy with the sale of my home of eighteen years, the move to a rental apartment in a town with a good public school, and Sophia's enrollment in junior year. In September, the question of what to do with myself was again facing me. Since the spring I had been discussing with Marie the prospect of returning to university to complete my Ph.D.

If there was ever anyone who knew about these things, it was Marie. After a long career with Exxon, she had returned to college for a master's and, at fifty, completed a doctorate. A teacher and dissertation counselor at Colombia's Teachers College, she was the most accomplished, knowledgeable and supportive woman I had ever known. Her optimistic and heartening communication with me was priceless when all else failed me.

After exploring the possible avenues open to me, I found that if the resumption of an incomplete doctorate appeared simple from the outset, the reality was far more daunting. Without elaborating on the matter, it turned out that, few if any of my hard-earned past credits would be accepted by any institution after such a long absence from academics—twenty years. The graduate advisors at New York University, my old school, were the least encouraging. They contended that the program had fundamentally changed, and that they only considered students who committed to the entire four or five-year Ph.D. program directly after the completion of their undergraduate degrees. In other words, a student with an existing master's degree or beyond would not be welcome in the program.

I ended up registering at Rutgers University, whose rules were less stringent. The dean of the Politics Department assured me they might take a few of my Ph.D. course credits that correspond to the current curriculum, but that I had to take more quantitative-research-related classes. Moreover, nearly two-thirds of the required courses had to be taken at Rutgers to merit the university's certification.

It was agreed that I would start immediately by registering for one core course called "Research Design in Political Science." The topic was really a euphemism for "Introduction to Advanced Statistics," which I labored through and completed with a "B" despite its tediousness. Clearly, this was not what I had anticipated, and by the end of 2005 I was in as much disarray about my future as ever.

All of 2006, and the first four months of 2007, witnessed my rise and fall as an aspiring independent stock-option trader—a half-baked idea I had after watching one of those extravagant infomercials promising easy fortune on TV one Sunday morning. After the initial euphoria of quick gains and fast money, I proceeded to lose all of my investment and much more, while feeling all the debilitating obsessiveness of an addicted gambler whose moods fluctuate with her gains or losses of the day.

For months, my daily routine consisted of staying glued to my computer, watching the up-and-down ticks of stocks being traded on the various exchanges with CNBC talking heads in the background. Before long I was hooked, always on edge, and depressed, and yet I continued to maintain the irrational conviction that it was only a matter of time before I mastered the tricks of the game. Despite the odds against me, I would in effect control my trades to such a degree that I would be able to minimize my losses while maximizing my gains with the assistance of sophisticated technical graphs and fool-proof methods taught in seminars by professional traders.

My qualified take on that stint—which I have since determined was nothing more than a well-oiled scam to sell expensive seminars and trading products—is that, like thousands of other ambitious wannabe traders, I had to concede that I'd been a total chump. Most depressing was the sad realization that I had yet again hit bottom in mental distress and muddled perception. The stock option trading was a pathetic attempt at finding an easy way out of my financial predicament. It was providential that it had failed so miserably.

34

Overcoming Fear

March 2008

The sun was high up in the sky. Spring was in the air even as the budding trees had yet to blossom. I was fixing my second cup of coffee since my cottage-cheese-and-fresh-fruit breakfast that late morning. My laptop was left open, waiting, on the coffee table in the living room. I had just re-read my previous chapter, tweaking at it at the margins, when the shrill tone of my house line pulled me away from my thoughts.

"Wafa, the reason for my call is to tell you about a fascinating book I'm reading," began my friend Naziha as soon as I answered the phone and we'd asked each other about our kids.

I had met her twelve years earlier at an Englewood Cliff's gym. A gorgeous young brunette from Morocco, she'd been looking for a new place to live and my mother had offered her second bedroom for rent. For the next two years, she shared our lives, becoming a cherished member of the family, until she met the man who became her husband and then the father of her two children.

"I don't know why," said Naziha, "But I immediately thought of you. I'm sure you'd love it."

"Really? What is it called?" I asked, intrigued.

"It's called *A New Earth*. It's by Eckhart Tolle. You need to get it right now!" she said emphatically.

"*A New Earth*," I repeated. "What is it about?"

"In short, it's about finding your life's purpose, living in the present," she explained. "But it's much more than that. I've been engrossed by it! It's truly amazing, Wafa. Oprah's been conducting a free weekly web-seminar to discuss the book with the author and answer readers' questions since the beginning of March, one chapter a week, for ten weeks. You can still download and watch the episodes you missed. I'm hooked, I swear. At the risk of sounding corny, it helped me find peace and happiness."

She was so enthusiastic I had no doubt I would follow her advice.

"Wow, that sounds great! It's weird you called me, you know. It's been so hard for me to write lately. I can't concentrate due to an incessant stream of negative thoughts and I'm always struggling with anxiety! I started taking yoga classes and trying meditation again since December. It's helping, but I definitely need something else..."

After the New Year I had resumed my writing, but it remained a sluggish, painstaking process, fraught with procrastinating schemes. Every little distraction was causing me to lose my focus, and remorse had become a habitual prowler. Meanwhile, I had not made any further attempt at looking for employment. I was stuck in a rut that felt tiresome even to me.

"Yeah, I know what you mean!" said Naziha. "Please get this book right away. My heart tells me you're ready for it. We'll talk again soon, and you'll tell me what you think."

I did not hesitate. I went online and ordered the book, then downloaded the previous webinars. Naziha had been inspired to call me, and she was right; I was ripe for Tolle's message. Lord, was I ready for it! Without any other material change in my life, it turned my outlook around almost overnight. And it became the spark that ignited a voracious appetite in me for all things of the spirit. With urgency and passion, I flung myself entirely into my new endeavor. Everything took second stage, while my snail-paced writing slowed down to a near standstill.

I proceeded to read dozens of tomes on spiritual awareness, some illuminating and others less so. Naziha and I had many more long and animated discussions on the phone about our readings, many of which she had recommended. Her command of English was impressive and the depth of her perception was invaluable to me in those early days. The only problem was that she did not live nearby and was rather busy with her school-age children and part-time work.

I realized I had to meet other like-minded individuals but had no idea where to start, until one night during a conversation about living in the moment with Elisa, my daughter's best friend.

"Oh my God," she laughed, shaking her long blond hair, "You sound just like my mom!"

I had known Elisa since she was a toddler. Her parents and older brother had been living in the Versailles before I moved in. Barely nineteen months older than Sophia, the two grew up together like sisters and spent a lot of time in each other's company.

"Really? Yvonne's into this kind of thing?" I asked.

"Oh, yes. You should call her. I'm sure you'll find you share many of the same views. She's also a member of a Qi-Kong group that meets weekly."

I had no idea what Qi-Kong was then and although I had been vaguely aware of Yvonne's spiritual interest over the past few years, I had never shown any curiosity and she had never talked about it to me. So it came as something of a surprise when I called and asked her to introduce me to her friends to help me along with my spiritual initiation.

"I'll have to ask them first if you don't mind, Wafa," said Yvonne circumspectly. "But I'm sure it'll probably be alright for you to join the group."

Yvonne is as ostensibly different from me as can be, both in appearance and character. A red-haired, blue-eyed, Swiss-born, she is soft-spoken and reserved. Shy, almost timid, at first, she is capable of putting anyone in their place should she find it necessary. She speaks mostly French with me, though her accented English is impeccable and articulate. Although I felt she had viewed me with some degree of sus-picion initially, she quickly realized that I was dead serious and from then on, gently coached me, suggesting her own reading and practices.

The first time she invited me to one of her group's Monday nights meetings, I knew I had entered a new world construct, one guided by the light of consciousness. What a diverse and magnificent assembly! In addition to Yvonne, the group was composed of eight other members, each unique and brilliant in her own right.

Donna's radiant face greeted me as soon as she opened her door. She took me by the shoulders as if I were an old friend and grinned. And, in that moment, I saw the glim-mer of acknowledgment in her eyes as well as the depth of her compassion behind her smile, and my heart went out to her. A widowed single-mother of a young teenage boy, and an accom-plished musician, she hosted most of the sisters' gatherings in the comfortable basement of her Leonia home with grace and generosity.

Behind her was Loretta. A worldly and spirited Armenian-American, she was born and raised in the Middle East and was completely attuned to my Arabic heritage. Fluent in many languages and outspoken on matters of politics and society she quickly seduced me with her talent as a writer and spiritual disciple.

Soon, I fell under the spell of Queen Maya—as I like to think of her—a vivacious and generous Mexican goddess, full of joy and zest for life, who frequently opened her beautiful realm for some spectacular entertaining.

When I fell ill that summer with a frightening case of uveitis and some severe and undiagnosed knee and arm pain, it was Carmen who tended to me. She prepared some delicious Latin dishes to sustain me and she used her essential oils to massage and wheedle my aches away. Words are not enough to describe my gratitude and love for her gentle healing touch.

I must admit it took me longer to warm up to Pio's guileless ways, perhaps because of my own often unwelcomed bluntness.

"It mustn't be too bad if you're still living in the Galaxy," Pio scoffed when she first heard me complain about my financial situation.

I can still picture her trademark derisive smirk and smug little chuckle. And of course, she was right to be cynical; after all, she was only referring to the upscale complex I was still living in then. Still, I grew to love her dearly over time. At once resilient and vulnerable, aloof and devoted, Pio, the no-nonsense Chinese princess, is also the gate-keeper of the group and master of the art of dumpling making.

It was much easier with Anne. Considerate and insightful, she is a talented artist and a shamanic practitioner. I had never so closely felt the extraordinary vibrational effect of drumming until Anne invited the sisters to her home for a few entrancing

gatherings. Her distinctive handmade drums will forever reso-
nate in my heart and guide me throughout my journey.

And then there was Pat B., a Tolle's devotee and tennis
and swimming buff. Married to a lovable and hot-headed
man, I enjoyed watching their interaction and her masterful,
yet tactful, way of tempering his opinionated outbursts when
inappropriate.

And last but not least, the reticent and thoughtful Pat D.
who gave me a jar of honey on our very first encounter, an offering which signified her acceptance of me right there and then,
even though she had not expected me to be there and had not
planned for me in her gifting to her group.

These were the women who entered my life. It was only
fitting that they called themselves "Sisters of Light!" They had
all been awareness-seekers for years and they welcomed me, a
neophyte, with patient and open hearts—each and every one
of them having an auspicious influence on the evolution of my
awareness.

**

Still, my shift in consciousness began at a very elemental
level. I was going through my very first reading of *A New
Earth*, when I knew I had found the answer to my protracted
unhappiness. I began practicing being fully in the present
instead of in my head, which does take an awful lot of practice
for someone like me. Because my relapses were frequent and
disheartening, I had to learn to forgive myself while catching
my old mind patterns as often as I could.

Like everyone else, I had heard such affirmations before:
live in the moment, for that's the only thing real; the past is
gone, and nothing can be done about it; the future is but a
figment of the imagination and may not be counted on; the

only reality is the *Now*, even as it is but a succession of fleeting moments; and, finally, the present moment is life itself, everything else just illusion. But even as my reason understood the premise inherent in each of these statements, my behavior remained pretty much unchanged, marred by fear and doubt.

The *Now* was obstructed by a gushing torrent of thoughts in my head. I had to learn to acknowledge and recognize those voices that made up the so-called "monkey mind" and refuse to be consumed by the negative thinking associated with it. Such internal thought process, I became aware, was often not a civilized discourse, factually based, but rather a shouting invective made of narrow-minded past and future wiles, judgments, vilifications, umbrages, and the like.

The voices were always there and, when they were not, it was only because they had been overtaken by the vocal sounds on the radio, TV, internet, and other noisy technological stalkers of our time. The thoughts and emotions generated by such cacophony were sometimes joyful—like listening to music— but more often they were unhappy, dissatisfied, indignant, jealous, or angry.

The result was permanent stress, the most potent poison of modern life, a virus that had infested my own "operating" system since my early years. Is it any wonder that Westerners, who are the most materially endowed people in the history of humanity, are also the ones who suffer the most from mental and physical maladies not related to poverty?

I learned to tame the noise by introducing silence. I turned off radio, television, telephone, internet, even music, for predetermined periods of time throughout the day and attended to whatever I had to do in silence. The first few times, the intense feeling of it almost choked me; I could hardly stand it. I used to think I needed the sound of TV or radio in the background for company even if I didn't pay attention to the programming. Slowly the loneliness I initially experienced made way to a peaceful solitude.

I then inserted short moments of complete stillness and focused breathing throughout my day. At home, waiting at a red light or stuck in traffic, I trained myself to be still while taking and slowly releasing three to four deep breaths. Doing this immediately put my mind at rest and in the present. Slowly but surely, I extended those short breaks as I began enjoying the calming effect of my conscious breathing, the tingling energy through my fingers and body, the sensation of bliss. Soon, I went on a disciplined regimen of meditation twice a day, upon waking and before sleeping, and during moments of abrupt stress.

The random negative thoughts in my head did not magically disappear; I still experienced their intrusion, but I learned to brush them aside, refocus on conscious breathing and return to my state of *Being* without thought. This daily exercise became easier with time and practice, and quickly resulted in a dramatic transformation in my mental state and overall well-being. My perennial anxiety and fear subsided and eventually disappeared.

My quieter mind, solidly grounded in the present moment, made it possible for my thinking—when it was called upon—to be more creative, and instilled my writing with greater motivation and inspiration, though I soon realized it still lagged in direction and belief. My intellectual vacillations had less to do with the overall purpose of my task—I saw my book as vital to understanding myself through an in-depth look at my past in order to unveil the roots of my confusion—than with the need of expert guidance. In mid-summer 2008, I had reached midpoint in my memoir and I was bewildered by the technical complexity of it.

It was then, after a weekly Qi-Kong group meditation hosted by Pio, at her home, that I met Barry, the man who was to help me regain confidence in my own ability to write creatively and teach me the techniques of effective writing, what he nonchalantly called the "plumbing and midwifery" of the craft. A self-described "word guy" who loves what he does with a passion, a writing teacher, a published fiction and poetry author, college professor, and art photographer of "metaphors," he is one of those people who make apprentices immediately feel at ease.

As soon as I joined his writing center at the end of September, I knew he had been put in my path by a guiding hand. His warmth, engaging demeanor, and endearing smile helped me overcome my doubt and get on with my cherished project. Most critically, by reading aloud selections of my writing in his well-attended weekly workshops, he exposed the strengths and weaknesses of my narrative, providing me with a panel of critics, including him, who voiced their approval and/or suggestions without a hint of disparagement. My craft improved immeasurably.

**

All wasn't bliss, unfortunately. The following six months, I, along with the rest of the world, entered an ever more precarious monetary condition that only kept getting worse as the global economy and stock markets began, and then persisted in, an unprecedented downslide.

By March 2009, the overall U.S. economy was in full-fledged recession, and stock indices had reached their lowest point since 1996, obliterating all gains of the previous *thirteen* years. Lax government regulation begun under Clinton after his repeal of the Glass-Steagall Act, cheap money, and a capitalist laissez-faire creed run amok, all contributed to the global financial crisis of 2008. But it was also the unbridled greed and nefarious dealings of a Wall Street generation high on its own narcissistic fumes that threw the world economies over the precipice. Like houses of cards stacked on top of each other, they stumbled and plummeted in a frightening debacle reminiscent of the Great Depression. Millions lost their jobs, homes, and businesses.

Savings that I once felt would last me at least another couple of years evaporated, while premature and heavily penalized withdrawals from my retirement account—down over fifty percent—had been my only option since the beginning of the year. Even so, I stubbornly persisted in my mystifying denial. My only refuge was my spirituality and daily meditation.

That is not to say I did not experience lapses or suffered occasional meltdowns. On one such occasion, I was explaining the causes of the financial crisis to my daughter as I watched her prepare her lunch, when she asked me if that was the reason I had given up on returning to work on Wall Street.

"No, I don't think so. I'm pretty disgusted by the greed, sure. But, look, I don't want to take a job to just make a living anymore," I said. "I don't even want a well-paid career that will leave me wanting again in a few years. Yes, I know, in these crazy times, it does sound extravagant, indulgent, whatever, but let me explain myself. All my life I've struggled to fulfill other people's expectations of me, even believing they were my own. All my life I've taken on jobs for the sole purpose of making money and earning a living. Don't get me wrong, I know I have to earn a living, but I want to do it with a career that fulfills me even if it makes me very *little* money. I can say this knowing full well that I have been blessed with a very lucrative career in the past, which now allows me to take my time and find out once and for all what it is I want to dedicate myself to, even at the cost of all my savings."

I paused and, for a second, mulled over my declaration. Sophia looked at me in consternation, not expecting to hear a lecture.

"There, I said it... Money no longer equates with success in my eyes, let alone happiness. I'm aware that my ostensible idleness has been viewed with amazement by my friends and relatives, and you. Some even think it's simply laziness, which it categorically is not. I know you believe me when I tell you that it's been an ongoing puzzlement for me as well. Well, not anymore!" I chuckled and went on: "It's ironic and pathetic at the same time, isn't it? At fifty-something, I'm going through what you're experiencing at twenty." My voice faltered.

I looked at my daughter's beautiful face. "When I was your age, I never had anyone to guide and support me in pursuit of my dreams. No one is to blame, it's just the way it was; I always had to work for a living. I feel I earned that right for myself now. Do you understand?"

Sophia nodded in silence. She had stopped doing whatever she was doing and, leaning over the kitchen island, was listening to me vent my frustration.

"If I have one piece of advice for you," I went on, "It's this: as long as I'm able to support you, you should find out for yourself and explore your options, allow yourself to fail and learn, and follow your wildest dreams now while you're still young and unattached. Only I must tell you, baby, that I may not be able to continue to provide you with the lifestyle you've grown accustomed to, and also forget about an expensive private college! We're soon going to have to adjust to new realities."

I paused to take a deep breath.

"But, Mom, it's not about me," Sophia finally interjected. "I'm actually ready to assume my responsibilities. But I know you, and you must be going through hell with the market crash and your unfinished book. It's been almost two years since you began writing it. Not to mention that you don't even know if it'll be published. You're not even looking for an agent. I thought you said once you could do that before you finish it."

"You're right, honey. But I need to complete it first for my own sake. It's not about being published; for all I know it may never be. And though I have every intention for it to succeed, I have no undue expectations, and I will not feel crushed if it doesn't. In any case, it's almost done. You know I've been working on it diligently since last fall when I joined Barry's workshop."

I smiled and pointed to the food on the kitchen counter. "I'm not letting you fix your lunch, I'm sorry. I got carried away. Here, let me help you."

"It's alright, Mom. You don't have to," said Sophia and with that she walked toward me and gave me a big hug.

She had watched me struggle over the years and she understood how vulnerable I was but also how determined to find the light.

Even so, Sophia had every reason to worry; my situation was alarming and reminiscent of an earlier time in my life. On the other hand, these times were also radically different from an awareness perspective. I had been on a spiritual journey for less than a year, but I had already gained life-altering insight, infused with acceptance, detachment, and trust.

The previous week, on the last Monday of January, during our meeting, Donna expressed the sentiment that we should all confide and support each other openly. Loretta, then, spoke of "shadows" in our lives, secret looming fears that prevent our growth, and added that money was one of the biggest of all shadows. Both encouraged us to talk about our personal situations and ask for support if needed. They suggested that we put our thoughts in writing and be prepared to share them with the group.

I knew how much that was true for me but had never faced up to it or even openly acknowledged it. Like a disease that spreads surreptitiously and infects every cell in the body until it's too late, money had always been a shameful topic that had affected every aspect of my life to the point of breaking me. It was high time for me to come clean and shed light on that shadow.

That cold February night, after we had greeted each other and settled down in a circle with our cups of fragrant herb tea, Donna gave the signal to begin telling our stories. When it was my turn to speak, I pulled out my sheet of paper and read out loud:

"For as long as I can remember, money has been at the center of my existence, as it was the dominant concern for my mother, and the source of my deepest insecurity—even when I had plenty of it—until now! Sure, it's a real practical problem, but it's no longer the fountainhead of all my fears. My burgeoning spirituality is responsible for my newfound ability to tame that monster and see it for what it is: the single greatest manifestation of the *ego*.

Somehow I've come to see my current financial situation as a direct challenge to my spiritual evolution; a test if you will, making the past six months perhaps the most defining period of my life. This may seem radical from the outset, but it's tantamount to losing all of one's earthly possessions in a brushfire, or standing at the brink of death, and emerging anew, like the phoenix rising out of its ashes.

I feel nearly cleansed of my oversized ego and its blind identification with form. In other words, if I were to lose all that I ever worked for, no longer possessed any material wealth whatsoever, and yet felt fulfilled and serene then I would know with certainty that I had reached my ultimate aspiration: true Awareness, freedom from financial angst, and deliverance from the ego. Today, I stand at the threshold of that realization. I've given up the struggle against forces greater than myself and surrendered in full acceptance of what is."

My voice grew faint as tears glistened in my eyes. Sitting on a pillow directly on the carpeted floor, surrounded by my sisters' compassion, I felt submerged with love and gratitude.

My articulated recognition that cold moonless evening in Donna's basement came to me like a revelation; I felt as if touched by grace, free at long last. Though I had written that statement a couple of days before, reading it publicly turned it into a solemn pledge that I knew made it the reality I would abide by for the rest of my life, my mantra.

Before long, my new and improved attitude was going to be tested in a serious way.

35

Awakening

One quiet evening, barely a few days after I had declared myself free from financial angst, my landlord called me to announce he was raising my rent because of an increase in condominium fees. I was already under pressure to pay my current rent, let alone afford an increase, and I expressed my concern to him. That didn't sit well with him.

"I'm sorry, but we all face enormous difficulties right now and you agreed to an increase should the maintenance go up. So I'll hold you responsible until the end of your lease in September," he warned me.

"I understand, Frank, but the fact is that I'm broke, and I may not be able to afford staying until the end of my lease. I'm already relying on early withdrawals from my IRA."

If I had hoped for sympathy, I was rudely awakened.

"Better you than I," he burst out rudely. "I just had a baby, and my wife is not working for now. I'll expect full rent starting next month." He sounded irate but also alarmed.

I hurried to reassure him. "I know my responsibility, and I'll do everything in my power to find a new tenant to take over my lease. I won't leave you in the cold," I promised. I hung up with him and breathed slowly.

"Who was that?" asked Sophia from behind me.

"Our landlord. He's raising our rent," I said evenly, turning to face her.

"Really? Can he do that? I can't believe you're so calm about it," she said.

"Yes, he can. It was stipulated in the lease. He was furious, and nasty, too. But he was right and I understand his predicament," I sighed.

"What are we gonna do?" she probed nervously. "Can we afford it?"

"To be honest with you, no. It's already been a tall order. Now it's getting impossible." I paused and caressed her cheek. "But don't you worry, honey. I'm sure, we'll find a solution. Haven't we always been just fine?" I reassured her.

She shook her head and returned to her room.

I walked to my bedroom, sat in silent darkness, and closed my eyes. Breathing deeply, I exhaled away all thoughts, envisioned myself bathed in warm, glowing energy, and swiftly entered the realm of stillness. Right now, I thought intently, I have a roof over my head and food in my fridge. My daughter and I are healthy and have loving friends and relatives. Soon, a wonderful opportunity will appear which will solve all our immediate problems. Thank you, Lord, for all our blessings. A smile appeared on my lips as I concluded my intention and let my body melt away while bathing in the light of my soul. After a few minutes, I pulled myself back and returned to the kitchen to prepare dinner, as if nothing had happened at all.

A couple of weeks later, my friend Annette called me.

"Wafa, what are you doing this summer?" she asked me.

"As a matter of fact, I really don't know, Annette. I've got one priority, and that's the fast completion of my book. After that, I have to look for a job, I suppose," I said.

"Would you be interested in working with me in Sag Harbor this summer? I need someone to work at the store part-time. I'm renting a house, so you could also live with me. You'll only pay a small rent, and you'll be able to write on your days off," she said.

I grinned widely. "Gosh, I'd love to, Annette, thank you," I answered.

Her offer—a temporary job and a place to stay in one of the most charming villages on the East End of Long Island—was irresistible and the opportunity I had been waiting for without knowing what form it would take.

Annette was a longtime friend of my sister's. They had met around 1990, when they both worked at Norma Kamali's store on East 56th Street in New York City. They'd become fast friends, and their friendship had extended to their close families. We then lost touch in the late nineties and had not reconnected until the fall of 2008, over a decade later thanks to Facebook, when both Annette and I were divorced with children.

Annette managed the two main retail stores of Urban Zen, an organization founded by Donna Karan, which advocates "patient well-being, children empowerment, and preservation of culture." Needless to say, I immediately saw Urban Zen's dictum "Raise awareness; inspire change," as a portentous sign, synchronicity at work again!

My next mission was to look for a new tenant for my landlord and find a place for my daughter to live in Manhattan where she was attending college and working part-time. I had decided to simply put all my belongings in storage until I determined what my options would be in the fall.

Within two weeks, I got a message from my landlord informing me that he had contacted his realtor and listed the apartment for sale. "Hopefully," he wrote, "The unit will sell quickly, as I was forced to price it below what I paid for it." By mid-April, he had a serious offer, followed by a contract.

On May 5, I started working part-time in Sag Harbor and driving back home to look for a roommate for Sophia. A week later, I found her a bright corner room with a separate bathroom in a cozy Upper East Side apartment. I began praying for the closing to happen by the end of the month, since my landlord would not release me from my lease, contending that no deal was done until the cash was in his hands.

Because of the lending freeze that followed the financial meltdown, stories of buyers waiting ad infinitum for mortgages abounded. Incredibly, though, he closed on June 1, and Sophia and I moved out on May 30. Clearly, the universe had fully cooperated and facilitated the entire process with hardly a bump.

I was certain my life had taken on a new meaning.

"What are you going to do *after* the summer?" I was asked by friends time and time again when I announced my short term plans.

"I have no idea but I'm confident something else will come along in due time," I told them, adding with a serene smile, "I have pledged to accept uncertainty in my life without fear and with gratitude for all my blessings."

"Wow," they said. "It takes a lot of courage to do that."

"I don't think so. At least, I don't see it as anything to do with courage. In my mind, courage implies danger, and I've never been in any peril. I prefer to call it trust, since there is no hint of anxiety in me anymore. I keep reminding myself that I'm resourceful and there are countless opportunities out there. I trust things will happen exactly the way that's best for me."

In truth, I reveled in my newfound freedom. I felt exhilarated even as I gently stirred myself to relinquish control, relish the unknown, even welcome uncertainty. Every morning, as I opened my eyes, I reaffirmed my gratefulness for being alive, healthy, and blessed with so much abundance and natural beauty around me. I then sat in meditation and re-emerged anew steadfast in the conviction that my spirit, mind, and body were opening up to the universal energy field and its endless creativeness. I knew such a field was part of a unified whole which was also within me. Connecting with that field through stillness and presence, the manifestation of my intentions and desires becomes possible. The simple ritual made me feel as if I walked on water, floating through my days in joyfulness.

This was precisely the kind of leap of faith I could never have taken had I not undergone a profound shift in belief. To be sure, there were many spiritual laws I continued to struggle with. One of the most challenging to me was the practice of non-judgment, the third essential element to successfully master the law of all possibilities—the two others being meditation and communion with nature. As humans, our entire mindset is conditioned to judge, criticize, label, and otherwise close ourselves to the inherent and exceptional qualities of that which is before our eyes, the world in its pristine state. We do this because of our fear, insecurity, and all-consuming need to dominate our environment. When that need gets out of control and affects our relationships with others, it leads to wide divides of resentment and, eventually, alienation.

My relationship with my daughter, which was frequently beset with conflict and confrontation, testified to that fact. Certainly it had benefited from my daily routine of *Being* without thoughts, from silence and meditation, but it suffered from my tendency to criticize, manipulate, and control her behavior, which I mistakenly confused with a caring motherly instinct.

As I wrote about my rapport with my own mother and the pain I had inflicted on her during my teenage years, I began to see more clearly the angst my own daughter was experiencing. Since I had ushered spirituality in my life and benefited from its transformative power, I explained to her as best I could what it was I was trying to accomplish and even gave her a copy of *A New Earth* to read.

"Mom, I'm nineteen, seriously... you think I'm going to read this?" She rolled her eyes and shoved the book aside.

Ignoring her scorn, I persisted. "It's just that I can relate to the kind of anxiety you experience day in and day out. I've been there; I know how unbearable life can feel at your age. Why don't you just give it a try, it'll spare you years of misery," I pleaded.

I felt very helpless in those days watching her gain weight and struggle with wild mood swings.

"Listen, Mom, I'm old enough to live the way I want to. It's my life, after all, and when I'm in need of advice, I'll ask you. I know I'll make lots of mistakes but they will be *my* mistakes, not yours. That's how I'll learn... As much as you want to, you cannot protect me or 'save' me from myself, even with all your experience."

Time after time, her level of maturity and clarity rarely failed to impress me. Still, I found it nearly impossible to witness her pain and not put in my two cents' worth, but also, inevitably, my criticism.

"You spend hours watching tabloid reality TV and on the internet when you're not working... You don't exercise, and you keep eating all that junk food. How can you expect to lose weight and feel good about yourself?" I complained.

Remarks like that enraged her, and she'd swing back at me with ferocious comments meant to hurt and take revenge for the wound I had just inflicted her.

It took me a long time to be able to let her be, and, even then, it was difficult. She was aching to be on her own, to free herself from my domineering presence. And I became well aware of the necessity for me to let her go, even as it filled me with apprehension.

All my life, I'd had to care for someone other than myself; first, my mother, then my daughter. Their needs superseded mine, even as I embraced my sandwiched position and its huge responsibilities to the point of complete identification with my roles. And suddenly, I had to learn to drop the role playing, catch the automaton in me, and just *Be*.

When the opportunity came up for us to part ways, much sooner than I had anticipated, Sophia was thrilled to move on her own to the big city, and I knew I had to let her go gracefully, keeping my advice to myself and learning to love and support her from a distance. Living apart for the first time presented us both with another test of personal and spiritual growth. Sophia wanted me off her back but not out of her life. What she yearned for was to be loved unconditionally for who she had always been, not the vision I wished her to be.

She needed to be recognized as my equal, not my inferior, and that meant accepting her completely as she was, without judgment, and always, not intermittently. It meant learning to listen to her in silence and compassion without rushing to find solutions for her, allowing her instead to come up with her own answers. It meant letting her experience suffering too, no matter how hard it was for me to watch. For, as Tolle writes, "the fire of suffering becomes the light of consciousness." I gradually recognized that it is only through the acceptance of suffering, not just pleasure, and the surrender to the evanescence of all aspects of life, that serenity and peace are achieved.

For true consciousness to emerge, I reminded myself of the ancient Greek aphorism "Know thyself." As a guiding rule, I had to be willing to observe my thoughts and actions, recognize the kernel of truth behind others' criticism of me, accept it despite the pain that exercise entailed, and finally transcend that suffering to experience true freedom, freedom from my ego. Inherent in my criticism of my daughter and my desire for her to behave according to *my* wishes, was the belief that I was right and she wrong. By rejecting her objections and criticism of me, I simply assumed I was blameless, which of course I was not.

When I moved to Sag Harbor, my environment became my best teacher. My journey so far had taken place in a very safe and controlled setting, my own home. I had learned to be present and aware, but my ego had not yet actually been put to the test except, on occasion, by my daughter. The real challenge was yet to come.

Everything I had known, from my home, to my friends, to my occupations, I had carefully orchestrated from an advantaged position. By relinquishing it all, I surrendered to a whole new reality. I lived in someone else's house, worked under someone else's authority, and met people who viewed and labeled me as a subordinate. Swallowing my pride, rebuffing my ego, recognizing that the very traits I loathed in others were often also mine, were all vital, albeit painful lessons.

I wept and moaned in disbelief as I admitted as much to gentle ears. How was it that those same remarkably strong, intelligent, and independent women whom I instinctively loved and admired also turned out to be controlling, self-righteous, and egotistical? For the same reason that their soul, their true *beingness*, like mine, was overtaken by their ego and identified with form—material success, intellect, sophistication, worldliness; they and I had been cast in the same mold. How could I judge them when they were the mirrors I could now clearly see myself in? Didn't they weep too in incredulity when, periodically, their armor was pierced and their hearts torn, often by the very people they cared most about?

And so my journey took on a new meaning, one that was epitomized by Gandhi's statement, often repeated, seldom understood: "You *must be* the change you want to see in the world." All of us wander around wishing for circumstances and people in our lives to be different and conform to our needs, all along ignoring that it is we who must change first, and everything else will follow. My relationship with Sophia was a living proof of this.

The more inclined I was to listen while fully present, admit to my flaws, and willingly receive her criticism of me—even as each of her rebukes felt like daggers in my flesh—the faster she acknowledged her own failings. Every time, we would look at each other with renewed respect and apologize. Because old habits die hard, it took us months of engaging, relapsing, retreating, and connecting again before she could begin to think of me as a trusted ally who would never betray her.

"It's hard for me to confess this, Mom, because I'm afraid you'll use it against me later," she had often complained in the past.

By and by, Sophia turned to the very books I had offered and she'd rejected just months earlier. Concepts that once sounded impenetrable began to make sense to her, and slowly she experienced the transformative changes in herself she had witnessed in me. Nothing in this world feels like the love and wonder a mother feels when her child takes her first flight on the path to awareness, *nothing*! Like a peacock parading in a sweep of brilliant plumage, I was swollen with pride even as I realized that it was my willingness to carry my own cross that had led her to pick up hers.

**

My summer in picturesque Sag Harbor began early and ended late. The part-time job I was hired to do turned into a full-time occupation that lasted till the last day of the year. The main sales associate had abruptly accepted another position elsewhere and it fell upon me to fill in. Unfazed, I stood on my feet from forty to fifty hours a week, often foregoing my lunch break altogether, in a fast paced, exciting, and beautiful setting. I had never worked in retail but soon I handled my responsibilities with ease and aplomb. I was in the moment, at peace and happy, and I met countless people making new friends almost every day. And while my income was small and my savings depleted, my heart was full to the brim, my consciousness expanding.

From this first opportunity, others followed effortlessly. The more I let go of my old fears—fear of the unknown being at the core of it all—the more I embraced uncertainty, and lived in the flow with the least effort and most detachment, the more things turned out for the best. Every day, I practiced and experienced the law of intention and desire, the law of giving and receiving, of cause and effect or Karma, and the closer I felt led to my purpose in life, or Dharma.

The universe opened its gateways wide for me to be all that I could be and more. This is my journey; it is life itself, laden with setbacks and lightened with small triumphs, and it will go on until my dying breath.

Today, what I know with absolute certainty, and from the depths of my being, is that there always was a reason for me to stubbornly resist looking for a job solely on the basis of income. At first, it was an inexplicable, irrational feeling, yet it was so profoundly ingrained that I could not find it in me to thwart it yet again and settle for the road most traveled. I was willing to use every last penny of my savings and retirement assets to fulfill what could be seen as an elusive goal, a fantasy. I somehow knew that if I were to accept a position only to support my privileged lifestyle and protect my assets, I would forever relinquish the light I was blindly seeking. I had to make a living with purpose, all in the service of a higher principle and with the passion that inhabits me!

I now know that my human form is only a vessel my soul temporarily inhabits. I know that my purpose in life is two-pronged: My primary, *inner* purpose is simply *to be*, and exist in full awareness and presence. My secondary, *outer* purpose is that which my human form is here *to do* and accomplish in my earthly life. The challenge is to reconcile the two, *doing* while *being*, regardless of what shape and actions the doing takes, for it will likely change throughout a person's lifetime.

From my early teens, I have been consumed with issues of social justice, peace, and freedom. I pursued my education filled with the expectation of one day applying my talent and efforts to my ideals regardless of income considerations. That dream faded as I took multiple shortcuts and succumbed to the lure of financial success in the land of opportunity. I have now come full circle.

I no longer consider a lucrative career on Wall Street solely as the blind pursuit of money over all else, particularly Being. If material success represented as much for me in the past, it only did so because of what I was missing, my inner purpose. George Soros, Bill Gates, and Warren Buffett, three of the greatest philanthropists and wealthiest men on the planet, are testament to how the combined pursuits of inner and outer purposes are not only compatible but also the road to great abundance and personal fulfillment.

A successful career can take any form at all, as long as one partakes in it in full awareness, in alignment with one's inner purpose, and not merely to satisfy the ego. "Finding and living in alignment with the inner purpose is the foundation for fulfilling your true purpose. It is the basis for true success," writes Tolle. In that sense the seamstress, the custodian, and the surgeon are all one and the same, if they perform their task in full presence, full awareness, full acceptance, without ego. Peace and joy are sure to follow.

EPILOGUE

Dharma

It has been only two years since I first took my leap of faith and three years since I began writing my book. I have never set foot in an Ashram or spiritual retreat, never traveled to India or Nepal or Tibet, never met or took counsel from a guru or a sage, and I am very far from being either myself.

My journey so far has been inward, a self-exploration based principally on silence, meditation, and acceptance as well as on the daily exercise of non-judgment, detachment, and faith. All the books I read have essentially emphasized these same basic principles. The key for me has been my willingness to put them into practice, no matter how hard, until they became second nature, a way of life.

At the risk of sounding contradictory, I can say with certainty that I'm aware the person I am shall never completely know the unfathomable me, only *what I am not*. And yet, even such infinitesimal inkling is enough to fill me with peace. My life's ultimate purpose is not only to persevere on the path of dis-identification with everything I once held essential to my happiness—for I now know it is all in me, always was—but also to invest my talent and effort to help spread the word far and wide in any way I am able. I am convinced our humanity needs every voice to begin to heal.

Yet, forever, I shall remain mindful and stay alert to life's ruses, for every step I take on that yellow brick road will lead me to a new dragon—one of the many manifestations of the ego—the slaying of which I have to undertake again and again, if I am to move to higher grounds. It will not always be a smooth journey, and I've already been acquainted with the sour taste of unforeseen setbacks. Such is the nature of evolution that it is often a messy process, fraught with stumbling blocks.

Ultimately, the most startling revelation about my awakening was that it had little to do with my separation from my mother's alter ego, or the "re-building" of my own fractured self. Instead it meant the *dissolution* of my ego—the ego that depends on the vision of others to exist, the self-indulgent little "me"—and the awakening to my true self, the "I" beyond the ego.

Still, spiritual books alone would not have accomplished the transformation I experienced without the simultaneous and cathartic process of exposing and relating the account of my life intertwined as it was with my mother's.

On that fateful night of April 2007, my departed mother had indeed channeled her desire for me to write her story, foreseeing all along that it would lead me to the unearthing of my own narrative, which in turn would pave the way to my true purpose. For if during her lifetime, she never knew how to experience the lasting inner peace and joy that awareness brings, she witnessed it in me, and that must have allowed her to finally rest in peace.

Hence, my memoir has gone from a narcissistic exercise in solipsism and self-pity to a tool for self-observation and tangible insight. Like an archeologist looking for clues and secrets of the past through chipped stone axes, I have gone through my life, digging out of the sands of oblivion old skeletons and lost memories, some of which were still causing me inexplicable physical ailments.

And like an archeologist, I had to dust off those relics and strive to match them with others in an effort to complete the puzzle of their origin and significance. Transcending my pain and tears and anger, I have cleansed and pieced together those vestiges of my past and displayed them in plain sight for everyone to see, for they no longer define who I am, if they ever did. The truth will set you free, they say. Since I figured that out, I have lived my life one moment at a time with added fervor while eating the stars.

Last night, I sat in darkness, oblivious of time, mesmerized by the starry firmament and full moon shining over snow in the backyard.

The cypresses lined up, and tall pines towered high—all stood still as they witnessed the flutter of a guiding angel's wings cast a passing shadow under the silvery light.

I thank thee, Sweet Mother, for leading me to the joy of being and true meaning of bliss!